MONTANA

=== *and the* ===

NFL

MONTANA

═ and the ═

★ ★ ★ ★ ★ ★ ★

BRIAN D'AMBROSIO

THE
History
PRESS

Published by The History Press
Charleston, SC
www.historypress.net

Front cover, clockwise from top: courtesy Milana Lazetich; courtesy University of Montana; courtesy Marion County Historical Society; courtesy Shane Collins; courtesy Jerry Kramer. *Back cover, top*: courtesy University of Montana; *middle*: courtesy Jan Stenerud; *bottom*: courtesy Marion County Historical Society.

First published 2017

ISBN 978-1-5402-2564-1

Library of Congress Control Number: 2017938351

To Dad and to our future trip to Canton together
To Sophia and her wonder, joy, personality and laughter

CONTENTS

ACKNOWLEDGEMENTS

Thank you to all the gentlemen profiled in this book who were gracious with their time and courtesy to make it come to fruition. Special thanks to Raúl Allegre; Ken Amato; former NFL personnel and Butte resident Bob Beers; Doug Betters; Ed Breding; Joel Carlson of the University of Montana, for his inestimable help with images and contacts; Artie Crisp, for his time and enthusiasm; Ed and Joe Cummings; Barry Darrow; Casey Fitzsimmons, Scott Gragg; Rick Halmes of the Montana Football Hall of Fame; Sharon Hawkins; Mick Holien, for his knowledge and time; Lex Hilliard; football historian Steve Jubyna; Bill Lamberty of Montana State University; Milana and Pete Lazetich; the Marion County Historical Society; Bob McCullough; Sam McCullum; Mark McGrath; Steve Okoniewski; Brian Salonen, for his friendship and kindness and fine example; Kirk Scrafford; and Mike Tilleman.

INTRODUCTION

Millions of fans tie their identities to their football teams' successes. Intense, vicious, competitive and marinated in strong feelings of camaraderie and revelry, the game of football yields much power over American society. It's the pride of small towns, the discussion on the front porch of universities and, by far, the country's most popular and profitable sport.

Montanans, too, take football seriously at all levels, from Pop Warner to high school contests played under Friday night lights to the raucous weekenders at the University of Montana and Montana State. Football is so rooted here we almost take it for granted. In Montana, it's a lifestyle for some and entertainment for others. To scores of folks, football is family time or an escape from everyday life. Deeper still, there is a special pride Montanans hold when one of their own reaches the pinnacle of the sport and earns a spot in the National Football League. Indeed, sparse populations produce big loves, and to send someone to the biggest stage from the smallest of population centers is extraordinary. The franchise is often irrelevant, for Montanans will cheer on a kid from Cut Bank or Choteau or Missoula, no matter if he is a Denver Bronco, Seattle Seahawk or Carolina Panther.

The vast state of Montana has been dubbed "Big Sky Country" for its mythic mountains, picturesque routes, crystal-clear lakes and glaciers. But it is also where Ryan Leaf and Brock Osweiler were groomed to become franchise quarterbacks and, by reason of the small percentage of Montanans in professional sports, ambassadors of their school, college and state. Russell

McCarvel, Osweiler's football coach at Flathead High School in Kalispell, recalled telling the seventeen-year-old that he had a particular obligation to represent not only himself but his community. McCarvel recalled telling Osweiler, "What you need to do is make sure that someday, when some kid is watching you on TV at Applebee's when he's older, he turns to his friend and says, 'You know what? I played with that guy, I blocked for him, and he was a great guy.' Because people from Montana love cheering for their own."

Football is a brotherhood, and that brotherhood is stretched tighter in Montana. Montanans have succeeded in reaching the country's number-one sport, and the state has influenced the lives and careers of at least ninety NFL players, dating to the earliest days of the league's inception, when UM running back and tackle Christian Bentz played with the Detroit Heralds in 1920, Missoula-born Herm Sawyer played with the Rochester Jeffersons and Flathead Indian Nick Lassa joined the Oorang Indians in the NFL's third season in 1922.

"It's going to be a small book, I'm sure," was the typical response from folks when I mentioned to them that I was researching and writing a book about Montana's NFL connections.

But that's not the situation.

Indeed, Montana's connections to the NFL are extensive, including a player on the earliest Green Bay Packers team (Butte-born Jack McAuliffe), a player on the first San Francisco 49ers squad of 1964 (running back Earl "Pruney" Parsons, who was born in Helena), one on the first Oakland Raiders team of 1964 (guard Wayne Hawkins, born in Fort Peck) and one of the most dominant offensive linemen of the 1940s (Anaconda-born Francis Cope, who earned all-decade honors as a New York Giant).

We've given birth to or sharpened the skills at the college ranks of several Super Bowl participants and even an NFL Player of the Year (defensive end Doug Betters, Miami Dolphins, 1983). Our links are, perhaps not surprisingly, quirky. "Frosty" Peters set a record of seventeen field goals in a football game, all by dropkicks, when he was a freshman at the University of Montana in 1924, against Billings Poly. Frosty later starred for the University of Illinois and spent time in the NFL. Connections include the first pure kicker inducted into the Pro Football Hall of Fame (Jan Stenerud) and the receiver who caught the first touchdown pass in Seattle Seahawks history (Sam McCullum). Montana has links to some of strangest, most surprising and most memorable plays and games in the history of the league, from the "Music City Miracle" on January 8, 2000—Stevensville's Joe Cummings was on the field when the Buffalo Bills lost to the Tennessee Titans—to

Montana State alumni Ken Amato snapping for the Titans' Rob Bironas's record-setting eight field goals in a game (October 21, 2007) to inaugural New Orleans Saints' lineman Mike Tilleman blocking for Tom Dempsey's NFL record 63-yard field goal (November 8, 1970).

For purposes of conciseness, the book includes only players who were born in Montana, raised in Montana or attended high school or college in Montana and then went on to play in the National Football League. Players who elected to settle in Montana after retirement are not included. Many former NFL players, including Drew Bledsoe and Tom Newberry, reside at least part of the year in Montana, with the highest density in the western part of the state. Migrating to Montana seems to have precedent; one of the earliest players was Jack Colahan, a member of the 1928 New York Yankees. Colahan was born in Minnesota but was married in Dillon in 1926 and is sourced as living in Butte until at least 1935.

Many Montana athletes came close but never suited up for a regular-season NFL game. For every one who made it, there are a number of players who didn't, such as Caleb McSurdy, a standout linebacker with the UM Grizzlies from 2008 to 2011. McSurdy signed with the Dallas Cowboys and debuted strongly in the first preseason game in 2012, but he injured his Achilles' heel in practice the next week. He was placed on injured reserve and never returned.

The 1966 Glasgow High School graduate and UM track star Roy Robinson was drafted in the ninth round in 1970 by the Atlanta Falcons and made it to the last cut. Following his discharge by the Falcons, Robinson received a tryout with the Denver Broncos, but his lack of self-discipline and failure to handle the intense pressure undid him. "I didn't agree with what was going on so I walked out of camp and never had another chance again in the NFL," said Robinson, who has won more track-and-field state championships than any other high school athlete in the history of the state.

A number of the greatest collegiate players in Montana sports history could not crack the roster of an NFL club. Glendive running back Don Hass had a special blend of speed and toughness at Montana State University that helped him etch his name into the record books. Hass ran for 1,460 yards and a school-record twenty touchdowns in 1966, and he gained 1,245 more yards in 1967. His 2,954 career yards are third all-time at MSU, and his twenty-nine career touchdowns and 101.5 yards-per-carry average rank first. Hass signed as a free agent with the Dallas Cowboys, but he did not last through training camp before being cut.

"There are guys like Caleb McSurdy or Don Hass, who are guys who they described as can't miss, and then freak injuries jumped out or they were not drafted and they didn't make the NFL and that's a frustrating thing to see," said Mick Holien, the radio announcer of the Montana Grizzlies from 1985 to 2016. "But then there are guys like Scott Gragg who went high and who you knew was going to be drafted and Guy Bingham and Rocky Klever had long careers and that pretty much made a statement of how good the college programs are in Montana. Heck, [Montana-born Grizzly] Mike Tilleman won the comeback player of the year in the NFL and now he has a successful business. It all goes back to the character thing we have in Montana."

Indeed, players from Montana who have gone on to establish themselves in the NFL lack any semblance of entitlement and take nothing for granted. Football has taught Montana kids to fight for what they want, and the sport has taken some talented, dedicated athletes further in life. Football has been good to them—and they have represented us through football.

"The Montana kid is going to give you something that a kid 1,000 miles away may not," said Bill Kollar, a graduate of Montana who played several years in the NFL and is currently employed as defensive line coach for the Denver Broncos. "I never saw any sense of entitlement from Montana kids. They know they represent their state, their college institution and their family, and that's the bedrock of the success. It's a deep relationship."

"The mentality is different here than in the Dakotas, or Idaho," said Holien, "and the mentality of what it takes to make it, to succeed, is different here. In the mid-1960s, if you were scouting or even living in a place like Spokane, when you looked at Montana, you figured the places in Montana just weren't good for producing football players. Back then there was such a disparity between levels of play at Montana colleges and elsewhere, but even someone like Mike Tilleman had a great career."

The profiles contained in this book emphasize the joys and struggles, challenges and hurdles, comforts and delights of reaching the NFL and representing the state of Montana at the highest level of the sport. The unpleasant truths haven't been dodged in the conversations, and the book examines the hotbed controversies and persistent concerns surrounding the safety of current players and the responsibility of the league to assist former ones.

Greater knowledge of head injuries and their effect on deceased stars such as Junior Seau forced a re-examination of the sport. Indeed, football is under assault because of its concussions, domestic violence, player discipline, Colin Kaepernick's political stance and the escalating perception of some that it's too costly to watch and too dangerous to play.

Ten years after he threw one of the most celebrated passes in Pittsburgh Steelers history, wide receiver Antwaan Randle El (2002–10) has trouble walking down stairs. He is dealing with post-football mental and physical struggles at age thirty-six. He said that if he could go back, he wouldn't play football. He said he would have stuck with baseball. "Right now," he told ESPN, "I wouldn't be surprised if football isn't around in 20, 25 years."

Bo Jackson, who suffered from hip necrosis, which required surgery for an artificial hip, told *USA Today* in January 2017 that, in retrospect, he would've passed on football. Some stars are even walking away in the prime of their careers. In 2016, Miami Dolphins running back Arian Foster retired from the NFL at age thirty after years of injuries. "This is a beautifully violent game, and the same reason I loved it is why I have to walk away," Foster told *Newsweek*.

Still, there is an incredible number of people who love football and see it and its better values as timeless and universal. Perhaps they are more interested in the three hours of action of the game itself than thorny issues of player safety, activism and misbehavior—all will, ultimately, be forgiven. The sport faced a crisis in 1905, when at least eighteen people died while playing. President Theodore Roosevelt stepped in, encouraging safety changes and the forward pass. There's no reason to think the NFL won't adapt and sustain itself in time for its 100th season in 2019.

Indeed, no matter its risks, football's rewards are undeniably alluring. "When I played, there was a 70 percent chance of a player ending up broke, physically disabled and divorced," said Stevensville native Joe Cummings, who played linebacker in the NFL from 1996 to 1999. "If I asked you, would you want to take a job where you would end up broke, disabled and divorced, and it would only last until you were twenty-eight, would you want the job? Probably not. But what if I told you that that job was playing in the NFL, and getting to be on ESPN, etc.? The draw to be on that stage is still too big."

If the product endures and if the country's most popular league expands, perhaps the time will come when the state of Montana hosts a National Football League team. Crazier things have happened in the history of league expansion. In fact, when NFL owners voted in 2016 to move the Rams back to Los Angeles, *Newsweek* opined that "they fumbled their chance to create a small-market behemoth akin to the one in Green Bay." The magazine's alternative market selection: Billings, the largest city in Montana.

"If NFL commissioner Roger Goodell were searching a map for the epicenter of the Lower 48 that has yet to be colonized by an NFL franchise, he would place a thumbtack in Billings. The closest NFL franchise is Denver, which is 554 miles—or about the distance between Jacksonville and New Orleans—south. The nearest NFL franchise to the west, the Seattle Seahawks, is 817 miles away, while the nearest to the east, the Minnesota Vikings, is 840 miles away."

It reasoned that the town of Green Bay, Wisconsin, "home to the most devoted fans in the NFL and approximately 105,000 people," attracts its spectators from the city of Milwaukee and all through Wisconsin. Billings, with a similarly sized population of about 109,000, could theoretically lure supporters from throughout the Treasure State as well as its four boundary states (Idaho, North Dakota, South Dakota and Wyoming), none of which is home to an NFL franchise.

Sweet dreaming? Perhaps. But until that time arrives, Montana football fans will continue to derive gratification from the sight of seeing one of its home-grown high school kids or college stars run, throw and tackle in an NFL uniform. Any NFL uniform will be adequate.

1
1920s–1950s

FRANK SCOTT AKINS
BORN: March 31, 1919, Dutton, MT
DIED: July 6, 1992, Redding, CA
COLLEGE: Washington State
POSITION: Running back
NFL EXPERIENCE: 1943–46
TEAM: Washington Redskins

Dutton-born Frank Akins played as a running back for the Washington Redskins in the 1940s. He attended high school at John R. Rogers in Spokane and played college football at Washington State University.

Selected in the thirtieth round of the 1943 NFL draft, Akins, five feet, ten inches and 210 pounds, played four seasons with the Redskins, gaining 1,142 yards on 244 carries.

In 1943 and 1944, Akins saw action as a punter and as a special teams star, leading the league with four blocked punts in 1944. In 1945, he carried the ball 147 times, the most in the league that season, finishing with 797 yards, second only to the Philadelphia Eagles' Steve Van Buren's 832 yards. Akins had a total of 854 yards from scrimmage. In his best season, 1945, Akins averaged 5.4 yards per carry and scored six touchdowns. That year, Akins finished with 79.7 rushing yards per game, second to Van Buren's 83.2, and he was voted first team All-NFL by *Pro Football Illustrated* and International News Service. He touched the ball 156 times, second only to Van Buren's total of 180.

A newspaper account from October 24, 1945, refers to "benchwarmer" Frank Scott Akins, "the Spokane sporting goods salesman, who has been spending the better part of the last two seasons sitting on the Washington Redskins' bench, leads the National League today in ground gaining." The following day's *Billings Gazette* noted that the former substitute back had sparked the Redskins to become the leading offensive team in football and acerbically added that Akins had once "trekked back to Spokane to sell sporting goods and tell customers about games he didn't play in."

In the 1945 National Football League championship game, Akins, quarterback Sammy Baugh and the 8-2 Redskins faced quarterback Bob Waterfield and the 9-1 Cleveland Rams. Held on December 16, 1945, at Cleveland Municipal Stadium in front of 32,178 fans, the match boasted two opposing quarterbacks who could have dueled for the honorific title of professional football's dandiest personality.

Waterfield, the twenty-five-year-old Rams rookie, attracted the public's attention because of his marriage to actress and leading "sex symbol" Jane Russell, whom he had known from Van Nuys High School. Nicknamed "Slinging Sammy" for his ability to chuck a baseball, the thirty-one-year-old Baugh spent the 1945 season commuting back and forth from his west Texas cattle ranch in Rotan to play for the Redskins on weekends. Baugh was an outstanding quarterback, safety and punter during a sixteen-year career with the Redskins that ended after the 1952 season.

One hour before kickoff, a biting wind swirled off of Lake Erie, plunging the thermometer into negative temperatures. The mercury climbed a few degrees above zero by kickoff, but it never reached more than six degrees that afternoon. According to International News Service, the league had a plan to weatherize the stadium and field and took precautions to stay "girded for the climactic battle." "Nine hundred tons of straw that cost $7200 spread over the stadium surface lent the helpful promise that the expected throng of 55,000 might see a football game instead of an impromptu version of the Ice Follies."

In the first quarter, Akins suffered a broken nose after being hit by Rams guard Riley Matheson. He refused to leave the game and was contained to 16 yards on six attempts. Anaconda-born Milan Lazetich was one of the Rams' starting offensive guards.

On the strength of two touchdown passes from Waterfield, the Rams earned a 15–14 victory. Police dispatched special details to the Union Terminal and Hotel in Cleveland to aid and thaw out frozen fans huddled inside buildings outside the stadium.

John Dietrich wrote in the *Plain Dealer*: "It was a triumph not only for the Rams...but also for professional football. When more than 32,000 fans...will struggle through zero weather to see a football game, there is no longer any question. The pros have arrived to stay." Each Ram took home $1,408.74, $20.00 more per man than the winning Giants pocketed in 1944. The Redskins made $902.00 each.

In 1946, Akins picked up 146 yards on the ground. He ended up in Shasta County, California, coaching Anderson High School football in the 1960s. He died in 1992 in Redding, California.

EDWARD ROSS BARKER
BORN: May 31, 1931, Dillon, MT
DIED: September 6, 2012, Lakewood, WA
COLLEGE: Washington State University
POSITION: End
NFL EXPERIENCE: 1953–54
TEAMS: Pittsburgh Steelers (1953); Washington Redskins (1954)

Edward Ross Barker, the son of Edward R. Barker Sr. and Julia Barker, attended grade school in Aberdeen, Washington, and his high school years were spent in Sunnyside, Washington. Barker was a natural athlete excelling in football and track; in 1949, he was the state champion in the high jump.

Barker attended Washington State University (WSU), where he was a walk-on athlete and became the premier pass receiver on the Pacific coast. He set several receiving records at WSU, within the Pacific Coast Conference (PCC) and in the nation. In 1951, Cougar quarterback Bob Burkhart established a new PCC record with fifteen touchdown passes, while end Barker set an NCAA receiving record with 847 yards.

Barker played in the 1952 East-West Shriner Game at Kezar Stadium in San Francisco. In 1953, he was a first-round draft pick for the NFL's Los Angeles Rams. He went on to play one year at left end with the Pittsburgh Steelers and one year with the Washington Redskins. He played six games with the Steelers in 1953, hauling in seventeen passes for 172 yards and one touchdown, and he saw action in twelve contests with the Redskins in 1954, totaling 353 yards on twenty-three catches and three touchdowns. After football, he began a twenty-year career with the U.S. Air Force.

According to his obituary, he was stationed in "Washington, Guam, Puerto Rico, Louisiana, Korea, California, Florida and Okinawa" and "was proud of his military service." After Barker retired from the military, he began another career as a real estate agent in Lakewood, Washington, and "enjoyed traversing the woods of eastern Washington, Idaho and Montana for that perfect buck and bull elk."

In 2011, Barker was inducted into the Washington State University Football Hall of Fame. He died in 2012.

Christian Bentz

Born: December 20, 1891, Artis, SD
Died: January 10, 1981, Spokane, WA
Colleges: Northern State University; Montana
Positions: Offensive tackle; running back; kicker
NFL Experience: 1920
Team: Detroit Heralds

Christian Bentz was captain of the 1917 University of Montana Grizzlies team and was Montana's first All-American. He lettered at tackle from 1914 to 1917 and was selected to Walter Camp's All-Service team in 1918. When the Bobcats looked like winners and the Grizzlies didn't seem to have a chance back in 1918, it was Bentz who galloped down the field with four minutes to go and presented Montana with the winning touchdown. He raced 15 yards to a touchdown "with four Bobcats hanging on to him for dear life," according to one newspaper account.

"He was 235 pounds, and that was huge for the time," said Mick Holien, radio announcer for the Montana Grizzlies from 1985 to 2016. "He kicked, anchored both offensive and defensive line, and he carried the ball on goal line situations. He also coached in 1917 after Montana coach Jerry Nissen got sick. They called him 'Blitzen.' He was named All-Northwest three times in four years, but I don't have anything [records or data on his life] after he left UM."

Every generation of Grizzly football dating back to the 1920s has produced a handful of NFL players—some of them Pro Bowlers and many of them journeymen. Bentz is the first Grizzly and person connected to Montana, either by birth or college, to play in the NFL. According to NFL archives, Bentz is credited with appearing in one game and being active for two on the roster of the Detroit Heralds in 1920, though details are nebulous. (An article from the *Fort Wayne Sentinel* of November 11, 1920, with a team roster and brief background data for each player, identifies Benz as "tackle, All-American service team in 1918.")

"Bentz is one of those off-the-wall guys who is hard to find info about," said football historian Steven Jubyna. "He was considered to be a great lineman. He then spent time in the military. He's listed as playing one game [for the 1920 Heralds], but I haven't been able to find any reference to him playing for Detroit, outside of the sites that copy the football websites. He seems to have no connection to the city of Detroit, and he was already twenty-nine. Considering that Bentz seemed to have no connection to the Detroit area, what circumstance enabled him to play one game there?"

In the summer of 1936, Bentz, "now a Lemmon, SD banker," made his first visit to the campus since he graduated in 1918. According to the June 4, 1936 *Helena Independent Record*, Bentz spent time getting reacquainted with track coach Harry Adams and other alumni. "He's still big brawny and husky voiced. His hair is gray. But he's yet one of the heroes of the year when Montana tied Syracuse university pretenders for the national championship."

Bentz died in Spokane in 1981.

JOHN D. BERTOGLIO
BORN: May 14, 1899, Butte, MT
DIED: July 22, 1973, Homosassa Springs, FL
NFL EXPERIENCE: 1926
TEAM: Columbus Tigers

John Bertoglio was a standout athlete at Butte High in the 1920s, leading the Bulldogs to the state football title in 1924 with eighteen touchdowns. He finished his career with thirty-nine touchdowns, the most ever by a Bulldog. He tallied twenty touchdowns during the 1923 season, which still stands as a record at Butte High. He also scored a school record six touchdowns in one game, against Deer Lodge. Bertoglio also won the long jump at the 1923 and 1924 state track meets. The Bulldogs won the 1924 competition.

According to NFL records, Bertoglio played seven games for the Columbus Tigers in 1926. Individual rushing statistics at that time were unformulated, although he is credited with one rushing touchdown against the Brooklyn Lions on October 23, 1926. He died in Florida at the age of seventy-four.

Mal Bross

Born: December 7, 1903, Great Falls, MT
Died: February 8, 1989
College: Gonzaga
Position: Running back
NFL Experience: 1927
Teams: Los Angeles Wildcats (1926) (AFL); Green Bay Packers
(1927)

Born in Great Falls in 1903, Matthew Bross, "a product of the Great Falls sand lot and high school gridirons," was a star halfback at Gonzaga University and a running back for the Green Bay Packers in 1927.

Nicknamed "Mal," Bross starred on the Lethbridge Elks' baseball team of 1924 as a third baseman. He was an honor student and, as a junior, accorded "signal honors" for high standing in several branches of education. He graduated from Gonzaga in June 1926.

Bross then signed with the Los Angeles Wildcats, a traveling team based in Chicago, part of the newly minted and short-lived American Football League. Formed and folded within several months, the league was started by a sports agent named C.C. Pyle whose application to join the National Football League was rejected.

According to one newspaper account, Bross most likely caught the eye of the Wildcats while playing for Gonzaga. At the time, it was common for college teams to scrimmage or compete in full-contact exhibitions with professionals. "Organizers of the Los Angeles pro team undoubtedly pegged Matt when he played with the Gonzaga team against the Los Angeles A.C. eleven. The young Mr. Bross was not only the main gear in the defeat administered the club squad, but he brought the fans out of their seats during the fray with a 95-yard dash that brought a touchdown."

Coached by Jim Clark, the 1926 Wildcats went 6-6-2, and Bross's versatility as a rusher and receiver earned him distinction. Montanan and UM grad Ted "Chief" Illman was also on the team as a wingback, tailback and blocking back.

According to NFL statistics, Bross found a temporary home in Green Bay in 1927, where he played in two games and started in one of them. Bross was not the only Montana-connected player on the 1926 Wildcats to join an NFL roster. After leaving the Wildcats, Illman signed with the Chicago Cardinals.

Both Bross and Illman were finished with professional football after one season. Perhaps the competition was too fierce, or they may have quit on their own accord, as the nascent sport compensated them poorly, was regarded as low-brow by the general public and was largely ignored by the media. An archival letter written by Benny Friedman of Michigan and later the New York Giants, who was regarded as one of the best backs of his time, notes the public attitude toward the sport of football in 1927. "In 1927 we played 23 games with 17 men. Nobody was newspaper conscious—we were the poor relations, being pro football players, having to fight for publicity. In fact, I traveled a day or two ahead of the team when we played away from home to visit newspaper offices for publicity."

Few records of any football contracts from the 1920s exist to use as references; "most agreements were by handshake," as Friedman noted, and professional football references were not officially kept until 1933.

TINY CAHOON

BORN: May 22, 1900, Baraboo, WI
DIED: February 3, 1973, San Francisco, CA
COLLEGES: Montana; Gonzaga
POSITION: Offensive tackle
NFL EXPERIENCE: 1926–29
TEAM: Green Bay Packers

Ivan "Tiny" Cahoon played college football at the University of Montana and at Gonzaga. Under head coach Gus Dorais at Gonzaga, he was part of the school's undefeated team in 1924. After graduating from Gonzaga in 1925, Cahoon taught and coached at Libby High School in western Montana for a year and returned to the mountains to honeymoon in 1926.

The 220-pounder played tackle for the Green Bay Packers from 1926 to 1929. Cahoon's rookie season was the Packers' seventh year in the National Football League. The team posted a 7-3-3 record under player-coach Curly Lambeau, earning them a fifth-place finish. The season marked the second year the Packers played at New City Stadium, renamed Lambeau Field in 1965. (The Green Bay Packers have played home games in eight separate stadiums since their inaugural year in 1919.)

Cahoon was placed on several All-Pro teams at tackle while with Green Bay. A knee injury ended his pro career after four seasons.

He coached high school football at Nicolet in West DePere in Wisconsin while a member of the Packers and later coached high school in Green Bay, college ball at Monmouth College in Illinois and the American Football

League's (AFL) Milwaukee Chiefs in 1940 and 1941. His AFL team won nineteen games, lost six and tied one in two seasons.

Cahoon entered the U.S. Army during World War II and coached football service teams. In 1951, he returned to Gonzaga University as an ROTC instructor. He died in San Francisco in 1973.

In an interview with the *Spokane Daily Chronicle* in 1953, he lamented "how they've streamlined football" with "two-platoon" products, which meant that there were now specialists for every job.

"Yep," he said. "Times are changing. I remember the time I played 18 straight games without relief. Finally I went out with a knee injury. Any way you look at it, and preferably from a seat on the midstripe, that's 1,080 minutes of battle without substitute help."

FRANCIS COPE

BORN: November 19, 1915, Anaconda, MT
DIED: October 8, 1990, San Jose, CA
COLLEGE: Santa Clara University
POSITION: Offensive tackle
NFL EXPERIENCE: 1938–47
TEAM: New York Giants

Francis Cope played college football at Santa Clara University. He was a tackle for the New York Giants from 1938 to 1947, earning Pro Bowl honors in 1938 and 1940 and first team All-Pro honors in 1945.

By the 1930s, a solid foundation had been put into place for the NFL to grow. The decade saw the league adopt major rule changes, divide into divisions and establish a championship game. The league also began to showcase the talents of its stars. The first Pro Bowl game was played in 1939.

Coverage of the NFL increased in newspapers across the country. The *Green Bay Press Gazette* helped recognize players' accomplishments by picking All-Pro teams in 1930 and 1931. Starting in 1932 and continuing through the early 1940s, the NFL's official All-Pro teams were picked annually by the coaches in the league.

Although his finest years came in the 1940s, this star lineman from the West Coast made an immediate impact with the Giants. His contributions as a rookie helped the Giants win the championship with a 23–17 win over the Green Bay Packers. By his second season, he was gaining attention as one of the NFL's best left tackles.

Left: Anaconda-born Francis Cope excelled at left offensive tackle for the New York Giants from 1938 to 1947, earning Pro Bowl honors in 1938 and 1940 and first team All-Pro honors in 1945. *Courtesy Pro Football Researchers Association.*

Below: Typical of the players of his era, Francis Cope (36) frequently played on both sides of the line of scrimmage. He was named to the NFL 1930s All-Decade Team. *Courtesy Pro Football Researchers Association.*

The bulk of Cope's career was spent at left tackle; he paved the way for running backs Merle Hapes and Bill Paschal. He was named to the NFL 1930s All-Decade Team. The Pro Football Hall of Fame's Selection Committee picked the All-Decade Team of the 1930s retroactively in 1969 in celebration of the league's first fifty seasons.

Don Stewart Cosner
Born: February 16, 1917, Malta, MT
Died: November 17, 2004, San Antonio, TX
College: Montana State
Position: Wide receiver
NFL Experience: 1939
Team: Chicago Cardinals

Born in Malta in 1917, Don Cosner attended Montana State University and played professional football for the Chicago Cardinals in 1939. That year, the Cardinals finished fifth in the West Division with a 1-10-0 record. They were coached by former fullback Ernie Nevers. According to NFL records, Cosner played in one game, with no other fine points available. According to his obituary in the *San Antonio Express News*, he retired with eighteen years of service in the U.S. Air Force.

Aldo Forte
Born: January 20, 1918, Chicago, IL
Died: August 29, 2007, Palm City, FL
College: Montana
Positions: Offensive guard; offensive tackle
NFL Experience: 1939–47
Teams: Chicago Bears (1939–41; 1946); Detroit Lions (1946); Green Bay Packers (1947)

Aldo Forte was born in Chicago and played on Fenger High School's famous 1934 team, known as the "Little Giants." Doug Fessenden was Fenger's head football coach from 1930 to 1934 before becoming head coach at the University of Montana in April 1935. Fessenden served two separate stints at Montana, from 1935 to 1941 and again from 1946 to 1948.

Aldo Forte and other stars from the "Little Giants" went with Fessenden to Montana, where most attained national collegiate fame.

Left: Born in Chicago, Aldo Forte graduated from the University of Montana and played as an offensive lineman in the NFL between 1939 and 1947. *Courtesy University of Montana.*

Opposite: Aldo Forte became an all-league guard twice (1940, 1941). In 1940, he was a member of the Bears team that astounded the football world by defeating the Washington Redskins for the championship, 73–0. *Courtesy University of Montana.*

Forte, who graduated with a bachelor of arts degree, was drafted by the Chicago Bears in the twenty-first round of the 1939 NFL draft. He became an all-league guard twice (1940, 1941) and was a member of the 1940 Bears team that astounded the football world by defeating the Washington Redskins for the world championship by a score of 73–0.

World War II intervened in Forte's career; he served four years in the navy in the Pacific theater and was awarded the Asiatic Pacific Medal with two stars, the Philippine Liberation Medal with two stars, the American Theater Ribbon and the World War II Victory Medal. After the war, he played with the Detroit Lions and Green Bay Packers, affirming his reputation as a tremendous blocker. His football ability carried over to his knack as a scout in spotting good football candidates for the Bears and Lions and as the Lions' coach in several capacities.

He started with the Lions in 1950 as an assistant coach and retired from the team in 1965. During this time, Detroit won three championship games, back to back in 1952 and 1953 and again in 1957.

On May 28, 1958, while serving as line coach for the Lions, Forte was honored in the Turf Penthouse at an informal gathering of former Montana State University football players of the 1938 era. One night earlier, he was the guest speaker at the annual Montana State University athletic awards dinner in Missoula.

The Detroit coach reviewed the previous football season (8-4, top spot in the West Division) and had words of praise for Lions quarterback Bobby Layne. "He is the best two-minute quarterback in football," Forte said. He explained that Layne is at his best in the last two minutes before the half and in the final two minutes of the game.

In an essay titled "Football and Its Progress," written by Forte in 1963, he detailed the changes in the game that he'd witnessed: "As in practically all other fields of activity, football has progressed to the point of specialization unknown or even anticipated in 1938. Even the shape and air pressure contained in the football is vastly different today, which is concurrent with the trend toward the forward pass."

While coaching in Detroit, he founded and oversaw a steel mill supply company in Michigan. After he retired from coaching, Forte moved to Florida, where he died in 2007.

EDWARD P. HIEMSTRA
BORN: March 8, 1920, Columbus, MT
DIED: August 28, 2012, in Bozeman, MT
COLLEGE: Sterling
POSITION: Offensive guard
NFL EXPERIENCE: 1942
TEAM: New York Giants

Ed Hiemstra was born to immigrant parents from Friesland, Netherlands. According to his obituary, "while just a small boy he developed a strong work ethic from his hard-working farming parents, which he carried throughout his life." The family of nine moved to a dairy farm in Nampa, Idaho, in 1929. Ed completed his schooling there, competing in football and track.

Sterling College in Kansas welcomed him to its athletic program, where he excelled in football, basketball, baseball and track. His performance in the Kansas all-star game led to a contract to play for the New York Giants in 1942. That team was captained by legendary Mel Hein, who played fifteen seasons for the Giants (1931–45) and never missed a single down due to injury. Starting at right tackle for the Giants that season was the Anaconda-born Francis Cope. Bill Edwards of Baylor was the team's starting right guard. The October 15, 1942 edition of the *Chicago Tribune* references Hiemstra, weighing in at a comparatively skeletal 180 pounds, as one of Edwards's possible replacements "from little Sterling College in Kansas."

According to several sources, Hiemstra was "a stellar rookie" who planned on a long career in pro ball, but Uncle Sam had different plans. He was drafted into the U.S. Army Air Corps in 1943, where he "directed physical training programs and coached the Troop Carrier football team in 1945."

After football and the military, Hiemstra coached football and track in Nampa, Idaho, before he moved to the mining town of Kellogg, Idaho, where he coached football, basketball and track along with teaching woodshop and U.S. history. He also worked as a logger, drove an ore truck for the mine and volunteered at the YMCA. In basketball at Kellogg, "his teams won five district, three regional and four state titles." His final years of coaching and teaching found him in Oregon, where, after thirty-nine years of service, he retired. In 2003, Hiemstra returned to "his beloved Montana," where he got married and lived out the remainder of his life. He died in Bozeman in 2012.

TED ILLMAN

BORN: November 27, 1900, Glasgow, MT
DIED: March 29, 1962, Missoula, MT
COLLEGE: Montana
POSITIONS: Fullback; defensive end
NFL EXPERIENCE: 1928
TEAMS: Chicago Cardinals; 1926 Los Angeles Wildcats (AFL)

Ted Illman played in five games for the Chicago Cardinals of the NFL in 1928. *Courtesy University of Montana.*

Ted Illman went to Glasgow and Deer Lodge High Schools and earned nine letters at the University of Montana (football, basketball and baseball). Nicknamed "Chief" because of his Sioux heritage, Illman excelled at football, basketball and baseball at UM. As captain of the Grizzlies, he was one of the most valuable defensive men on the squad. At 175 pounds, his weight and ability to punch the line put him in real fullback class. A 1924 press clipping refers to Illman as a "great fullback" and "one of the best the University has had."

In 1924, Illman scored five times in a 106–6 drubbing of School of Mines. He was captain of the team in 1925, a year in which Montana traveled 7,288 miles during the season, second only to Washington

State College. He was named to the Walter Scott all-state collegiate team as Montana joined the Pacific Coast Conference, where it would remain until 1950. In 1926, he played professionally for George Wilson's Wildcats, barnstorming the country playing against other professional traveling teams.

Illman played in five games for the Chicago Cardinals of the NFL in 1928. In 1920, the Cardinals had become a charter member of the American Professional Football Association, which morphed into the NFL in 1922 for a franchise fee of $100.

"WILD" BILL KELLY

BORN: June 24, 1905, Denver, CO
DIED: November 14, 1931, New York, NY
COLLEGE: Montana
POSITION: Back
NFL EXPERIENCE: 1927–30
TEAMS: New York Yankees (1927–28); Frankford Yellow Jackets (1929); Brooklyn Dodgers (1930)

William Carl "Wild Bill" Kelly was born in Denver on June 24, 1905. His father, James Kelly, a farmer and a liquor merchant, died at the age of thirty-eight of pneumonia. In 1909, his widow took four-year-old Bill to Butte, Montana, where she married Otis Johnson Price, a Northern Pacific Railroad worker. In 1916, Bill, his mother and stepfather lived at 738 North Fourth Street in Missoula, "a rough area on the north side," according to one newspaper description.

In 1921, he led Missoula High to its first state football championship and guided the basketball team to its first state title. He competed in track and field, played baseball and earned a reputation as a self-taught boxer.

Kelly enrolled at the University of Montana in September 1923. On December 8, Montana was allowed to become the ninth member of the Pacific Coast Conference, joining California, Washington, Stanford, the University of Southern California (USC), Idaho, Washington State, Oregon and Oregon Agricultural College (now Oregon State). Kelly scored 193 points in helping guide the freshman team to an undefeated season.

Official pro football records were not kept until 1933, thus, details of Kelly's professional career are murky. On October 14, 1927, his name appeared in the starting lineup for the New York Yankees, listed as a quarterback and credited with two touchdowns. The Yankees won over the

"Wild" Bill Kelly is the only Montana Grizzly player to be named to the College Football Hall of Fame. He played in the NFL from 1927 and 1930 and died at age twenty-six from alcohol poisoning. *Courtesy University of Montana.*

Buffalo Bisons, 19–8, at Buffalo. Kelly played in eleven games as a fullback, halfback and quarterback in 1927. One of his teammates was Harold "Red" Grange, nicknamed the "Galloping Ghost," who turned professional in 1925 and played ten years of pro football.

On November 9, 1927, Kelly's nickname of "Wild Bill" appeared in the sixth paragraph of a story that lacked basic game data, roster info or future schedules of either squad. According to the Pro Football Researchers Association archives, "with Kelly in the lineup the Yankees had a 7-3 mark at midseason. Suddenly, Kelly was sidelined for five games, most likely due to injury. The team lost every game he was absent."

Kelly, who was known to eat massive quantities of peanuts and candy bars, returned to Missoula for the winters of 1927 and 1928. He earned extra income from endorsements. One national advertisement for the cigarette brand Lucky Strikes reads, "After trying them all, I have decided on Luckies. They have never hurt my throat and they taste just right." The ad was signed, "W.C. Bill Kelly."

In 1928, Kelly again played for the New York Yankees. The Yankees lost their first six games but finished with a 4-8-1 record. Indicative of the era's roughness, the *New York Times* of December 3, 1928, reported, "The New York Giants were penalized five yards for kneeing Kelly."

In 1929, Kelly became a member of the Frankford Yellow Jackets, the forerunners of the Philadelphia Eagles. Ray Flaherty (1903–1994), a Gonzaga graduate who played with Kelly on the 1927 Yankees and later with the New York Giants from 1928 to 1935, recalled Kelly in a letter. Kelly liked Missoula while he attended Montana "but liked to party in Butte." Flaherty continued: "He was rugged, very confident of his ability and did not like anyone who would not give their best effort. He talked a great deal about Butte and the good times he had there when in college. He would bring alcohol from Butte by the gallon and serve it to his friends just for the fun of it."

Flaherty references a serious knee injury Kelly received in 1927 and his salary as approximately $3,500 for a season. "Kelly never had it operated on, and the cartilage bothered him. For that reason, Kelly never had the chance to show his real ability," wrote Flaherty.

Ed Halicki (1905–1986), one of Kelly's teammates on the 1929 Yellow Jackets, later recounted in the *New York Times*, "If Kelly were playing today, he would be one of the greatest. The game of today was made to order for him." George Wilson (1901–1963), halfback in the AFL and NFL in the 1920s, told *Collier's*: "He's the hardest man to tackle I ever met. He can dodge and turn and spin in amazing fashion. He's a real football player if one ever lived."

Kelly's final professional football game as far as available records indicate was December 15, 1930, with the Brooklyn Dodgers defeating the Memphis Tigers at Memphis, 13–0.

He died on November 14, 1931, among eighty thousand spectators at the New York University–Fordham football game in Yankee Stadium. The five-paragraph death notice in the November 15, 1931 *New York Times* mentions that he had "consumed a large amount of peanuts and frankfurters"; the cause of death was listed as "acute indigestion." A certificate of death from the Borough of Manhattan in New York City indicated the cause of death as "acute alcoholism and coronary sclerosis."

A correspondence in the Montana Historical Society archives written by former teammate Joseph Cochran to a writer researching Kelly and the genealogy of early American football players is particularly telling. "At first, I was not going to answer your letter because of what happened to Bill. He was a hero at Montana and perhaps that's the way he should be remembered. You'll have to decide what use you want to make of my letter about Bill. In Bill's tragic death there might be some message for the college society that basks in the glory of the football team and the individual heroes, but overlooks the fact that they are like the rest of us with conflicts, fears, frustrations, and weakness."

The inimitable Kelly, Montana's homegrown version of Jim Thorpe, is the only Griz player to be named to the College Football Hall of Fame.

JERRY KRAMER
BORN: January 23, 1936, Jordan, MT
COLLEGE: University of Idaho
POSITION: Offensive guard
NFL EXPERIENCE: 1958–68
TEAM: Green Bay Packers

Jerry Kramer is best known for playing with the Green Bay Packers when they won the first two Super Bowls, in 1967 and '68. The offensive lineman also played a big role in helping the Packers win seven world championships in the 1960s.

Any discussion of his career is also likely to include mention of the epic contests Kramer participated in, such as the "Ice Bowl" (1967 NFL

Jordan-born Jerry Kramer is best known for playing with the Green Bay Packers when they won the first two Super Bowls, in 1967 and 1968. *Courtesy Jerry Kramer.*

championship game), or his interactions with almost sanctified figures like Vince Lombardi.

Overlooked in the old game film and the glory of football lore are Kramer's origins in eastern Montana. He was born in Jordan, arguably one of the most isolated communities in the state (the nearest movie theater is in Miles City, more than eighty miles away). "My dad was not a college-educated guy, but a self-educated one," said Kramer, eighty, now living in Boise, Idaho. "My father was a strict German. He got to be quite a religious guy and studied his Bible. He just had a short temper and he got your attention pretty quick with the strap."

"We lived in the town of Jordan and we went through the Depression and my dad worked for the WPA [Works Progress Administration] and that pumped the money into the community and the economy."

Kramer is also related to a pair of memorable eastern Montana personalities. "There are two Hall of Famers in the Kramer family in Montana," he said. Bobby Brooks Kramer (1913–2005) was inducted into the Cowgirl Hall of Fame and Corwin "Bud" Kramer (1913–1979) was inducted into the Montana Cowboy Hall of Fame last year.

"Bobby Brooks and Bud were married and I remember Bud as a cowboy and me running along as Bud was on his high-riding pony. I remember trying to get alongside and Bud saying, 'You will ride on the pull of my boot, if you don't shut up and pull away!' Bud had a big ranch in Cohagen, a 150,000-acre ranch, that was half BLM [Bureau of Land Management] and half the Cohagen boys."

Kramer's family left Jordan when he was five, but he still remembers a series of little hills they called the "Toy Mountains"; even at the age of three or four, he would run up and down those hills with his siblings. He also recalled camping out and catching catfish on the Missouri River. There was some boyish mischief, too. "I set grandpa's house on fire after I discovered matches and tar paper and I lit it up," he said. "I remember I created a lot of havoc."

Then there was the time when, at the age of five, he "became quite smitten" with one of his cousins, a girl by the name of Donna.

> *I wanted to buy her something but I had no money and I went to the local garage to see if he had anything I could help out with. He was using horsehair stuffing. He told me about an old dead horse two miles down the road and he sent me to cut the hair off of it. That horse stunk. I walked out there and I cut the mane and the tail and stuffed it in a paper bag, hustled to the garage, and I made a nickel.*
>
> *I grabbed a brown sack at the drugstore, and bought candy, five or ten for a nickel, and planned on visiting Donna. I walked out of the drugstore, but Donna and her family were driving past me, heading to Roundup.*

After Jordan, Kramer said, he and his parents and five siblings spent about a year in Helena, where his father attended an electronics school. The family later moved to Utah and then to Sandpoint, Idaho. After his graduation from Sandpoint High School in 1954, Kramer was a standout player for the University of Idaho Vandals. The team later retired his uniform number (64).

He was drafted by the Packers in 1958. As a professional, his excellence was so enduring—and the team's victories so ritual—that he perhaps didn't always get the appreciation he deserved. He played on five Green Bay championship teams (1961, 1962, 1965, 1966 and 1967) and earned rings in the first two Super Bowls (1967 and 1968).

Kramer retired from football in 1968 and became involved in a wide variety of business endeavors, including projects in oil and gas exploration. He said he last traveled through eastern Montana around 2008, on the way to have a look at Williston, North Dakota, the center of the Bakken oil boom. "I've been involved with oil and gas several times," he said. "Everybody was doing good and it was an exciting time. We went from being out of energy and then past peak oil and now on the downhill slide, and one of the prolific producers in the world. My two sons, Matt and Jordan—he is named after Jordan, Montana—worked in the industry about ten years ago, and one is still involved."

Kramer talks freely about his career, recalling high moments and low, and he remains one of the most popular living Green Bay Packers. He recently spent a week at charity events throughout Wisconsin. One of Kramer's old teammates, Paul Hornung, a hall of fame running back with the Packers from 1957 to 1966, has sued Riddell, one of the leading makers of football helmets. Hornung asserted that the company knew of the dangers of brain trauma more than fifty years ago but failed to warn him and other players that their helmets would do nothing to prevent concussions.

"I'm not sure that anyone knew about the dangers back then and Paul has been having some difficulties lately," Kramer said.

> *He called me a few years ago and he said that he was having a hard time giving speeches and that he couldn't fulfill his obligations, and he asked me if I would, and I told him I'd check the calendar and try to fill in for him.*
>
> *It's a difficult thing to see. Paul would be at dinner and telling the same story three or four times and it was awkward and his faculties aren't what they once were. He was so bright—and he still is—and he's still fun. He's still getting around and doing all right.*

Another teammate was Willie Wood, a Packers cornerback from 1960 to 1971. Now seventy-nine, Wood suffers from dementia in an assisted living center and doesn't remember anything about his NFL career. The hall of famer, a victim of chronic traumatic encephalopathy, a degenerative brain disease, told the *Washington Post* in 2007 that he made less than $20,000 as a Packers rookie in 1960 and never made more than $98,000 in a year during a career that ended after the 1971 season. "Willie Wood was my roommate and one of my closest friends and it's terrible to see Wood the way he is," Kramer said.

> *The last time I saw him, I spent three to four hours with him in the afternoon and he didn't know who I was. He said, "Are you Jerry Kramer?" His girlfriend tried to alert him to the fact and he had a tough time believing that he had played himself. The toughest part of the journey is watching your teammates' disintegration.*

You are acutely aware of it. Doug Hart [Packers cornerback and safety, 1964–71] *is a friend and I got him to go to a Boys & Girls Club event recently. Over the last three, four years, he hasn't been able to be out by himself. But he can still golf, still shoot a shotgun, and he can still fish. But it's painful to talk about something he doesn't remember and he gets frustrated and stumbles along and it gets awkward. So, we stick to things like fishing together and giving each other a little crap about other things. Football? We don't go there.*

Kramer himself, despite the strain of approximately twenty-two major operations, moves about with vigor. "I exercise and try to eat fruit and be really more involved intellectually in the world and the things that are happening. I have a curiosity about things. I have had several stem cell injections and I chew that stuff up. I believe having the brain active burns up energy and calories and may burn up the substances that clog your mind when you have dementia problems."

Kramer doesn't dwell on his failure to be inducted into the Pro Football Hall of Fame, though his yearly omission invariably sparks lively discussion elsewhere. He was rated no. 1 in the NFL Network's list of top ten players not in the hall.

"I really enjoyed the game and it's been a wonderful ride," he said. "I had limited expectations coming from Sandpoint and I didn't really understand what was happening. I didn't know how to negotiate, or discuss what I might be worth. I didn't maximize that position. But the game still rewarded me with recognition and wonderful moments—far beyond anything I could have imagined as a youngster."

NICK LASSA

BORN: July 11, 1898, Flathead Valley, MT
DIED: September 4, 1964, Missoula, MT
COLLEGES: Haskell Indian Nations University, Carlisle Indian School
NFL EXPERIENCE: 1922–23
TEAM: Oorang Indians

Nick Lassa's life yields only clues.

He was Native American and from Montana. Perhaps he was a member of the Blackfoot tribe—"a Blackfoot from Montana," as one clipping read. Other sources propose that he was a Cherokee or a Flathead. "He's actually

Left: Nick Lassa and the Oorang Indians debuted their first NFL game, October 1, 1922, a contest with the Dayton Triangles at Triangle Park. *Courtesy Marion County Historical Society.*

Below: Montana native Nick Lassa, *seated, second from right, front row*, was a member of the Oorang Indians of the NFL in 1921 and 1922. *Courtesy Marion County Historical Society.*

the high and mighty one and only chief of the Flathead Indian tribe in Montana," reads the September 7, 1922 *Columbus Citizen.*

Lassa certainly attended and played college football at the Carlisle Indian School and Haskell Indian Nations University. He is said to have to been sent to Carlisle at the age of fourteen for his education and "during the war he served overseas with an Indian detachment." The *Fort Worth Star-Telegram* referenced Lassa in its news brief of the Haskell-Texas Christian game of 1921. "The Indians were supposed to get beat but the weather turned cold and Haskell got hot so the contest ended 14 to 0 in favor of the Redmen.... Lassa wore a derby downtown and played football with his hair tied in a topknot with a white cloth."

In 1921, the Haskell team won five out of nine games scheduled, with a team averaging "scarcely heavier than an ordinary high school aggregation." A newspaper clipping from November 1921 refers to Lassa as "a giant guard" and "a 206 pound guard performing" at a weight above the Haskell average, which was slightly above 166 pounds. He was removed from the lineup at the end of the season due to injury.

Lassa played as a guard in the National Football League in 1922 and 1923 with the Oorang Indians, an all–Native American team based in La Rue, Ohio. Formed by Walter Lingo, owner of Oorang Dog Kennels, in 1922 to help market and promote a breed of dog known as the Airedale, the Indians team was organized by Jim Thorpe, arguably the greatest all-around athlete the world has ever known.

Thorpe, star of the 1912 Olympics, served the team as a player-coach. Lingo hired Thorpe for $500 a week to coach his football team and run his large Airedale terrier business.

The team lived in La Rue at the Airedale kennel. Lingo bought the rights to his pro franchise for $100, "half the price of one of his trained Airedales," according to his own brochure. During his team's debut season, he "sold over 15,000 dogs."

Without a home field, the Indians were relegated to traveling, playing in major cities such as New York, Chicago, Philadelphia and Pittsburgh. The team entertained the idea of playing home games but nixed the thought "because the area was too rural." The Oorangs played football, baseball and basketball, each in its own season. In a March 5, 1920 Kansas newspaper, Lassa is referred to as "heavyweight wrestling champion at Haskell and a member of the R.O.T.C. team."

When the team formed, Lassa was purportedly the first player to arrive in La Rue. The *Lima News* described Lassa's unique arrival:

The squad mascot was a coyote, brought from Montana by Nick Lassa, nicknamed Long Time Sleep because he was so hard to rouse in the morning.

Besides practicing football the Indians are running these Airedales at night. When the Airedales start yipping, Jim Thorpe's hounds start howling, Lassa's coyote lends his voice and the bears used in training the Airedales start growling, the place sounds like a circus zoo. Folks who have the idea that an Indian is a savage, taciturn, individual, should watch these Indians at play.

Other nicknames on the squad included Wrinklemeat, Long Time Sleep, Laughing Gas, Xavier Downwind, Dick Deerslayer, Baptist Thunder, Joe Little Twig and Bear Behind the Woodchuck.

The Oorang Indians played their first NFL game on October 1, 1922, a contest with the Dayton Triangles at Triangle Park. According to newspaper reports, "tickets were $1.75 and over 5,000 spectators showed up." During intermission, Lassa and his teammates "would change into Indian garb and put on a show with the Airedales." Along with "chasing bears and treeing coons, the players threw tomahawks and shot rifles, did Indian dances and re-enacted World War I battle scenes that included Native American scouts and code talkers."

One of the NFL's original eighteen teams, including the Chicago Bears, the Green Bay Blues and five teams from Ohio, including the Dayton Triangles, the Oorang Indians squad lasted two seasons, 1922 (nine games) and 1923 (eleven games), of which Lassa played every game.

Aside from football, Lassa is said to have enjoyed wrestling, making "up to $50.00 for wrestling matches throughout the area." He wrestled a bear as part of a halftime show at one of the Indians' games. "Lassa would usually win between 10–20 dollars per match and that money would allow the whole team to go out partying all night," according to one account. "The chief, when the spirits have put him in the proper mood sometimes puts on the Tribal ghost dance or the Snake dance, according to the way the spirits have worked."

After the team folded in 1923, Lassa stayed near LaRue, earning his living as a professional wrestler and a circus strongman and working for Lingo and several other farmers. An Ohio newspaper from December 27, 1927, shows a photo of Lassa, "Chief Long Time Sleep" and Thorpe, as well as two members of the "World Famous Indians" basketball team in advance of their contest with the Isaly Dairies on the floor. "Chief Long Time is a Flathead. That is an Indian tribe and is spelled with a capital f. The chief is the last in a long line of medicine men, being the direct descendant of old Chief Ki-Ki-Che. The chief therefore should get class A rating in any list of first families."

Lassa is said to have left the area in the early 1930s. He reportedly "gave up drinking, raised a family, and became a respected member of his community."

Lassa died on September 4, 1964.

BILL LAZETICH

BORN: October 16, 1916, Anaconda, MT
DIED: November 18, 2009
COLLEGE: Montana
POSITIONS: Wide receiver; defensive back
NFL EXPERIENCE: 1939; 1942
TEAM: Cleveland Rams

Brothers Bill and Milan Lazetich were standouts at Anaconda High School in the late 1930s and early 1940s. Bill went on to play at Montana and had a short pro football career with the Cleveland Rams before joining the military during World War II. He was chosen in the sixteenth round of the 1939 NFL draft by the Detroit Lions. It would be decades before another UM player would land a place on an NFL roster, when Mike Tilleman did it in 1965. But it wasn't for lack of attempts, as many Grizzlies were drafted in the interim yet couldn't obtain a position in the league: Tom Kingsford, Bob Hanson and Ray Bauer (1951); Jim Murray and Hal Maus (1953); Don Brant (1956); Terry Hurley (1957); and John Gregor (1961).

"Dad was embarrassed one time by a Columbus newspaper," recalled Pete Lazetich, Bill's son.

Cleveland had sent him from Cleveland to the semi-professional Columbus Bullies [professional football team in Columbus, Ohio, from 1939 to 1941. The Bullies originally played in the American Professional Football League but joined the American Football League in 1940]. *For the article, they stated his name was "Wild" Bill Lazetich. He was put him on a horse in his football uniform and game pants, with no saddle, and they took a photo of him. He was in full uniform, bareback, with horse rearing up. The story went on and on about "Wild" Bill coming in from Montana and how he rode his horse to the*

Brothers Bill and Milan Lazetich were standouts at Anaconda High School in the late 1930s and early 1940s. Bill went on to play at Montana and had a short pro football career with the Cleveland Rams before joining the military during World War II. *Courtesy University of Montana.*

train station, got off, slapped the horse on the rear knowing that the horse would run right back to Montana. Dad had this frightened look on his face, and for years my mom would threaten to pull it [the photo] *out.*

Bill Lazetich had a memorable pair of encounters with Green Bay Packers legend Don Hutson. Perhaps no player dominated in the NFL like Hutson did during his eleven-year career. He was the league's first player to rack up large receiving stats. He retired holding eighteen different NFL records, including an incredible 488 catches and ninety-nine touchdowns.

"The Cleveland Rams had played against Don Hutson, and the first time they played," said Pete, "Hutson didn't score, and before the next game, there was an article in the newspaper, and the article was about this big rookie from Montana [Bill Lazetich] who shut out the great Don Hutson. Well, Hutson and the team must have read that article coming into the

Green Bay game, because Hutson burned him for four touchdowns in the first half."

During World War II, Bill, a tough boxer who always had a speed bag and jump ropes at the family ranch, served in the Pacific and saw extensive action with the highly decorated First Marine Raider Battalion. He rose to the rank of captain and was awarded the Purple Heart for wounds suffered in Okinawa. After recovering, he rejoined his troops and on August 30, 1945, became one of the first Americans to land in and occupy defeated Japan. Lazetich coached a Guadalcanal team of Marines that played two games in December 1944.

"He never spoke about it at all [the devastation of the war]," said Pete. "He said that after the invasion he was met by thousands of Japanese, all around him, bowing politely. He had a big Samurai sword in the basement he'd taken off a Japanese solder. He hated guns. We didn't even a have a bb gun in the house."

Bill Lazetich then coached football and basketball at Billings Senior High School, winning three state titles. He died at age ninety-three in 2009. "I was blessed that my dad was coach of football, basketball and track for forty years," said Pete Lazetich. "He was the only levelheaded guy in the family. He was always calm and proper and he wasn't goofy like the rest of us and he always had a coat and shirt and a white tie on. There were no theatrics with him to get his point across and he wasn't a screamer."

Bill, brother Milan and son Pete Lazetich were among a group of thirteen persons inducted into the inaugural Montana Football Hall of Fame at the Billings Hotel and Convention Center in the summer of 2016.

"I think it's great that they're bringing in some of the old-timers like my dad and my uncle," said Pete Lazetich. "They're the guys I looked up to."

MIKE "MILAN" LAZETICH
BORN: August 27, 1921, Anaconda, MT
DIED: July 9, 1969, Butte, MT
COLLEGES: Montana; Michigan
POSITIONS: Defensive guard; linebacker
NFL EXPERIENCE: 1945–50
TEAM: Cleveland Rams

Mike "Milan" Lazetich played one year at Montana before enlisting for World War II. When he came back, he served as a deputy sheriff in Deer

Milan Lazetich (*third from left of center*) played one year at Montana before enlisting for World War II. When he came back, he served as a deputy sheriff in Deer Lodge. *Courtesy Milana Lazetich.*

Milan Lazetich (27) was a member of the 1946 Cleveland Rams. *Courtesy Milana Lazetich.*

Milan Lazetich (77) finished his collegiate career at the University of Michigan before turning professional, playing for the Cleveland Rams. *Courtesy Milana Lazetich.*

Lodge. From there, he went on to finish his collegiate career at the University of Michigan before turning professional, playing for the Cleveland Rams.

"Pound for pound there was no one as tough as my uncle," said nephew Pete Lazetich.

> *He packed ninety years of living in forty-seven. One time a horse bit him in the back and he wheeled around with a quick forearm shot and dropped him, just like the character Mongo from the movie Blazing Saddles. He was All-Pro three teams and he was drafted number sixteen overall in* [round two of] *the 1945 draft. The guy drafted before him* [by the Cleveland Rams] *was the fifth overall,* [legendary wide receiver] *Elroy "Crazylegs" Hirsch. Milan was the best football player of the Lazetich family. He was a man's man.*
>
> *When* [St. Louis owner] *Daniel Reeves had his all-time Ram team, Milan was on it. The owner used to have parties and at a party for the last part owner of the Rams, Milan saw that there was a huge cake on the table and he kicked the cake into the coffin corner. Milan knew Frankie Yankovic* [America's polka king, father of "Weird Al"] *and the Yanks, and people came from all over the place to see them. The Rams were one of the first big sports teams to move out to California, and Milan was friends with Bob Waterfield and Jane Russell and all the movie stars.*

Rams quarterback Bob Waterfield was a budding star, as was his girlfriend, actress Jane Russell. The two eloped to Las Vegas in 1943 and were married for twenty-five years. Waterfield was the NFL's most valuable player as a rookie in 1945, and by then, Russell was a sensation at the box office and a popular magazine pinup girl. "Jane Russell came up to Montana and Milan and Bob and her went hunting, and the cars in Anaconda lined up for miles to see her. [Chicago Bears owner] George Halas had such respect for Milan for being a tough guy, and Halas gave him five hundred dollars and a train ticket back to Montana when he cut him [Milan tried out with the Bears in 1952], and Halas was notoriously cheap, and Halas giving him five hundred would be like giving someone five hundred million. Milan was shot [as a football player] when he got there to Chicago."

Milan regaled his nephew Pete with a number of stories of his encounters and exploits in the National Football League, many of which Pete recalls with eager alacrity. Pro football was much more vicious in the 1940s, a gang fight in shoulder pads, devoid of the high-tech veneer its violence has taken on today.

Pete said, "Milan told me about a run-in he had with Clyde 'Bulldog' Turner," a multi-position starter on the Bears from 1940 to 1952.

> *Turner had knocked Milan down at the goal line and Turner was standing over him and I think Milan coined the phrase "birdcage," because he responded by making fun of Turner's facemask, calling it a birdcage. Turner was gloating, standing over him at the goal line. I think you were allowed to wear a cage if you had a broken nose—and maybe Turner did. Milan said something like, "You don't see me wearing a birdcage!" Turner was incensed and the two got into a big fight during the game. After the game, the monstrous Turner, he was out there waiting by the bus for Milan. I asked Uncle Milan what happened next. He laughed and said, "What'd you think I'd do? I stayed in the locker room!"*

"Milan was tough, but smart," continued Pete. "His nose was broken so many times he could hardly breathe. Back then there were less guns and more fists. He was a beauty, and he had the tough guy look, with one eye shut and his face drooping."

"The guy who Milan most resembled physically was boxer Sonny Liston," recalled Ed Cummings, who was born in Anaconda and played professional football in the 1960s. "He was powerfully built with long strong arms. If Sonny had been white, the two could've passed for brothers. They had the same deep, threatening look. Milan was a tough, brutal man. When he came to town on a Saturday night in Anaconda, all of the bad guys left town. He'd fight two guys or three guys at once. He was my original basis for wanting to play pro football."

At times fun loving and family oriented, Milan knew how to throw and enjoy a party. One of his favorite pastimes was picking up a guitar and crooning impromptu country-style songs. Younger brother Eli was serious about music and didn't want to miss a note, but Milan was a showman.

Milan Lazetich died at age forty-seven in 1969.

"When Milan was playing for the Rams, he had a ruptured artery of some sort," said Pete Lazetich.

> *He had an operation and they sewed him back up. Ultimately, he had an aneurism of some sort but played the next season. He had the fever when he was young. When he was one year old, it blinded him in some way and he couldn't hear out of one ear well because of it. He snuck in to the service and once they realized he couldn't see then they released him. He had*

that old tough guy look, with one eye closed. His forty-seven years—liquor, booze, and partying—he hit it hard.

"He played in the days before face-masks, and leather helmets, and hardly any padding at all," said Milana Lazetich of her father, who died when she was six. "He had broken his nose about thirteen or fourteen times, and when I was a kid, I used to sit on his lap, and you could kind of twang it back and forth."

The memory of Milan Lazetich—"a schoolboy celebrity in Anaconda of Serbian descent," as he was once referred to by the *Butte Standard*—has forever been perpetuated for "fellow Montana Serbian boys with athletic ability." In the 1970s, the Serbian Fraternity of Anaconda renamed the center in the Serbian Church Home the Milan Lazetich Serbian Church Memorial Shrine.

VICTOR LINDSKOG
BORN: December 3, 1914, Roundup, MT
DIED: February 28, 2003, Fort Worth, TX
POSITION: Offensive center
COLLEGE: Stanford
NFL EXPERIENCE: 1944–51
TEAM: Philadelphia Eagles

Victor L. Lindskog, born in Roundup, moved to Cut Bank in 1938, where he met and married Doris Fee. During this time, he worked in the oil fields in the Hi-Line area. Lindskog chose a career in football, but he almost chose a career in professional boxing.

He became involved with American League amateur boxing. Ken Pardue, a local oilman, sponsored him to go to Santa Anna, California, to box under George Blake, a noted trainer in Los Angeles. Blake felt that Lindskog had the strength and stamina to develop into a heavyweight contender. "It came down to a matter of preference," said Lindskog to the *Philadelphia Herald* in 1967, "and I preferred football."

Lindskog had never played football before he showed up on the Santa Ana College campus in the fall of 1938, a refugee from the little town of Cut Bank, which had a district high school but no athletic teams. The only thing in the way of sports that Vic had ever done well was box; he was a swift, hard-hitting heavyweight with an AAU (Amateur Athletic Union) tournament background.

Roundup native Victor Lindskog, who played from 1944 to 1951 with the Philadelphia Eagles, was once referred to as "the best center in professional football." *Courtesy Pro Football Researchers Association.*

So unfamiliar with football was Lindskog that he had to be shown how to get into his uniform and told the rules and codes of the game. He was discovered after he caught the eye of a visiting Stanford Cardinal coach.

One assistant coach told the *Stanford Daily* that Lindskog distributed punishment equally to foe and teammate: "He hasn't any finesse but, man alive, I had to get him out of our defensive platoon. He was murdering the regulars. Every guy he tackled was shook up like he had been hit by Bronko Nagurski. Vic was decimating our ranks."

Soon, Lindskog found his niche as a blocking center while at Stanford. A little older than most of his teammates, Lindskog was married; he and his wife "never had it easy while I pursued my studies," Lindskog later said. He went to class in the mornings while his wife tended to their baby. At noon, Vic went home to look after Sonny while Doris worked in a store downtown the rest of the day. That continued until he graduated.

Lindskog centered the undefeated Stanford Rose Bowl team of 1940 and again in 1941. After beating Nebraska in the Rose Bowl in 1941, Vic stayed at Stanford as assistant coach in boxing and football.

He worked in the shipyards in San Francisco at night during World War II until he joined the Philadelphia Eagles in 1942. Thereafter he became "the best center in professional football," according to UPI. He played center and linebacker until 1947, at which time he was moved solely to center. He intercepted four passes and returned one 65 yards for a touchdown in 1944.

He was the starting center when the Eagles won world championships in 1948 and 1949. "Vic has a lot of power," halfback Bosh Pritchard once said. "He is not the biggest guy, but he knows how to deliver a blow. I can see where he must have been a pretty tough man in the ring."

Coach Earle "Greasy" Neale, according to the Philadelphia Eagles media guide, considered Lindskog "the greatest offensive center ever to play pro football." In 1949, when the Eagles drafted Chuck Bednarik from Penn, Neale put the rookie together with Lindskog on the practice field. The coach told Bednarik, "Here is the fellow who will teach you more about playing center than you ever dreamed was possible." Lindskog, always contemplating retirement, told the rookie, "I'll give it to you as fast as you can absorb it. You, Charlie, are my 'out' of pro football."

Neale once told a Philadelphia newspaper that it irritated him that Lindskog was named All-Pro only once (1951), while Clyde "Bulldog" Turner of Chicago was an All-Pro six times. "If Turner is considered the leading center, it must be due to his defensive ability. He can't hold a candle to Lindskog on the offense. He's the only center I've ever seen who can block the halfback out of bounds on an end run."

When he retired in 1952, Lindskog became an assistant coach with the Eagles, where he stayed until 1954. He became a head coach for the BC Lions of the CFL and finished his master's degree at Stanford in physical education with a minor in history.

He subsequently worked for the Los Angeles Rams as line coach under Bob Waterfield and became a scout in the NFL for Quadra, a consortium for which he scouted college football players for four NFL teams. While working there, Lindskog moved to the Dallas–Fort Worth area and scouted 127 schools in Texas and Oklahoma. When Quadra failed, he scouted specifically for the Seattle Seahawks (1977–79). From the Seahawks, he went to scout for the San Francisco 49ers, still living in the Dallas area. While there (1979–85), he was awarded Super Bowl rings in 1981 and 1984.

Lindskog retired from the NFL in 1985 and died in 2003.

JACK MCAULIFFE
BORN: May 21, 1901, Butte, MT
DIED: December 17, 1971, Butte, MT
COLLEGE: Montana; Beloit
POSITION: Halfback
NFL EXPERIENCE: 1926
TEAM: Green Bay Packers

A halfback on the Green Bay Packers in 1926, Butte native Jack McAuliffe was a member of Beloit's class of 1924. He was a true triple threat on the gridiron: expert at running, passing and punting. During his three football years at Beloit, McAuliffe was given all-state and all-conference honors.

He was center on Beloit basketball teams that won three successive state and Midwest Conference titles, compiling a 39-2 mark in three years.

The teams were undefeated in 1921–22 and 1923–34. On the track team, McAuliffe was a hurdler, pole-vaulter and member of the relay teams. Beloit track teams during that period won three state championships and two conference crowns as well as two state relay titles. He raised the state pole-vault record to eleven feet, nine inches in 1922 and to twelve feet, one inch in 1923.

McAuliffe is credited with playing in eight games for the 1926 Green Bay Packers, a squad coached by Curly Lambeau. The team ended the season at 7-3-3. The Packers were founded on August 11, 1919, by Lambeau and George Whitney Calhoun. In 1921, the team was granted membership in the new National Football League. The squad that McAuliffe played on was a part of the American Football League (AFL), a competitor to the NFL founded in the 1926 season and disbanded thereafter.

LAURIE NIEMI

BORN: March 19, 1925, Red Lodge, MT
DIED: February 19, 1968, Spokane, WA
COLLEGE: Washington State
POSITIONS: Offensive tackle; defensive tackle
NFL EXPERIENCE: 1949–53
TEAM: Washington Redskins

Red Lodge native Laurie Niemi was one of the all-time greats of Washington State Cougar football as a player and coach. He was named to the International News Service All-America team as a tackle in 1948 following

Red Lodge native Laurie Niemi was one of the all-time Washington State Cougar football greats as a player and coach. He played several seasons with the Washington Redskins. *Courtesy Pro Football Researchers Association.*

LAURIE NIEMI
WASHINGTON REDSKINS

his three-year playing career. He also won the coveted J. Fred Bohler Award for inspirational play his final year. He played five years in the NFL with the Washington Redskins, including two Pro Bowls, and later returned as an assistant Cougar coach.

In his rookie season with the Redskins in 1949, he began with a promising team trying to improve on its 7-5 record from 1948. Quarterbacked by thirty-five-year-old Sammy Baugh, the Redskins struggled at 4-7-1. The 1950 Redskins fared worse (3-9), and the records of subsequent teams weren't much better: 1951 (5-7), 1952 (4-8) and 1953 (6-5-1). Niemi was one of the Redskins' bright spots, earning Pro Bowl nods in 1951 and 1952.

In 1953, he was one of twelve players to return a fumble for a defensive touchdown, sharing company with players such as Dick "Night Train" Lane.

Niemi died in a Spokane hospital after undergoing surgery. He had been battling cancer for twelve years. Former teammates, friends, players and the 1966 WSU football team were among those at the services. He was forty-two.

According to NFL records, he is one of only two players named Laurie ever to suit up in the league. The other, Laurie Walquist, was a running back for the Chicago Bears from 1922 to 1931.

LEONARD NOYES
BORN: July 12, 1914, Butte, MT
DIED: December 24, 1985, Winston-Salem, NC
COLLEGE: Montana
POSITION: Offensive guard
NFL EXPERIENCE: 1938
TEAM: Brooklyn Dodgers

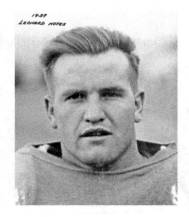

Noyes played five games in 1938 with the Brooklyn Dodgers, who played their home games at Ebbets Field. *Courtesy University of Montana.*

Leonard William Noyes, born in Butte in 1914, attended the University of Montana, where he excelled as an offensive guard, opening holes on the ground for speedy halfback Milt Popovich. A photo in the sports section of the October 30, 1937 *Montana Standard* depicts Noyes and several other teammates, including future NFL halfback and captain Milt Popovich and Anaconda-born fullback Bill Lazetich: "Mining and Smelter City Stars for Montana U." Noyes

52

Leonard Noyes was born on July 12, 1914, in Butte and went to college at the University of Montana, where he excelled as an offensive guard. *Courtesy University of Montana.*

was a standout on the 1937 team that outscored its opponents 111–28 on the way to a 6-1 record; a loss to Idaho kept the team from a Cotton Bowl bid. Noyes was an example of the lineman that typified the Doug Fessenden–coached squads, a solid compliment to a good backfield.

The 1938 National Football League draft was held on December 12, 1937, at the Hotel Sherman in Chicago. The draft consisted of twelve rounds and 110 player selections. It began with the Cleveland Rams selecting Corbett Davis. The Brooklyn Dodgers chose the six foot, 214-pound Noyes in round eight, sixty-third overall. Fellow Montana standout Popovich was scooped up by the Chicago Cardinals in the second round, fifteenth overall.

Close friend and teammate Aldo Forte, who was drafted by the Chicago Bears the following year, once related this story about Leondard Noyes. "Leonard and three all-Americans were trying to make the Brooklyn team. Four teeth and two All-Americans later, the Montana lineman had made the Brooklyn team," Forte told Harvey Munford in 1964.

Noyes played five games in 1938 with the Brooklyn Dodgers, who played their home games at Ebbets Field. Under coach Potsy Clark, the Dodgers finished third in the East Division that season at 4-4-3. After his football career, Noyes operated a service station in Billings. He died on December 24, 1985, in Winston-Salem, North Carolina, age seventy-one.

EARLE "PRUNEY" PARSONS
BIRTH: September 16, 1921, Helena, MT
COLLEGE: USC
POSITION: Running back
NFL EXPERIENCE: 1946–47
TEAM: San Francisco 49ers

Earle Parsons played three sports and earned all-state honors in football and basketball as well as being the high-point performer at the state track meet in both his junior and senior seasons for Helena High School. In football, he was named all-state in 1939 and 1940, the same two years he won all-state honors in basketball. Parsons was the state meet's top scorer as a senior.

Parsons went on to play football for Santa Ana Junior College in California for two seasons. He then transferred to the University of Southern California, where he helped the Trojans to victory in the 1944 Rose Bowl.

Parsons was drafted by the Philadelphia Eagles, played for the Los Angeles Bulldogs (an American Football League team competing from 1936 to 1948) and then played two seasons for the San Francisco 49ers.

After five years of petitioning the NFL for a franchise, trucking executive Tony Morabito spent $25,000, and the San Francisco 49ers were designated a charter member of the All-America Football Conference. The 49ers played their first game on August 31, 1946, against the Chicago Rockets. About forty thousand fans watched the 49ers claim a 34–14 victory at Kezar Stadium. After playing middling football most of the season, the 49ers ended their first season with three straight wins to post a solid 9-5 record. In the team's inaugural season, Parsons played in ten games and rushed for 362 yards, the team's third-highest amount.

In 1947, he gained 125 yards on the ground in eleven games in addition to 163 receiving yards. He is listed in NFL records as having started a pair of games his first season and none in his second.

He is a member of the Helena Sports Hall of Fame.

FROSTY PETERS

BORN: April 22, 1904, Creston, IA
DIED: April 17, 1980, Decatur, IL
COLLEGES: Montana State; Illinois
POSITION: Running back
NFL Experience: 1930–32
TEAMS: Providence Steam Roller (1930); Portsmouth Spartans (1930); Brooklyn Dodgers (1931); Chicago Cardinals (1932); Memphis Tigers (1932–34) (AFL)

Son of a railroader, Frosty Peters graduated from Billings High School in 1923. In 1924, he began college at Montana State. Peters gained national repute by converting seventeen of twenty-five dropkicks for the MSU freshmen in a November 1, 1924 game against Billings Polytechnic Institute (now Rocky Mountain College).

Peters's prowess—"a world record," according to the *Chicago Tribune*—propelled the Bobcats to a 64–0 win. The Bobcats helped him set up his dropkicks by falling short of the goal line instead of scoring. Montana State athletic director Schubert Dyche said, "We agreed that every time we got inside the 30-yard line. Frosty would drop kick one."

He brought that accurate toe along to play for the University of Illinois in 1925, where, as a freshman, he was heralded by some as a potential successor to Red Grange. Referred to as "Second Red Grange," Peters lettered in football for the Illini in 1926, 1928 and 1929. He also made fifteen dropkicks in another game.

Peters played for the Providence Steam Roller and Portsmouth Spartans of the NFL in 1930. He then played for the Brooklyn Dodgers in 1931 and the Chicago Cardinals in 1932. He played for the Memphis Tigers of the American Football League from 1932 to 1934, serving as player-coach (1933–34). He was later a player-coach with the St. Louis Gunners and spent time playing professional baseball in the 1930s.

To provide a perspective of how respected—or, perhaps, disrespected—pro football was as a profession in the late 1920s and early '30s, Bernard Crowl, a former teammate of Peters's on the 1931 Brooklyn Dodgers, told a newspaper: "I did not dare tell any future employer that I had played professional football. It then had a reputation for having largely players who never intended to do anything beyond just play football, and that's putting it mildly."

Peters was a sergeant during World War II and spent time instructing trainees at an army air force technical training command detachment at the University of Michigan. While working as an umpire, he was assaulted by a double-A manager in 1946. Peters then resigned, stating, "when an umpire gets socked and they fine the guy only $100 and five days, it's an open invitation for everybody in the league to start punching you around."

RUSSELL HAROLD PETERSON
BORN: August 25, 1905, Midale, Saskatchewan
DIED: October 10, 1971, Cascade County, MI
COLLEGE: Montana
POSITION: Tailback
NFL EXPERIENCE: 1932
TEAM: Boston Braves

Born in Canada and raised in Miles City, Russell Peterson attended Custer County High School. He played football at the University of Montana and, later, in the National Football League for the Boston Braves.

Peterson was second team all-league tackle from Miles City in 1929. He played from 1928 to 1930, when the Grizzlies were playing in the Pacific Coast Conference.

At age twenty-seven, he played as a lineman for the Boston Braves. On October 2, 1932, the Braves played their first game, against the Brooklyn Dodgers, at Braves Field, a baseball park on Commonwealth Avenue at Babcock Street in Boston (now the site of Boston University's Nickerson Field). The Braves lost the contest, 14–0, and ended their inaugural season with a record of 4-4-2, fourth place in the National Football League. Peterson is credited with playing in three games.

In 1933, the Boston franchise dropped the name "Braves" and began using the name "Redskins." In 1936, the East Division Redskins hosted the West Division Green Bay Packers. The game was moved by owner George Preston Marshall from Fenway Park in Boston to the Polo Grounds in New York City to boost attendance. The Packers won the title game, 21–6. Despite the glory of his team's first winning season, days after the title game, Marshall announced that the Redskins would be relocating to his hometown of Washington, D.C., for the 1937 season.

MILT POPOVICH

BORN: December 28, 1915, Butte, MT
DIED: June 23, 2005, Butte, MT
COLLEGE: University of Montana
POSITION: Halfback
NFL EXPERIENCE: 1938–42
TEAM: Chicago Cardinals

Milt Popovich was born on December 28, 1915, in Butte, the son of Joko and Josephine Popovich. Milt was the youngest of eight children born into the Popovich family. He was one of only three Popovich children to live past the early teen years.

Milt attended local schools on the east side, including the Grant and Washington schools. "Popo" was a prominent athlete at Butte High School, competing in football, basketball and track. He played on the 1932 and 1933 state championship basketball teams at Butte High School. He also was on the 1933 track team when it took the state crown. Milt scored twelve points at that state meet, the most of any athlete competing.

It was in football, however, that Milton, known also as the "Butte Bullet," made his name. He returned the opening kickoff and ran 89 yards for a touchdown in the 1933 city title game against Butte Central. It was the first time such a feat was achieved in the long, bitter rivalry between the schools. Popo was named first team all-state the following season.

After graduating from Butte High in 1934, he took his talents to the University of Montana, where he was a star running back for the Grizzlies. In the 1935 season opener at the Los Angeles Coliseum, the mighty University of California Trojans suited up three full squads, compared to the Grizzlies' fourteen total players. Popovich scored two touchdowns, but both were nullified by penalties. The Trojans won, 9–0.

Popovich ran two punt returns back for scores in a win over Montana State in the annual Bobcat-Grizzly game, played in Butte in 1936. His 102-yard kickoff return against Oregon State is a Grizzly record. He led the Grizzlies to a 7-1 record in 1937 and was named an All-American. Popovich played in the 1937 East-West Shrine football game and the College All-Stars vs. Washington Redskins game in Chicago the following fall.

He then played seven years with the Chicago Cardinals (currently the Arizona Cardinals) of the National Football League. According to NFL records (not always reliable when referencing its early decades), Popovich

Milt Popovich in 1937

Courtesy of UM athletics

After graduating from Butte High School in 1934, Milton Popovich took his talents to the University of Montana, where he was a star running back for the Grizzlies and later for the Chicago Cardinals of the NFL. *Courtesy University of Montana.*

ran for 233 yards on seventy-eight carries in his career. He finished his career as a player-coach for the Seattle Bombers.

After football, Milt devoted his working life to the service of Butte as a fireman and Silver Bow County commissioner. According to one obituary, as a firefighter for twenty-seven years, Milt "fought all the big fires that charred Uptown Butte including, the Butte Hotel fire, Currie Tire, Al's Photo Shop, J.C. Penney and the Medical Arts Building." He retired from the department in 1973.

He maintained his interest in football by serving as an assistant coach for the 1948 Class A state champion Butte Central Maroons and the 1951–52 Butte Buzzies.

Popovich was one of the original members selected for the Butte Sports Hall of Fame in 1987. In 1993, he was inducted into the University of Montana Grizzly Sports Hall of Fame. In 2000, he was chosen by *Sports Illustrated* as one of the fifty "Greatest Sports Figures of the Century" from each of the fifty states.

HERM SAWYER

BORN: October 18, 1898, Missoula, MT
DIED: September 1968, New York, NY
COLLEGE: Syracuse University
POSITION: Offensive back
NFL EXPERIENCE: 1922
TEAM: Rochester Jeffersons

Herm Sawyer played football at Syracuse University in 1919 and in the NFL in 1922. Sawyer played as a back at Syracuse in 1919. That season, the Orangemen had a record of 8-3 and outscored their opponents 123–47. After graduating, Sawyer played in the NFL with the Rochester (New York) Jeffersons.

In 1922, he appeared as a wingback and blocking back in three games for Rochester, which had a record of 0-3-1 and finished in fifteenth place in the league's third season. Program guides list Sawyer at five feet, eight inches and 170 pounds. The Jeffersons were coached by Sawyer's former teammate at Syracuse, offensive lineman Joe Alexander. The team finished 0-4-1.

The Rochester Jeffersons played from 1898 to 1925, including a stint in the NFL (1920–25). While several variations and splinter groups of organized football have existed since the 1890s, the NFL recognizes August 20, 1920, and Canton, Ohio, as the date and location of its origins.

Rochester would play four games in 1923, losing every game and scoring just 6 points while allowing 141. In 2014, the Chicago Bears joined the Jeffersons as the only teams in NFL history to allow fifty points in back-to-back games.

KEN SNELLING

BORN: December 11, 1918, Musselshell, MT
DIED: September 17, 1994, Ruch, OR
COLLEGE: UCLA
POSITIONS: Fullback; linebacker
NFL EXPERIENCE: 1945
TEAM: Green Bay Packers

A Musselshell native, Ken Snelling played high school football in Ruch, Oregon, and attended college at UCLA. He lettered as a fullback in 1941 and 1942. He was the school's leading scorer in 1942 and among four players to lead the team in scoring in 1941. Snelling was part of UCLA's first football victory over USC.

In 1942, the Bruins, led by Bob Waterfield, beat USC for the first time in nine tries, 14–7. Waterfield completed only two of six passes in the game, but one went for a 42-yard touchdown to Baldwin. That play and a touchdown run by Snelling built a 14–0 UCLA lead. The defense did the rest.

Snelling was picked in the eighth round (fifty-eighth overall) in the 1943 NFL draft by the Green Bay Packers. He was a member of the 1945 Packers, coached by Curly Lambeau. That team finished 6-4, good for third place in the West Division.

STEPHEN SULLIVAN
BORN: July 1, 1897, Butte, MT
DIED: August 17, 1969, Concord, CA
COLLEGE: Montana
POSITION: Tailback
NFL EXPERIENCE: 1922–24
TEAMS: Milwaukee Badgers (1922); Hammond Pros (1922); Evansville Crimson Giants (1922–23; 1924); Kansas City Blues (1924)

At six months of age, Stephen Sullivan lost his father. From his youngest days, he was the breadwinner supporting his widowed mother. He started his athletic career with Butte High in 1914, playing center in 1914 and in the backfield in 1915 and 1916, years in which he captured all-state honors. In 1915, the Purple and White squad was the Intermountain Conference champion after a remarkable season that was topped off with a 7–0 victory over West Side High School of Salt Lake City. Sullivan was a halfback on that team, which included such scholastic stars as Harry "Swede" Dahlberg.

Sullivan played with the University of Montana in 1917, 1919, 1920 and 1921 as halfback. He was a member of the only Montana team to defeat the University of Washington. In 1920, Montana played the Washington Huskies in Seattle. It was considered a practice game for the Huskies. The stadium was decorated with a large banner derisively announcing that it was, according to the *Missoulian*, "the last practice game of the season." Sullivan had a horrendous first quarter and was benched. Washington was ahead throughout the game until the last half, when the Grizzles moved out in front and stayed there. According to one newspaper account, "Mr.

One the earliest Grizzlies to make it to the NFL, Stephen Sullivan played on three separate teams over the course of the 1922 season. *Courtesy University of Montana.*

Mad Sullivan was responsible. He was in every play. He piled up yardage; he blocked, tackled, ran interference and acted as a spark plug." Montana won, 18–14, and "rocked the football world that day when the final score was posted and printed."

The captain of the 1921 team was a mainstay of the Grizzly backfield for four seasons. "Fast, aggressive, and possessing an indomitable fighting spirit, Steve was a reliable ground-gainer on offense and a veritable wall on the second line of defense," wrote the *Sentinel* newspaper. He was selected on the All-State and All–Northwestern Conference Elevens and was given All-American mention by Walter Camp, a player, coach and sportswriter who created football's line of scrimmage and system of downs.

By 1923, sports had entered a "Golden Era." Bobby Jones had become a household name in golf. Red Grange, the "Galloping Ghost" of Illinois, had etched his name into the book of football immortals. And Finland's Paavo Nurmi had lowered the world record in the mile to 4 minutes and 10.4 seconds. One of the earliest Grizzlies to make it to the NFL, Sullivan played on three separate teams over the course of the 1922 season: the Milwaukee Badgers (two games), the Hammond Pros (two games) and the Evansville Crimson Giants (one game). He returned in 1923 to play in four games overall for the Pros, an Indiana-based traveling team existing in the National Football League from 1920 to 1926, before he was traded to the Kansas City Blues. He started 1924 with the Blues before returning to finish the season for the third and final time with the Pros.

The Kansas City Blues became the Kansas City Cowboys in 1925 and folded after two seasons. Located on the north side of Milwaukee, the Badgers, an organization notably composed of several black players, existed from 1922 to 1926. The Evansville Crimson Giants lasted two seasons (1921–22).

In 1922, Sullivan, while still an active ballplayer, began his coaching duties at Butte Central High School. Indeed, Sullivan retained a strong affinity for Butte and a longtime residency there. In 1924, he unsuccessfully ran for sheriff of Silverbow County on the Democratic ticket. His political advertising trumpeted that he was born and bred in Butte and that, "admired by all, he has no enemies." In the 1930s, he became a judge and a presiding official in the International Greyhound Racing Association. He moved to California in the late 1940s and died there in 1969.

PAUL SZAKASH
BORN: May 5, 1913, Chicago, IL
DIED: October 24, 1984, Missoula, MT
COLLEGE: Montana
NFL EXPERIENCE: 1938–42
TEAM: Detroit Lions

Paul Szakash's parents, John and Mary, had come to the United States and Roseland, Illinois, from Hungary as teenagers, met in Chicago and married in 1904. Paul attended St. Catherine of Genoa Grammar School and then Fenger. He was Fenger's fullback in 1929 and 1930, graduating in June 1931. His prowess on the football field earned him a ticket to Montana University. This *Missoulian* quote from 1937 captures Szakash's athletic grace: "Paul Szakash will be remembered as the smashing fullback who played every minute of every game in the 1935 season. He received plenty of good publicity on the coast, including several All-American honorable mentions. An appendix operation kept Paul out of the entire 1936 season—that cost Montana many first downs and touchdowns." Szakash was also a standout in baseball at Montana. Of the forty-one players on the 1937 Montana team, eleven were from the Chicago area, including future NFL'er Aldo Forte.

Paul Szakash was a standout in baseball and football at Montana. He was selected by the Detroit Lions as the fifty-sixth pick in round seven of the 1938 National Football League draft. *Courtesy University of Montana.*

He was selected by the Detroit Lions as the fifty-sixth pick in round seven of the 1938 NFL draft, held on December 12, 1937, at the Hotel Sherman in Chicago, the city where Szakash was born. The draft consisted of twelve rounds and 110 player selections. It began with the Cleveland Rams selecting Corbett Davis. Over four seasons with Detroit, Szakash carried the ball twenty-three times, including twenty in his rookie campaign. He saw time as a fullback, blocking back, linebacker and defensive end. Teammates of his with the Lions were ironman center and future Pro Football Hall of Fame inductee Alex Wojciechowicz, a two-way threat who played at center on offense and at linebacker on defense, and Byron "Whizzer" White, a Rhodes scholar who later became a U.S. Supreme Court justice. All three were rookies in the National Football League in 1938.

Szagash was a lieutenant in the U.S. Marine Corps for four years during World War II and later an assistant coach at Montana. He married a Missoula native in 1938, and the couple raised three kids and operated a frozen food business there.

1960s–1970s

DOUG BETTERS

BORN: June 11, 1956, Lincoln, NE
COLLEGE: Montana; University of Nevada
POSITION: Defensive end
NFL EXPERIENCE: 1978–87
TEAM: Miami Dolphins

Doug Betters spent ten years in the NFL, all with the Miami Dolphins as a part of the squad's heralded "Killer Bees" defense. The six-foot, seven-inch defensive end played one season with the Grizzlies before finding a role with the Nevada Wolfpack.

"I had planned on becoming an offensive lineman when I came to Missoula and I was going to be an offensive lineman or tight end," said Betters, "but some folks got hurt on defense."

"I learned fast that it was better to be the hammer than to be a nail and the offensive linemen were getting nailed all of the time. The personalities between offensive and defensive linemen are different. The offensive linemen always seemed to have lockers that were orderly and in place and the defensive guys' locker room seemed thrown in there and a mess."

Betters transferred to Nevada-Reno following his junior season to play for John L. Smith, who had been an assistant at UM. Miami selected him in the sixth round of the 1978 NFL entry draft. He played in two Super Bowls, once recorded four sacks in a single game (of the Buffalo Bills' Joe Ferguson, in 1983) and was the NFL Defensive Player of the Year in 1983.

Doug Betters spent ten years in the NFL, all with the Miami Dolphins as a part of the squad's heralded "Killer Bees" defense. *Courtesy Doug Betters.*

"I would have loved to have had my name on the Miami roster with Montana [as my college, instead of Nevada] following that [defensive player of the year award]," said Betters, who retired from pro football in 1988.

Betters's love affair with Montana began in college, when he worked as a whitewater rafting and fishing guide at Glacier National Park. It deepened when he was with the Miami Dolphins. He would return to Montana every chance he could to head out into the wilderness dirtbiking, motorcycle riding, fishing or downhill skiing.

In 1998, Betters hit his head in a ski accident at the Big Mountain resort in Kalispell, Montana. The tip of his ski became caught, and he fell, landing on his head. He was skiing alone and, admittedly, at a high speed when the accident occurred. Betters, forty-one, was rushed to Kalispell Regional Medical Center. (Around the same time, Doak Walker, a former Heisman Trophy winner and an All-Pro with the Detroit Lions, was injured in a ski accident in Steamboat Springs, Colorado. He died eight months later as a result of paralyzing injuries.)

"There are a lot of people who are able-bodied who still have issues with it and I've lost a lot of friends who just wanted to get away from it," said Betters, who is paralyzed from the torso down. "People see anybody who is disabled or kids with Down syndrome, and those guys are just invisible. It's harder for people who knew me as a professional football player. [Former offensive lineman and friend] Randy Cross comes to visit every year. Cross said, 'It's mind-blowing, but I'm getting used to the new version of you.' I'd done it [skiing at Big Mountain] one thousand times and had been skiing for thirty-five years."

Years earlier, Betters witnessed the death of Paul Schafer, a Bobcat tailback from 1968 to 1971 who died from injuries sustained in a similar skiing collision.

"Schafer had an outstanding career," recalled Betters.

> *He carried three* [Montana] *Grizzlies on his back with a dislocated shoulder, shot grizzlies, and hunted lions in Africa. He hit a tree and it killed him. I remember picking up his skis, his gloves and his hat. A pine tree snag snapped off and killed him. His eyes were fixed and dilated and I started CPR and he never regained consciousness. I remember thinking that if he would have survived it would've been worse, because he would have been in a wheelchair and broke his vertebrae. At the time, I thought if I had a choice that I'd be better off dead than to have been in a wheelchair. Two years later—ironically—I had my accident.*

Still, Betters, who lives in Whitefish, retains a strong optimism that the advancement of stem cell research will help him once again walk, and he's grateful for his wife, his health and the cherished access he is provided to the natural world.

"I'm lucky that I have what I have," said Betters. "There was a cop who was shot in Missoula in 1998 by a young punk kid who was passing a bum check at a pawn shop. He shot the cop with your standard Saturday night special, and afterwards, the cop, he couldn't even scratch his own nose. He passed on from respiratory failure, and he couldn't even off himself."

Betters is able to fly-fish from a twenty-foot boat equipped with a standing contraption to support his lower extremities, and he retrofitted a 1978 Cessna to enable him to fly over places such as Glacier National Park. He has the freedom of his favorite truck and a Mustang that has been fitted to meet his specifics.

"I always love getting out," said Betters.

JON BORCHARDT
BORN: August 13, 1957, Minneapolis, MN
COLLEGE: Montana State
POSITION: Guard; tackle
NFL EXPERIENCE: 1979–87
TEAMS: Buffalo Bills (1979–84); Seattle Seahawks (1985–87)

Born in Brooklyn Park, Minnesota, Jon Borchardt was an All-America line selection in 1978 and earned all-conference honors as a junior and senior. The six-foot, five-inch, 260-pounder played on the line for the 1976 national championship team, when Montana won the NCAA Division II championship at the Pioneer Bowl in Wichita Falls, Texas, beating the Akron Zips, 24–13.

Borchardt was chosen in the third round of the NFL draft by the Buffalo Bills in 1979. He played nine seasons in the National Football League, six on the line for Buffalo and three for the Seattle Seahawks.

When Borchardt arrived in Buffalo, he was coached by Chuck Knox, who had arrived in 1978 and left the Bills after the strike-shortened 1982 season. He was later re-acquainted with Knox, who coached the Seahawks from its eighth season, in 1983, to 1991.

"Knox was a winner," said Borchardt. "He prepared you to win. He was a straight shooter. He'd tell you if you screwed up or if you did good. He was coach of the year three times with three different teams. I did it in reverse. I moved to Seattle while I was in Buffalo and asked to be traded there."

As a backup on the Seahawks offensive line, he played alongside former Bills teammate Reggie McKenzie, a former mentor, who had led the way for O.J. Simpson to become the NFL's first 2,000-yard rusher in 1973. McKenzie is the current general manager of the Oakland Raiders. "Reggie taught me a lot," said Borchardt.

Borchardt said that playing inside the warmth and comfort of Seattle's domed stadium was a welcome contrast to the frequent blizzards in Buffalo. No matter the location, in the NFL, there are few jobs and plenty of applicants. "You have to stay in shape all year round. There's always some young kid coming along you have to watch out for."

For more than twenty years, Borchardt, who retired from professional football in 1987, worked as sales development manager of Microflex Products for 3M, an American multinational corporation based in a suburb of St. Paul.

EDWARD BREDING

BORN: November 3, 1943, Billings, MT
COLLEGE: Texas A&M
POSITION: Linebacker
NFL EXPERIENCE: 1967–68
TEAM: Washington Redskins

After playing college ball at Texas A&M, Edward Breding was drafted in the fifteenth round of the 1967 NFL draft. He spent the 1967 and 1968 seasons with the Washington Redskins, appearing in twenty-eight games as a middle linebacker, starting five of them.

Indeed, Breding learned the rules of engagement from Sam Huff, one of the NFL's greatest all-time linebackers. Huff played thirteen seasons with the New York Giants and the Redskins (1956–69).

"Huff was so nice and a gentleman all of the time, except when he was playing," said Ed Breding. "He had the right built, broad shoulders, to really smack somebody. He had kind of skinny legs. But he moved good. He had the instincts in him to know where the runner was coming and go there before he got blocked."

In fact, it was Breding, a rookie on the Redskins, who stood in Huff's middle linebacker position on October 23, 1967. Redskins coach Otto Graham told the *Daily Times* on the morning before kickoff against the Baltimore Colts that Breding "is tough, and eager—and inexperienced." That brought a big smile from the face of Colts quarterback Johnny Unitas, who tried to capitalize on such an advantage.

"Here comes third down," recalled Breding recently.

I'm sure that Unitas is going to throw it, and I called a blitz, the kind where the middle and strong side linebacker blitz. Their center picked up the tackle on my right side and I squeezed by and I got through the hole and I tackled Unitas for four- or a five-yard loss. I reached down and helped him up. I was more in awe of tackling somebody famous like that. It was a special moment. I helped him up and I didn't say anything, and he had one of those dishpan helmets. Unitas wore a single bar across his helmet as far as the facemask goes. I almost apologized.

Football opened up a wider world of relationships and contacts for Breding, who was born in Billings but attended high school and college in Texas. "Being a player from Texas, there were no black players. So it was new to me to meet a guy named Spain Musgrove [Redskins defensive end, 1967–69], a big old black kid, a huge guy, and he was my partner and roommate. Generally, they would put two black guys together or two white guys together in a room and since the math didn't work out, so they put he and I in a room. He would stay loose and play around with high fives and low fives, and he was a neat guy."

With rookie John Didion being groomed as Huff's backup, Breding, nursing a severely broken ankle that badly diminished his lateral movement, was released on waivers on September 10, 1969 as the team ended its preseason out-of-town drills. Vince Lombardi, one of the country's most popular figures in and out of sports, coached the Redskins one year before he died in 1970. A training camp under the immortal Lombardi was an experience for Breding. "Lombardi was every bit as tough as they said he was," said Breding. "He demanded respect and he got it. The veterans wanted him and he had their respect, too. Lombardi wasn't close to any of the players, either. He was different from Otto Graham, who was the coach for my two years, and both were losing seasons. Graham was a quiet guy."

Breding arrived in Winnipeg to play for the Canadian Football League (CFL) less than twenty-four hours after Washington lopped him off its roster. "It [CFL] is like a cross between soccer and the American game. You run a lot more. Those backs in motion really speed it up."

Reflecting on his NFL experience, Breding noted the monumental gap between the average paycheck a player today collects and one received by a player in his era. "Geez, back in those days there weren't any salaries," said Breding. "My first year was the NFL-AFL merger and I made $32,000 a year and in my second a little more than that. [Quarterback] Sonny Jurgensen was the highest-paid guy on the team at $120,000. We were offered a $100 bonus if we'd take out the quarterback, like hired killers. Quarterbacks now are prima donnas, you can't touch them. Jorgensen was always partying, a wild guy, and he could throw a football behind his back to someone forty yards down the field and he could still be accurate. He was terrible in camp because he would stay out late."

At seventy-three, Breding ranches on a sixty-two-hundred-acre plot of family land in Shawmut, where he raises black Angus cattle and helps rear several grandkids.

"I've got an income ranching," said Breding. "I love to make the grandkids oatmeal in the mornings. It's a wonderful way of life."

ED CUMMINGS

BORN: June 29, 1941, Anaconda, MT
COLLEGE: Stanford
POSITION: Linebacker
NFL EXPERIENCE: 1964–65
TEAMS: New York Jets (1964); Denver Broncos (1965)

Ed Cummings grew up in Anaconda in the 1950s, idolizing Montana Grizzlies such as Stan "The Ram" Renning. Cummings graduated in 1959 from Anaconda High School, where he compiled an outstanding record in several sports. He then played college football at Stanford University, where he earned first-team All-America honors as a fullback in 1962.

Cummings said that he learned values, toughness and even intelligence through the game. "The risk of going to Stanford was worth taking because I didn't want to look back at forty, asking why I didn't take the chance," he said. Cummings excelled at both fullback and linebacker for coach "Cactus" Jack Curtis just as the one-platoon era was coming to an end. He was not only an All-American on offense, but he also led Stanford in tackles as a junior and senior in 1961–62.

Cummings was selected to compete in the East-West University game and was chosen to compete in the East-West Shrine Football Game in 1962 (along with UM grid standout Terry Dillon).

Following the Shrine Game, Cummings went to New York to try out with the Giants. "The first day I showed up to practice with the Giants, the competition looked at me and left," said Cummings. "I was trying for the middle linebacker slot, and Sam Huff was holding down that position. He walked out of training and didn't come back for two weeks. I guess he figured I wasn't any competition. During the first major tackling drill, I damaged my right shoulder in a bizarre accident and the next day they cut me. In today's world, you couldn't do that to a player. Back then, they could."

The day Huff returned to the Giants' camp, Cummings was cut from the team. With the outlook for a slot on the pro team poor, he decided to enroll at the New York University School of Social Work at Columbia University. During his first year at Columbia, he walked into the office of the New York Jets of the American Football League and asked to try out as a free agent. This time, he found himself playing middle linebacker.

I met with coach Weeb Ewbank and told him I wanted a tryout. I got the game ball once when we beat the Chiefs and I played behind [linebacker turned professional wrestler] *Wahoo McDaniel, who was really something. There are so many stories about Wahoo that could not be printed. At one point, he had somehow carried an automobile on his back after using a hacksaw to hack the car into parts in Oklahoma. He was a lot of fun. I was traded to Denver just about the time Joe Namath was drafted from Alabama by owner Sonny Werblin. The headline of the New York Daily News said, "Werblin Pays Namath $400,000, This Will Ruin Professional Football."*

Cummings played with the New York club for one season and then returned to Columbia to finish his graduate work. The next season, he was traded to the Denver Broncos and played with them for a season. He suited up for a total of eleven games with the Jets in 1964 and fourteen games with the Broncos in 1965, starting in the last eight.

"Football is a brutal game," said Cummings.

However, you just don't realize it when you are out on the field hitting. The emotional effects make you very high and you get a real thrill out of just hitting someone. Football is like being ten years old and having $1,000 in your pocket all of the time.

I had a dispute with Denver over a bonus I thought they should have paid me. My lawyer sent one letter to the Broncos and they paid me the $1,500 bonus. The lawyer got $500 and I put $1,000 toward law school. My original salary with the Giants was $9,500, for the Jets was $9,500 and the Broncos $10,500. Cattle get more respect than we did. We paved the way for today's players.

Cummings returned to his home state and entered law school at the University of Montana. He obtained his degree in 1969. "It was nice for myself, for my family and for Anaconda," said Cummings, seventy-five, who retired from practicing law in Missoula and currently runs a ranch in the Bitterroot Valley. "The important thing is having a chance to make an impact on kids. They can see, here's another Anaconda guy who's done all right."

Three decades later, Ed's son, Joe Cummings, starred at Stevensville High and Wyoming before playing linebacker for the San Diego Chargers and Buffalo Bills. "Joe was a much better athlete than I was and he had much superior size and he was a very good NFL linebacker. I had no desire to make a career out of pro football. I wanted to do it and then when I did do it I lost interest."

Barry Darrow

Born: June 27, 1950, Peoria, IL
Colleges: University of Montana Western; Montana
Position: Offensive tackle
NFL Experience: 1974–78
Team: Cleveland Browns

"Occasionally, I'll receive a photo in the mail to sign for someone from as far away as Asia," said Barry Darrow. "It's nice that the celebrity never goes away." *Courtesy Barry Darrow.*

Barry Darrow has watched many of his former teammates and friends succumb to physical and psychological health issues. Inevitably, the conversation with him comes around to player safety and head trauma and the league acknowledging on Capitol Hill in March 2016 a link between football and degenerative brain disorders such as chronic traumatic encephalopathy (CTE).

His former linemate on the Cleveland Browns, Tom DeLeone (center in the league from 1972 to 1984), suffers from dementia as a result of his playing career. Teammate Gerry Sullivan (guard, 1974–81) was highly respected by his colleagues until his career unraveled when his behavior became erratic, vacillating between "manic hilarity and extreme anger," according to Darrow.

Darrow has been a vocal opponent of the NFL's retirement and disability board's treatment of former players, which he deems "unfair, inadequate and unreasonable."

"The figures of CTE are startling," he said. "When you look at the cadaver brains that are being dissected, 90 to 95 percent have CTE, and that's after playing at all levels, including high school. I think the indictment of the NFL hasn't been strong enough and that the NFL operates like a drug cartel and organized crime ring and they don't care about individuals."

Despite all of this, Darrow said that he was glad that was able to live out his dream of playing professional football despite being hampered by knee problems since high school in Great Falls (as a sophomore, he dislocated and severely bent his left knee at a brutal angle). Being six feet, six inches and 235 pounds as a high school kid left Darrow with limited choices. "We were poor growing up," he said. "We had limited means, though we had no concept of it until you get into high school and you realize that everyone else has a muscle car."

Darrow was grateful to earn a scholarship to the University of Montana Western in Dillon, where he had a "partial ride" and a job where he mopped the floor of the dormitory and did other duties. He quickly became a starter on the Bulldogs' offensive line as a freshman, but he needed to switch programs "to reach the next level," he said. After seeing the Grizzlies go undefeated in 1969, he tried out for the team. He was a starter when the Grizzlies posted another 10-0 regular season record in 1970.

Drafted late in the 1973 NFL draft by the San Diego Chargers, he fared better than fellow Grizzlies Jim Hann (linebacker) and Cliff Burnett (defensive end), who were drafted earlier yet failed the secure a roster spot. Between 1974 and 1978, he started in forty-seven out of a potential seventy-one games at tackle for the Cleveland Browns.

Claude Humphrey [defensive end, 1968–81] *was inducted into the Pro Football Hall of Fame last year and at the induction they showed a clip of him beating me for a sack. I remember it clearly. So I did get my own day of infamy. It was in Atlanta* [on October 17, 1976], *and* [Montana native] *Mike Tilleman played as defensive tackle and Claude was All-Pro and that sack was on a screen left and I took a 12-step drop. It's hard to block someone of that caliber on a 12-step drop.*

Now, the funny thing is we decided to have [running back] *Greg Pruitt run right at him and doing that calms someone like Humprey, a defensive end who is a good, aggressive pass rusher, right down. Pruitt got 191 yards and we won, 20–17 and I gave him the game ball. He said, "I'm going to give it you! You deserve it!" I have two game balls against NFL hall of famers and All-Pros, the other against Jack Youngblood and we had to handle him. That's not usual for an offensive lineman to get the game balls.*

Following a second knee surgery at the pro level, Darrow was traded to New Orleans in the winter of 1979. At the age of thirty, fed up with feeling as if he were simply a commodity for a big business, Darrow returned to Missoula. His parents are both native Montanans, sans the first four months of his life, which were lived in the Midwest. It's always been home.

I made a whopping $26,000 my first year in the NFL and after Cleveland I really didn't have the heart to play anymore. I was lucky to make over

$50k a year. The quarterback of the Browns [Brian Sipe], he made $150k, and that was a big deal. Sipe made $13 million by going to the USFL, and he was making $150k in the NFL. I was one of the old linemen who kept him alive, and what did I get paid? We played for the love of the game and everyone had the same attitude. Back then, it was not about money or notoriety.

The biggest factor to retirement was that they were bouncing me around from pile to pile and my feet hurt so damn I could hardly stand up, because of a life of wearing football cleats. When the ground froze, the pegs would come up through the soles of my feet. There is nothing like being a huge guy, doing manual labor of the extreme kind, in ballet slippers.

Yet retirement was still a bumpy mental transition for Darrow. "It's a lot like having PTSD [posttraumatic stress disorder], the loss of the camaraderie and the loss of friends you've succeeded or failed with, your peer group disappears." Darrow returned to UM for his teaching certificate and spent five years teaching and coaching, first at Big Sky High School in Missoula for three years and then in Stevensville. In 1987, he began working at Montana West Lumber, a Great Falls–based lumber brokerage firm that has an office in the Bitterroot. Montana West has two mills, and Darrow now sells remanufactured products such as paneling and flooring.

"Occasionally, I'll receive a photo in the mail to sign for someone from as far away as Asia," said Darrow. "It's nice that the celebrity never goes away."

TERRY DILLON
BORN: August 18, 1941, Waukesha, WI
DIED: May 28, 1964, Tarkio, MT
COLLEGE: Montana
POSITION: Defensive back
NFL EXPERIENCE: 1963
TEAM: Minnesota Vikings

Terry Dillon came to Montana from Hopkins, Minnesota, to play offense and defense. In his first year as a Grizzly, he was second on the team in rushing and scoring. Besides being an offensive threat, Dillon proved himself a hardnosed defensive player. In his senior year, he led the team in tackles and assists. In 1962, Dillon held the all-time MSU rushing record for a single season. He played on the 1963 College All-Star team that beat the

Top: UM star and Minnesota Vikings defensive back Terry Dillon drowned in the Clark Fork River while working on a construction project in the Missoula area. His body was found on July 17, 1964, by a fisherman. *Courtesy University of Montana.*

Bottom: Postcard announcing the Minnesota Vikings signing of UM star Terry Dillon. *Courtesy University of Montana.*

Green Bay Packers, 20–17—the final time a college team would beat a professional team in that series.

Dillon was drafted in the nineteenth round of the 1963 American Football League draft by the Oakland Raiders. He did well in summer camp before an ankle injury ended his chances of cracking the roster. He was put on waivers and released. He was signed by the Minnesota Vikings, working out with the "Taxi" squad, before getting his chance at midseason, starting the final seven games of the year at defensive safety.

"After returning [to Montana] from his first year as a pro, he came not as someone to bow down to, but Terry Dillon," recalled Dan Foley, editor of the *Montana Kaimin*. "He didn't say much about his accomplishments as a pro, and when he did it was only with the greatest of urging."

On May 28, 1964, Dillon was operating a gasoline-powered cement carrier and working on a bridge construction project twenty-five miles west of Missoula when part of the temporary decking gave way and he fell seventy-five feet into the swift-running, swollen Clark Fork River.

Witnesses said Dillon, a strong swimmer, started swimming for shore, fighting the current, but he disappeared approximately twenty feet from the bank of the river. Search parties, boats and divers scoured the river and shore for Dillon's remains for several weeks. Authorities found some bridge decking and a man's boot about four miles from the construction site.

His body was found on July 17, 1964, by a fisherman about seventeen miles downstream from the bridge. Dillon had planned to be married soon and complete a degree in business administration. Coach Norm Van Brocklin of the Vikings said that Dillon, who had already signed his 1964 contract with the Vikings, "had a real future in professional football. He gave the Minnesota Vikings the best play they had at defensive safety in three years."

In 1965, linebacker Rip Hawkins received the first "Terry Dillon" award given by the Minnesota Vikings in honor of their deceased teammate. The award symbolizes Dillon's qualities of dedication, self-sacrifice and ability. Grizzly football coach Hugh Davidson suggested retiring jersey no. 22, the number Dillon wore as a Grizzly. The Montana State University Department of Athletics agreed to retire the number in Dillon's memory.

PAT DONOVAN
BORN: July 1, 1953, Helena, MT
COLLEGE: Stanford
POSITION: Offensive tackle
NFL EXPERIENCE: 1975–83
TEAM: Dallas Cowboys

Pat Donovan was among a crop of football stars at Helena Central who moved to Helena High in 1970 after the closing of their Catholic school. At six feet, five inches, he was a key part of his high school football team as a tight end, played in two state championship basketball games (winning one) and helped his track team by winning shot and discus titles in both his junior and senior years. In addition, he was fast enough to anchor his 880 relay team. Donovan graduated with three school records in the shot, disc and javelin.

Billings Senior High School star Pete Lazetich enticed Donovan to enroll at Stanford University, where he received a bachelor of science degree in mechanical engineering and was twice named All-American. (Donovan was chosen for Stanford University's All-Century team, along with Lazetich.)

Donovan was taken as a defensive end by the Dallas Cowboys in the fourth round of the 1975 NFL draft. Three days into training camp, however, the Cowboys switched him to the other side of the line. The new strategy was to groom Donovan as a potential successor to Rayfield Wright. (Wright, a six-time Pro Bowl selection and member of the Pro Football Hall of Fame, is in deteriorating mental health. He is among more than forty-five hundred players who have sued the NFL, contending that the league concealed for years what it knew about the dangers of repeated hits to the head.) "Rayfield was getting older and so they kind of needed somebody on the offensive side and nobody on the defensive side," said Donovan. "Dallas was more interested in drafting athletes at that point and they were especially interested in position players."

Though Donovan wasn't happy with the transition, he chose to adapt to it. "Defensive players aren't ever interested in playing offense. Defensive end is a lot of fun to play, but I figured I'd just check it out and see what came of it. The problem is, training camp your rookie year is no time to learn a new skill."

After nine seasons, Pat Donovan retired in 1983. He earned four All-Pro selections at offensive tackle. *Courtesy Helena Sports Hall of Fame.*

The 1975 campaign was the Cowboys' sixteenth season in the National Football League and their sixteenth under head coach Tom Landry. He coached the Cowboys for twenty-nine seasons (270-178-6). Landry went 0-11-1 in his first year (1960), but the coach hit his stride with a vastly improved squad in 1966, kicking off a streak of twenty consecutive winning seasons that included eighteen postseason appearances, thirteen division championships and five NFC titles.

"They hadn't made the playoffs in 1974 [with an 8-6 record]. It was the first time in umpteen years they hadn't, so it was slated as being a rebuilding year. We had 103 rookies in training camp, so they were obviously going to make a move. That was probably the reason I made it because it was a rebuilding year."

In 1975, Donovan, in a backup role, was one of a dozen rookies who lifted the Cowboys to Super Bowl X, which they lost, 21–17, to the Pittsburgh Steelers. That draft class included Randy White, Thomas Henderson, Bob Breunig, Ed "Too Tall" Jones and Herbert Scott.

When the Cowboys won Super Bowl XII two years later, defeating the Denver Broncos, 27–0, Donovan started at right tackle after replacing Wright, who had injured a knee. In the first night Super Bowl (kickoff was at 5:17 p.m.), the Cowboys won their second Super Bowl in a game that was not nearly as close as the 27–10 final score implied.

"There was a lot of trepidation on their part and I'm sure everybody was nervous about me stepping in for Rayfield. That's because I'd really only played on special teams. My defensive background I suppose helped that, and being a little quicker than most of the offensive linemen. But I was covering punts and kickoffs and all that stuff for two years and then started my third year."

In 1978—the first sixteen-game season in the NFL—Donovan became the starter at left tackle and helped Dallas reach Super Bowl XIII (a loss to Pittsburgh, 35–31). From 1979 to 1981, both Donovan and left guard Herb Scott—dubbed the "Dynamic Duo"—finished with Pro Bowl honors. At left tackle, Donovan combated and neutralized the aggression of some of the sport's quickest, most relentless rushers.

"Even if a guy gets only one sack, that could be the end of your quarterback if you've got a right-handed quarterback. But Roger Staubach was incredible. He had that third eye and just phenomenal mobility, which made him correspondingly easier and harder to block for. You never knew where he was so you were always on your toes. It was instinctive. He would just take off and he rarely made the wrong choice."

Donovan credits running back Tony Dorsett's athletic explosiveness as one of the things that made his job easier and ultimately made his career more noticeable. "Tony Dorsett just broke the game wide open when he came to the team. He was another guy you never knew where he was going to end up."

After nine seasons, Donovan retired in 1983, ending with four All-Pro selections at offensive tackle. The Cowboys made the playoffs all nine seasons, with six NFC championship game appearances and three conference titles.

He worked in real estate development in the Dallas area for several years and then returned to Montana in the late 1980s to develop real estate, including a private golf community in Whitefish called Iron Horse. Donovan concentrates on other real estate projects and is a partner in the Sotheby's International Real Estate company in Whitefish, but he otherwise maintains a quiet profile. He rarely watches sporting events these days.

"Whitefish is a super, super fun place. If you're an outdoors person, we're twenty miles from Glacier National Park and sixty miles from Canada. We've got lots of lakes and rivers and golf and there's a ski hill four miles away."

In 2000, *Sports Illustrated* listed Donovan no. 4 on Montana's greatest sports figures of the twentieth century.

RICK DUNCAN
BORN: August 14, 1941, Mattoon, IL
COLLEGE: Eastern Montana
POSITIONS: Kicker; punter
NFL EXPERIENCE: 1967–69
TEAMS: Denver Broncos (1967); Philadelphia Eagles (1968);
Detroit Lions (1969)

The Eastern Montana Yellowjackets represented Eastern Montana College in football from 1947 to 1978. Eastern Montana College is currently known as Montana State University, Billings. Originally Eastern Montana Normal School when it was founded in 1927, its name was changed in 1949 to Eastern Montana College of Education. The four-year school merged with Montana State University in 1994.

Duncan and Bill Wondolowski are the only two Yellowjackets who went on to compete in the National Football League. Duncan played two games with Denver in 1967, tallying nine points. He missed three out of five field goal attempts and converted all three point-after attempts. He punted five times in a game for Philadelphia in 1968, netting a 45.6 average. He appeared in one game for Detroit in 1969, punting three times, averaging less than 26 yards a boot.

RON EAST
BORN: August 26, 1943, Portland, OR
COLLEGES: Montana State; Columbia Basin College; Oregon State
POSITIONS: Defensive tackle; defensive end
NFL EXPERIENCE: 1967–77
TEAMS: Dallas Cowboys (1967–70); San Diego Chargers
(1971–73); Cleveland Browns (1975); Atlanta Falcons (1976);
Seattle Seahawks (1977)

Ron East attended Lincoln High School in Portland, where he trained in football, wrestling and track. He was Oregon's state javelin champion as a senior.

He accepted a scholarship to play at Oregon State University, but after being considered "too small to eventually become a starter," he enlisted in the U.S. Marine Forces Reserve. After boot camp, he transferred to Columbia Basin College in Pasco, Washington, where, as a defensive tackle, he received

In 1999, journeyman NFL'er Ron East was inducted into the Montana State University Hall of Fame. *Courtesy Ron East.*

all-conference honors and led his undefeated team to the conference championship.

In 1966, he transferred to Montana State University, where he helped the Bobcats win the Big Sky Conference championship and received all-conference honors. He also was the Big Sky javelin champion in 1966.

East signed as an undrafted free agent with the Dallas Cowboys in 1967. He was the fifth defensive lineman on the depth chart and a backup for defensive tackles Bob "Mr. Cowboy" Lilly and Jethro Pugh. According to a biographer of Tom Landry, the legendary head coach would later say, "Ron East was the most aggressive player he ever coached."

On May 19, 1971, a major three-team swap known as the "Bambi trade" was announced. The agreement involved the Dallas Cowboys, Los Angeles Rams and San Diego Chargers and centered on two wide receivers named Lance. The Rams sent tight end Billy Truax and wide receiver Wendell Tucker to Dallas for wide receiver Lance Rentzel. The Cowboys then dealt defensive tackle East, tight end Pettis Norman and offensive tackle Tony Liscio to San Diego for wide receiver Lance "Bambi" Alworth.

San Diego proved to be a better location for East, who was a three-year starter at left tackle in a defensive unit that included an aging Deacon Jones, Dave Costa, Lionel Aldridge and Coy Bacon. East's footnote to NFL history took place on October 15, 1972. Miami Dolphins quarterback Bob Griese's ankle was dislocated and his leg broken in game five of the team's 1972 perfect season when he was sacked by East and Jones. Griese was replaced by veteran Earl Morrall, who carried the Dolphins to Super Bowl VII before relinquishing the starting job back to Griese.

East started all fourteen games for the Cleveland Browns in 1975 at left defensive end. After a season with the Atlanta Falcons, East finished as a starter on the Seattle Seahawks in 1977, the squad's second season in the league.

In 1994, East was inducted into the Northwest Athletic Conference Hall of Fame. In 1999, he was inducted into the Montana State University Hall of Fame.

TERRY FALCON
BORN: August 30, 1955, Culbertson, MT
COLLEGES: Minot State; Montana
POSITIONS: Offensive guard; offensive tackle
NFL EXPERIENCE: 1978–80
TEAMS: New England Patriots (1978–79); New York Giants (1980)

Terry Falcon, "an easy-going man from tiny Culbertson," according to one media guide, played in the class C ranks. He spent two seasons playing for Minot State in North Dakota before transferring to UM.

"I was about six-four and 245 pounds," said Terry Falcon, the son of a signal maintainer for the railroad. "I was a fullback, and when I got to Minot they told me I was a tight end. Then one week into practice one of the starting tackles was in a big pile-up. He broke his ankle, and the next day they said, 'Falcon, you're not a tight end anymore. You're a tackle.' Apparently, all tight ends are just one injury away from being a tackle."

At UM, Falcon sat out the 1975 season, then was injured midway through the 1976 campaign. Even with just a half season of playing time, Big Sky coaches were impressed enough with what they saw to name Falcon, a business administration major, to the All–Big Sky second team offensive unit.

At the University of Montana in 1977 are (*left to right*) Murray Pierce, Ron Lebsock, offensive coordinator/line coach Dave Nickel, Terry Falcon and Ben Harbison. *Courtesy University of Montana.*

Falcon continued in professional football after the New England Patriots selected the Montana product in the 8th round (198th overall). Falcon told one newspaper that, as excited as he was to embark on a higher level, leaving the Grizzlies "is like losing a friend." As a Patriot, Falcon appeared in eight games in 1978 and ten in 1979, all on special teams. In his second season, he was placed on the injured reserve list with a knee injury he suffered in a game against Buffalo. He underwent surgery on his left knee to repair ligament damage.

"Mike Haynes, who's in the Hall of Fame, is a great friend of mine and we've connected with each other in the last couple of years. I lived with him for a while when I was with the Patriots. Just being around him is a lot of fun. We won the Eastern Division in 1978, my first year, and got in the playoffs. So I got to experience that. When I was at New England, Bill Belichick was the linebackers coach, and Romeo Crennel was the defensive backs coach, and Bill Parcells was the defensive coordinator."

The New York Giants signed Falcon after his contract with the Patriots elapsed, and in 1980, he started a pair of games at guard. Phil Simms started thirteen of sixteen games that season under Ray Perkins. The team finished last in the NFC East at 4-12. Also on that roster was Havre-born Mike Friede, who started in four games at wide receiver.

"I was a starting right guard for a time in New York, and ended up playing against Dallas." said Falcon. "They had Randy White and John Dutton at defensive tackle."

Falcon was cut the following preseason. He has enjoyed a long career as a high school coach and administrator in Montana. At age sixty, he is now the assistant principal at Poplar High School. "I tell everybody, I wanted to get out of here. And now forty years later I'm back. We've got good people to work with and fantastic teachers. It's been great here."

CURT FARRIER
BORN: June 25, 1941, Yakima, WA
COLLEGE: Montana State
POSITION: Defensive tackle
NFL EXPERIENCE: 1963–65
TEAM: Kansas City Chiefs

Curt Farrier played several seasons at Montana State as a defensive tackle before being selected by the Kansas City Chiefs in the tenth round (eightieth overall) of the 1963 AFL draft. Farrier, who as a three-year letterman for Montana State was the Bobcats' fastest interior lineman, was rated one of the top two rookies of the AFL Chiefs. Farrier, a six-foot, six-inch, 240-pound tackle, was the only rookie starter for the Chiefs in its first exhibition game with the San Diego Chargers. Farrier missed out on the Chiefs' AFL championship teams of the 1960s (they won in 1962, 1966 and 1969). He dressed in a total of twenty-nine games over three seasons as a backup. He would have played on the same defensive line as Buck Buchanan, the first player taken in the 1963 American Football League draft who played thirteen seasons as a Chief. Since tackle data is unavailable prior to 2001, the precise amount of time Farrier played, if any, is unclear. According to league statistics, generally accurate, he didn't start in a single contest.

MARK FELLOWS

BORN: February 26, 1963, Lodge Grass, MT
COLLEGE: Montana State
POSITION: Linebacker
NFL EXPERIENCE: 1985–86
TEAM: San Diego Chargers

Born in Lodge Grass, Mark Fellows's family moved to Choteau when he was in the fourth grade. Growing up on the Crow Indian reservation, Fellows said he always believed he had something to prove. Football seemed like the right outlet to channel his determination. He'd been a Bobcats fan since he was little because his dad often took him to home games.

"With football, either you like it or you don't because there is too much work and physical contact," he said. "Growing up on the reservation tempered me a little bit. I felt I had something to show."

He was a first team All–Big Sky and All-American his senior season at Montana State University. He was one of the defensive stars of MSU's run to the 1984 Big Sky and Division I-AA national championships. He recorded twenty-three sacks that season and finished his career with forty. Both remain school records.

He was drafted by the San Diego Chargers with the 196th overall pick in 1985. He played for the Chargers in 1985 and 1986, starting in several games. Fellows suffered a devastating hip fracture in 1985. While covering a kickoff in the second game of the season against the Seattle Seahawks, he was clobbered by a blocker. The force of the collision broke his hip and essentially finished his career. "I had two surgeries on it, and I have two Swiss stainless steel pins in it," he said. "It still aches, but I live with it. It's the nature of the beast. You want to play, so you're willing to risk [injury]."

Fellows, age fifty-three, remains tight with his alma mater and its football program and is a member of MSU's hall of fame. "I am a lot more proud of it now than I was then," he said. "When you're twenty-one years old, you don't appreciate it as much as you do later."

He continued: "Winning All–Big Sky and All-America was my deal. But when I go back to Bozeman, what people talk about are the championships. When you hear that, you have the feeling we did something right."

Fellows said he might have made a career out of football, perhaps even as a coach, had his dad not wanted him to return to Choteau to help on the family cattle ranch. He and his brother Mike run the day-to-day operations.

"Once I couldn't play anymore and I wasn't going to coach, I retired up here in kind of a quiet way," said Fellows. "That's the way I am: Either I have to get out of it completely, or I have to go into it. But it's hard to get away from it. I reluctantly helped out with a football camp here in Choteau. I still think about football when I'm on a horse."

WAYNE HAMMOND
BORN: January 30, 1953, Minneapolis, MN
COLLEGE: Montana State
POSITION: Defensive tackle
NFL EXPERIENCE: 1976
TEAM: Denver Broncos

Montana State defensive tackle Wayne Hammond was chosen by the Los Angeles Rams in the 5th round (112th overall) of the 1975 NFL draft. After being released by the Rams in preseason, he signed with the Denver Broncos in 1976. He is credited with suiting up for five games on the 9-5 team, coached by John Ralston. The Broncos defensive was anchored by linebackers Tom Jackson and Randy Gradishar. Otis Armstrong led the team with 1,008 rushing yards, and hall of famer Rick Upchurch set an NFL record by returning four punts for touchdowns and made the Pro Bowl. One of the greatest punt returners in NFL history, Upchurch had his best season in 1976, returning thirty-nine punts for 536 yards and a 13.7-yard average.

WAYNE HAWKINS
BORN: June 17, 1938, Jordan, MT
COLLEGE: Pacific
POSITION: Offensive guard
NFL EXPERIENCE: 1960–69
TEAM: Oakland Raiders

Wayne Hawkins was born in Jordan, Montana, and was delivered by the same doctor who greeted Jerry Kramer into the world two years earlier. Hawkins's mother and Kramer's mother were close friends, and both families moved elsewhere within a couple of years. Both boys went on to become dominant offensive guards in the NFL.

Jordan-born Wayne Hawkins was one of only twenty players who were in the AFL for the league's entire ten-year existence. *Courtesy Sharon Hawkins.*

A few years after Wayne's birth, the Hawkins family moved to California, and he attended Shasta High School in Redding. He played college football at the University of the Pacific.

Hawkins was selected by the Denver Broncos in the 1960 American Football League draft. He was one of only twenty players who were in the AFL for the league's entire ten-year existence. More than fourteen hundred men suited up and played at least one down in a regular-season AFL game; only twenty of them, including Hawkins, George Blanda, Jack Kemp and Don Maynard, lasted for the entirety of the league, from preseason in 1960 through Super Bowl IV after the 1969 season.

Hawkins started at right guard on the inaugural Oakland Raiders team, which was quarterbacked by both Tom Flores and Babe Parilli. The team posted a 6-8 record. From the start, the franchise was known for its loud, passionate, unruly, blue-collar fan base. That "Commitment to Excellence" spirit of Raider rebellion, of course, was fomented in the attitude of the swashbuckling, ducktailed owner Al Davis, who defied, antagonized and elevated the NFL for half a century. Hawkins played his entire career with Oakland through the 1969 AFL season. He earned AFL All-Star honors for five straight years beginning in 1963 and was a key offensive component on the 1967 AFL champion team that competed in the second AFL-NFL World Championship Game, known, retrospectively, as Super Bowl II. That game was played on January 14, 1968, at the Orange Bowl in Miami, Florida. The Packers won the contest, 33–14. On the winning side was longtime friend Jerry Kramer, who kept MVP quarterback Bart Starr protected in the pocket.

After his NFL tenure ended, Wayne trained in New York City as an investment broker and started other ventures, including the development of housing tracts in Hawaii and a foray into the world of wine.

The effects of the violent game of football have left Hawkins physically enfeebled. Following a series of erratic episodes and the emergence of short-term memory loss in the late 1990s, his doctor ordered a series of PET scans that revealed brain damage from the many concussions Hawkins had suffered as a player. According to his wife, Sharon Hawkins, "Wayne experienced approximately three to four concussions per season over a period of participating in football in high school, college and professional football."

One of Hawkins's most debilitating concussions was received in a game against the Kansas City Chiefs in 1963. "He sustained a Class III traumatic brain injury," said Sharon, a professional artist who struggles to be the sole family provider. "He was rushed to a hospital, slipped into a coma for twelve hours and awakened not knowing any personal information. A few hours later he was deemed fine. He flew to Oakland, saw a neurologist and was told he could play the following weekend in Denver. During the first half of that game, he sustained a concussion and yet played the second half."

Also in 1963, Hawkins endured a brutal blow against the San Diego Chargers when six-foot, nine-inch, 315-pound defensive tackle Ernie Ladd shoved his head into the goalpost. "Wayne was dizzy and continued to play the entire game," said Sharon, who has been married to her husband since 1952. "He complained of a toothache all evening. He saw his dentist on Monday where X-rays showed his jaw was broken from end to end. His teeth were wired together with a space in front for a straw. He continued to play with his jaw wired for several weeks of the season."

In the mid-2000s, Hawkins's short-term memory loss accelerated. He became lost while walking and driving, he lost credit cards and his NFL championship ring and he could no longer operate simple items such as a TV remote or a cellular phone. He suffered a devastating slip on ice, which broke several ribs and slammed his head on the concrete; the fall resulted in a "brain whiplash," stranding him unconscious for twenty minutes.

Sharon contacted the National Football League's Disability Office for financial assistance and at first was summarily ignored: "He has been out of football too long." In 2007, the NFL's Disability Board agreed to enroll Hawkins under Plan 88, numbered after John Mackey, the hall-of-fame Baltimore Colts tight end who died after losing his mind to CTE. Sharon said that Plan 88 now pays them $100,000 annually to cover living costs, to be raised to $133,000 a year in April 2017.

In July 2015, Sharon Hawkins moved Wayne, seventy-seven, to a senior living center in the southern California desert community of Rancho Mirage, where her husband was placed in the dementia unit for professional, round-the-clock care.

DONALD HEATER
BORN: June 22, 1950, Helena, MT
COLLEGE: Montana Tech
POSITION: Running back
NFL EXPERIENCE: 1972
TEAM: St. Louis Cardinals

Born in Helena, Donald Perry Heater achieved great success as a running back at Montana Tech. The six-foot, two-inch, 205-pounder, who was raised and went to high school in Thompson Falls, eventually made it to the NFL, dressing for a handful of games for the St. Louis Cardinals.

Heater was selected by the Cardinals in the sixth round (135th overall pick) of the 1972 NFL draft.

"Teams played six preseason games back then and I pulled a hamstring before the camp and it affected me," he said.

> *I played for four preseason games and we went through about ten running backs, and I was let go. While I registered for class* [at Montana Tech], *I got a call from Green Bay to try out, flew out there, and I watched them play St. Louis in the final preseason game of the season, which I didn't play.*
>
> *I was the last guy left in the hotel, watching TV, and my name came up as being waived* [by the Packers]. *No coach came up to me. I heard it on TV. I asked the Packers about it, but they said don't worry, just be ready to go practice. Soon after I was told that St. Louis had picked me up and I went back and played with St. Louis and made the forty-team squad.*

As a member of the 1972 Cardinals, Heater was on the field during kickoff and punt situations. He was cut halfway through the season after the team brought in Jim "Cannonball" Butler and a number of other, more experienced veterans. "At times I was disillusioned watching guys like [running back] Roy Shivers, who had had two knee operations in the two previous years, and seeing how his knee went completely sideways, and how they dragged him off of the field. Yet fifteen, twenty minutes later he was back in there. [Teammate and running back] Craig Baynham, he had his ankle, two knees, and a shoulder operated on."

Heater, who roomed with offensive guard Conrad Dobler and formed friendships with future hall of famers safety Larry Wilson and cornerback Roger Wehrli, said that he received "a few concussions" in his short stint.

"That's what they used to call getting your bell rung," said Heater. "I realized that it would be a better career for me in engineering."

Heater has surely put his mining and engineering degree to excellent use, working as an engineer and an employee of an offshore construction company in such far-flung places as Azerbaijan, Dubai, Peru, Jakarta, Singapore and Morgan City, Louisiana.

He retired in 2010 and lives in Thompson Falls. Heater remains the only Montana Tech alumni to reach the NFL.

BILL KOLLAR
BORN: November 27, 1952, Warren, OH
COLLEGE: Montana State
NFL EXPERIENCE: 1974–81
TEAMS: Cincinnati Bengals (1974–76); Tampa Bay Buccaneers (1977–81)

Bill Kollar grew up in Warren, Ohio, and attended Warren G. Harding High School, graduating in 1970. He then attended Montana State University, where he was a three-time first team All–Big Sky Conference selection and a two-time Little All-American.

"I remember I flew in from Cleveland during recruiting and I landed in Bozeman," said Bill Kollar. "I remember that the plane was low to the ground and instead of landing the plane went back up because something was wrong. It was the first time I'd ever flown and it was an exciting deal. Bozeman over forty years ago was a heck of a place and small town atmosphere."

As a junior for the Bobcats, he was named the Big Sky Player of the Year. Currently the defensive line coach of the Denver Broncos, Kollar was MSU's highest pick ever, in the first round. He earned All-America honors in 1973, and his MVP award in the 1974 Shrine Bowl college all-star game was the precursor to a long NFL career.

"Playing at a smaller school, you could just tell, once you end up playing, guys are guys, players are players, and I really enjoyed it," said Kollar. "Growing up in Marion, halfway between Cleveland and Pittsburgh, I was a big Browns fan and watching Jim Brown. Paul Brown was the coach when I got to Cincinnati, and playing for him was something else. In the 1970s, the uniforms, the pads were bigger, and everybody seemed slower back then and it seems like the further you go back in the videos, the smaller and the slower everyone ends up looking."

The Tampa Bay Buccaneers joined the NFL as a member of the AFC West in 1976. The following year, they were moved to the NFC Central, while the other 1976 expansion team, the Seattle Seahawks, switched conferences with Tampa Bay and joined the AFC West.

"I joined the Buccaneers in their second season," said Kollar. "We had Doug Williams and Lee Roy Selmon on defensive line and Dewey Selmon at inside linebacker, Richard Wood, who we called 'Batman,' who played linebacker for University of Southern California. In 1979 [the Buccaneers' fourth season], we probably had the number one defense in the league and we went to the NFC Championship game and lost to the Los Angeles Rams, 9–0. We had scored with three minutes left but the touchdown got called back because of a penalty."

Kollar began coaching as a defensive assistant and special teams coach for the Tampa Bay Buccaneers under coach John McKay in 1984. "After six years of playing, I blew my knee out and blew out my ACL and flunked the physical. McKay hired me in his last year when he resigned in the middle of the season."

He then spent three seasons at the University of Illinois and two years at Purdue University. He was the defensive line coach for the Atlanta Falcons (1990–2000), St. Louis Rams (2001–5) and Buffalo Bills (2006–8) before joining Gary Kubiak's staff in Houston in 2009. He served as the Texans' defensive line coach and assistant head coach from 2009 to 2014 and is credited with advancing star defensive player J.J. Watt.

In 2015, Kollar left the Texans and became the Denver Broncos' defensive line coach, where he reunited with Kubiak and work alongside Kalispell-born offensive coordinator Rick Dennison. In Kollar's first season, the Broncos defeated the Carolina Panthers in Super Bowl 50.

"It was my third Super Bowl, I'd lost one with Atlanta and the other with Rams and they were gut-wrenching. We had a good team and we were the underdogs and if we didn't win our last two games we wouldn't have made the playoffs and our wins in the playoffs against the Steelers and Patriots went right down to the wire. Those games are what builds the energy and makes the game so great."

Kollar said that he has warm feelings for the role Montana has played in both his professional and personal lives. "I enjoyed my time at Montana State and all of the great people and maybe there were a little bit more Montana people there back then. I met my wife in Bozeman, who is originally from Great Falls, and we've been married for 41 years."

In 1988, Kollar joined Sonny Holland, Jan Stenerud and Don Hass as the only Bobcats whose jersey numbers have been retired.

PETE LAZETICH

BORN: February 4, 1950, Billings, MT
COLLEGE: Stanford
POSITIONS: Defensive end; linebacker; defensive tackle; nose tackle
NFL EXPERIENCE: 1972–74; 1976–77
TEAMS: San Diego Chargers (1972–74); Philadelphia Eagles
(1976–77)

Following in the career path of his father, Bill, and uncle Milan, Pete Lazetich comes from the heartiest of rural frontier Montana stock.

"My grandfather, Petar Lazetich, was powerfully built and about five foot-nine and he worked in the Pittsburgh area in the coal mines," said Pete Lazetich.

As a young man, he excelled at broad jump events, and as lore has it, when he was sixteen or seventeen, he arrived over in Butte, where [as a newly arriving Serb] *he was looked down upon. One time, a brawl broke out because the Irish and Italians miners who were already established and higher on the pecking order were picking on a Serbian friend of his and my grandfather took on five or six guys and he threw one of them down a shaft as it was going.*

The worse thing for a man to be in Anaconda would be to be banned and blackballed from the Anaconda [Copper Company's] *smelter* [operations], *but as part of his penalty he was blackballed. He worked for a dairy farm near Warm Springs and he raised nine kids and one time in Butte in the 1920s, he wrestled a world champion wrestler from France for two and a half hours, and the Frenchman apparently cheated. He was using coal dust to neutralize the oil on his body. They finally called it a draw.*

Pete Lazetich, who played several seasons with the San Diego Chargers and Philadelphia Eagles, is a member of Montana's first family of football, following his father, Bill, and uncle Milan into the NFL.
Courtesy Pete Lazetich.

Pete Lazetich (71) obstructs a pass from Miami Dolphins quarterback Bob Griese. All four Miami Dolphins pictured—Larry Csonka (39), Bob Griese (12), Jim Langer (62) and Larry Little (66)—are in the Pro Football Hall of Fame. *Courtesy Pete Lazetich.*

Lazetich enjoyed the burly physicality of football more than its finesse elements; he liked to hit and to be hit, and he found high school football in the Montana the perfect battle ground. "Football got easier after I left high school in Montana," he said. "They had some tough teams across the state just at the high school level. Everybody is giving their all and kicking the shit out of me. My Billings Senior team had three guys that ultimately got drafted by the National Football League and our best record was 6-4."

Lazetich was a standout at Senior and played for two Rose Bowl champions at Stanford. Jim Plunkett was his teammate during the first victory, over Ohio State in 1971. He played pro football for five years with the San Diego Chargers and Philadelphia Eagles.

Lazetich was a member of the Eagles team later immortalized in the 2006 movie *Invincible* about lifelong football fan Vince Papale (Mark Wahlberg) who sees his wildest fantasy come true when he becomes a member of the Philadelphia Eagles.

> *Vermeil decided to have an open tryout and advertising that any one in Philly who thinks that they are a tough guy can try out. Vermeil did it as a lark, a publicity stunt. Do you think you are so tough? Papale is a thirty-year-old part-time schoolteacher and bartender and that was based on the first year I was there. Papale was fearless and he was the hometown hero and just like in the movie, it was storybook.*
>
> *I spotted the Lazetich jersey in the movie. It turns out it was a black guy with an Afro as an extra. My daughter looked at me and said, "Were you consulted about doing the movie?" We got such a kick out of that, and we started laughing so hard we had to leave the theatre. My one starting role and it was a black guy playing me.*

Many of Lazetich's memories intersect with some legends of football, characters whose names and tales and fables only amplify more loudly as time passes.

> *I played with the old, fat version of Johnny Unitas* [traded to the Chargers in 1973], *but by that time he was so old and beat up. He was the Will Rogers of football and he had the smile and the confident look in his eyes and he was a real gentleman. He was the nicest guy to know in the world and also one of the toughest. Unitas befriended me and he liked my Montana stories. Deacon Jones, man if there was ever a guy who would be a chief in Africa, he would have been it. Tim Rossovich used to light himself on fire. "Big" Bob Brown—no one knew how old he was, he was well into his forties. He delivered a forearm shot that people avoided. He was a mysterious fellow and he had a scar on his neck and upper cheek and that was because some kid shot him and blew out his cheekbone. He'd be chugging whiskey at practice, and nobody said a word. Hot day and grab the jug and empty room and take care of that bottle.*

Lazetich has lived in Reno, Nevada, for several decades, where he currently operates a messenger service, bales and packages hay on a small farm and takes long walks with his two dogs. "I think that per capita Montana produces more football players than any other state," he said.

"In college and the pros, people treated you special because you were from Montana and it had its own aura. It was like coming from a different planet to other people. It was a special place and always had a little glow over it, compared to Los Angeles or somewhere else."

BOB McCULLOUGH
BORN: November 18, 1940, Helena, MT
COLLEGE: Colorado
POSITION: Offensive guard
NFL EXPERIENCE: 1962–65
TEAM: Denver Broncos

Montanan Bob McCullough played in all of the Denver Broncos' fifty-six games between 1962 and 1965.

McCullough's father, Bob Sr., was a native of nearby Boulder and a traveling salesman and, later, sales manager at Montana Power and Equipment Company. A strong, precocious kid with a naturally husky frame, the boy attended grade school in Great Falls, returning to Helena at the start of sixth grade. He excelled as an all-star fullback for the Helena Crimson Bengals, playing at what is now one of Montana's most notable high school venues: Vigilante Stadium.

McCullough chose to play college football at the University of Colorado, where he had a successful run with the powerful Buffaloes under Everett "Sonny" Grandelius. He embarked on a professional path because it was "a lot of fun and all" and because the money was "a lot better than what most people made." The Denver Broncos were founded on August 14, 1959, as an AFL charter franchise and won the first-ever AFL game, beating the Boston Patriots, 13–10, on September 9, 1960. When McCullough arrived in Denver in 1962, the struggling franchise was helmed by thirty-five-year-old quarterback Frank Tripucka, who had entered the league in 1949.

> *But you certainly weren't going to go the rest of your life with it* [the money from football]. *The greatest players might have made 20,000 bucks. My first year with the Broncos, I negotiated a contract for $11,500 dollars and*

When Bob McCullough arrived in Denver in 1962, the struggling franchise was helmed by thirty-five-year-old quarterback Frank Tripucka, who had entered the league in 1949. *Courtesy Bob McCullough.*

they gave me a signing bonus of $2,500. That was far more than I was worth. I made $14,000 my first year. To put it in perspective, a highly paid electrical or engineering position straight out of college at the time made probably $5,500 to $6,000. Hell, when I was playing, Joe Namath signed a $400,000 contract, and papers said nobody was worth that.

As a rookie, McCullough earned the role of starting right guard, although he played at left guard throughout his second season. Other historical footnotes include McCullough's Broncos playing against the New York Jets in 1963, the final year that the Jets played at the Polo Grounds, as well as facing the Jets in their inaugural game at Shea Stadium on September 12, 1964. The talents he observed were ubiquitous, from Oakland Raiders cornerback Willie Brown to teammate Lionel Taylor, a nimble-footed wide receiver. Roommate Wahoo McDaniel's eccentricity stood out from the pack. A Choctaw-Chickasaw Indian, McDaniel's post-football career included a successful stint as a professional entertainment wrestler who engaged in top-billed events with gimmicked titles such as "Indian Death Match." "Nothing does him justice," said McCullough. "He was a nutty guy from Oklahoma. He was trouble from the word 'go.'"

McCullough remembers vividly where he was when President John F. Kennedy was assassinated shortly after noon on November 22, 1963, as well as the pervasive unsettled feeling two days later when the NFL decided not to postpone its scheduled games (Pete Rozelle said the decision was his biggest regret as NFL commissioner). "We were practicing for a game and we pulled into a hamburger joint and we heard it on the radio that it was reported that Kennedy had been shot. By the time we were finishing, we heard it again on the radio, this time announcing that he was dead. It was a grief-stricken time in the wake of his death."

Following his retirement from football in 1965, McCullough graduated from business school with a degree in marketing and worked as "a high-pressure stockbroker" in Denver for twelve years and then as a branch manager in Spokane for two years. After living close to the ocean in the Seattle area for approximately two decades, he returned to Helena in 2010. He still participates in Denver Broncos alumni and reunion events.

"It was unique at that time to be from Montana and to play for the Denver Broncos," said McCullough. "It seems like in any given town now in Montana fifty percent of the people are Broncos fans. It's still a big deal to people. Personally, I don't have a complaint about how it all went."

SAM MCCULLUM

BORN: November 30, 1952, McComb, MS
COLLEGE: Montana State
POSITION: Wide receiver
NFL EXPERIENCE: 1974–81
TEAMS: Minnesota Vikings (1974–75; 1982–83); Seattle Seahawks (1976–81)

In the summer of 1967, Sam McCullum's family of eight crammed into the station wagon in southern Mississippi and drove to northwest Montana.

McCullum's father, Mac, the son of a Mississippi sharecropper, was a sergeant in the air force and was commissioned to work at the radar base in Lakeside. Sam and the military family were accustomed to moving—they had lived in eight different states before Sam was in high school. All told, his father had spent twenty-six years in the military, employed at bases around the world, including Germany, France and Korea, and at U.S. locations in Alaska, Michigan, Montana and Washington.

But arriving in Lakeside as a sophomore at Flathead High School, McCullum felt like an outsider. He

Sam McCullum, a six-foot, two-inch, 203-pound wide receiver, played on special teams in his rookie season for Minnesota in Super Bowl IX, in New Orleans' Tulane Stadium. *Courtesy Sam McCullum.*

didn't know how to swim or ski, so he participated in sports as a way to make friends and to keep busy outside of school. "I think people knew that as one of the only black families in the town of Kalispell that we were only temporary," said Sam McCullum. "It took the community a while to realize that I wasn't just passing through or transient. When I started integrating and competing with guys in school who were trying to make teams, it became harder to accept me."

He was six feet, two inches, fast and athletic, and even though he had no experience playing organized sports, he developed into a three-sport athlete at Flathead High, where he made all-state in football, basketball and track. The following year, Sam's dad retired, and the enlarged family of ten moved to the east side of Kalispell. Mac worked at the Skyline Bowling Alley downtown. He set up a desk downstairs, where Sam said he would study late into the night. "My father was a very good role model in that respect. He preached to us a great deal about discipline and don't forget about your education," said McCullum. "He got his college degree in the military and my mother never finished high school growing up in the rural south."

As a junior, McCullum decided to try football for the first time. One season later, the speedy senior earned all-state and garnered college recruiting attention from Colorado State, Washington State, Montana and Montana State. McCullum gridded collegiately at MSU from 1970 to 1973, where he set Bobcat records of twelve touchdown receptions in a season and sixteen career TD catches.

"At Montana State I had a great time visiting Yellowstone, going to hot springs, and I learned to ski and I was accepted 100 percent."

He was drafted by the Minnesota Vikings in the ninth round of the 1974 draft and went on to play ten seasons in the NFL, with the Vikings and Seattle Seahawks.

McCullum, a six-foot, two-inch, 203-pound wide receiver, played on special teams in his rookie season for Minnesota, including in Super Bowl IX, at New Orleans's Tulane Stadium. The Pittsburgh Steelers captured the first of their six Lombardi Trophies with a 16–6 victory over the Vikings. (As of 2015, only eight players from Montana State University, including McCullum, and six from the University of Montana have appeared in the Super Bowl.)

"It was still quite a big game and quite a big to-do," said McCullum. "The streets of New Orleans were mobbed by die-hard Steelers and Vikings fans and I met Bill Cosby and Jim Brown and was mobbed by Steelers and Vikings fans. Now the whole world plans for Super Bowl Sunday."

McCullum's Vikings narrowly missed out on the Super Bowl the following year, and then in 1976, McCullum went on to play for one of the league's two new franchises, the Seattle Seahawks (the other was the Tampa Bay Buccaneers).

He holds the distinction of catching the first touchdown in Seahawk history. On October 17, 1976, McCullum caught a TD pass from Jim Zorn and helped Seattle win its first game, 13–10, over Tampa Bay. Both teams were 0-5 at the time. Zorn's 15-yard toss to McCullum and a pair of field goals by John Leypoldt in the first half were enough to earn Seattle the victory. "I didn't even think of collecting the football," said McCullum.

"The Buccaneers were more in disarray than we were. It helped us get our first win and we were both expansion teams. It would have [been] worth keeping just for that reason."

Job security in the NFL in the 1980s was still a fantasy; teams of that era shipped, shuttled and released players with zeal. "There was a such a tremendous turnover on the Seattle team, with new players coming and going every single week. It made it hard to discover who you were as a team. We'd have three hundred players go through the team in a season. It was unreal. You knew little about them [your teammates]. Sometimes, it would be older veterans showing up and every day new seats were assigned. It was hard to go to battle when the guy with you in battle just showed. There was no commitment."

Yet, McCullum's commitment helped him post statistical highs with the Seahawks in 1980 in pass receptions (sixty-two), yardage (874) and touchdowns (six).

McCullum served as the Seahawks' player representative and vice president of the NFL Players Association from 1982 to 1984. Among the most memorable events of the 1982 strike was his politically motivated firing by former coach Jack Patera and general manager John Thompson, which left McCullum embittered for many years.

> *I've learned to look at the situation differently and to move past it. The Seahawks saw an opportunity to weaken guys who were involved in the strike and labor situation and we were talking about the issue of player solidarity. As players, we were not allowed to walk across the field and shake hands with the opponent. We wanted all the players on both teams to shake before the coin toss. But in the NFL you were taught to hate your opponents. You were told that if you were too close to the opponent then you demean the game and that you could not be friendly with the other team, because if you did, then you wouldn't play as hard.*

The players in the NFL today have much more leverage and clout than did previous generations, thanks to the labor activities of men such as McCullum.

> *Coaches were the big stars back then and now the players became the stars. [As a result of the 1982 strike] players began to have the ability to control how their retirement was being invested and began to be able to choose the doctors who were operating on them. We started to have access to*

our own medical records and to be able to see them. We got to know about the chemicals and the things they treated us with, even things such as what the field was being painted green with. Whatever it was it hurt our skin and if we were scraped [with paint] we'd get inflamed glands. What are you treating the field with? What are you using for the painted lines, and the grease and the substances? We wanted a say in our environment, to control our own 401k and our own playing conditions.

Patera and Thompson both insisted that McCullum's firing was a "football decision," but the players association protested, and a federal law judge held that the Seahawks had unlawfully cut McCullum because of his union activities. A National Labor Relations Board administrative law judge ordered the team to reinstate McCullum, who had re-joined the Vikings, at full back pay.

McCullum spent two more seasons with the Vikings before retiring after the 1983 campaign. He finished his career with 274 receptions for 4,017 yards and twenty-six touchdowns.

McCullum, sixty-four, lives in the Seattle area. In 1993, he was inducted into the Montana State Hall of Fame. He was inducted into the Legends Wall of Fame in Kalispell in 2010.

"I look back on Kalispell as being the jump start of my athletic ability," said McCullum. "There were great coaches at the time who believed in me and helped me a great deal. The people in Kalispell who got to know me and my family, they treated us well. I'm very thankful."

RICK OGLE

BORN: January 14, 1949, Tacoma, WA
COLLEGE: Colorado
POSITION: Linebacker
NFL EXPERIENCE: 1971–72
TEAMS: St. Louis Cardinals (1971); Detroit Lions (1972)

Rick Ogle's family construction company business has operated in Bozeman for 125 years. His father was born in Billings and raised in Livingston; his mother was born in Baker and raised in Jordan. They met at Montana State, where Bill Ogle played basketball for the Bobcats. Ogle spent the first six months of his life in Tacoma, Washington, and has called Bozeman home ever since.

Bozeman native Rick Ogle (no. 52) played baseball and football and was good enough at the latter to be drafted by the St. Louis Cardinals in 1971. *Courtesy Rick Ogle.*

After graduating from Bozeman High School in the late 1960s, he left for college at Colorado.

"Bozeman was a small town when I left to go to college, about 13,000 in town and 20,000 in county. I grew up in a cabin in the mountains. It was idyllic. I can't complain. I tried to do everything at Bozeman High School. Being busy kept a lot of kids out of trouble."

At the University of Colorado, Ogle played baseball and football, good enough at the latter to be drafted by the St. Louis Cardinals in 1971. "Dan Dierdorf [hall of fame offensive lineman] was my roommate at St. Louis. I had played in the college all-star game in Chicago and after the game I was in camp. I lost my first roommate because he got cut. Dierdorf was a huge man and I remember looking at his big pair of shoes in the room. His? My God. He was a 17EEE and I was a 12B. He was born to play football. He was six feet, three inches, three hundred pounds, and nobody could hurt him."

Ogle played one season with the Cardinals, even starting the final few games of the year at outside linebacker. In his first game as a starter, he lined up opposite Green Bay Packers quarterback Bart Starr, one of the league's savviest, more experienced field generals. "There was a guy who I had watched and who I thought was the greatest who ever played the game. Starr came up to the line of scrimmage and he looked right at me and tried to take advantage of me as one of the young guys, and they did. They ran two plays right at me and then a flair pass. It was exhilarating to line up and play against a guy with that much history."

When Ogle and the Cardinals played the New York Giants in Yankee Stadium, the first thing Ogle did on arrival was head out to centerfield and absorb the feeling of one of the sports world's most memory-laden places. In that contest, Ogle played against quarterback Fran Tarkenton, and he burned his share of calories that day chasing the elusive scrambler all over the field.

Still recuperating from an injured knee, he was shipped to the Detroit Lions in a trade.

> *In Atlanta, I got clipped on a kickoff and tore my knee in half. It was a catastrophic knee injury. Detroit was a lot different than St. Louis— rough, and tough, and black and blue. St. Louis seemed more skilled. [Quarterback] Jimmy Hart could throw the ball 100 yards. Rioters had burned down part of the downtown that prior summer in Detroit and there was racial tension and it was still a strong economy bustling with jobs. You'd see the school buses with General Motors and American and Ford workers and they'd drive around to pick up employees and take them to the plant and to work.*

Ogle was released after one season with the Lions; after failing to latch on to another squad, he called it quits. For several decades, he's been operating a construction company in Bozeman, which was started more than a century ago by his relatives. He remains a rabid Bobcats fan. He said that the road to the NFL, while arduous, is one well worth the journey.

"There's no way I thought at their age I'd be playing in the NFL," said Ogle. "You can't put limitations on yourself. You cannot put ceilings on yourself. I encourage them to dream big and go after it."

STEVE OKONIEWSKI

BORN: August 22, 1949, Bremerton, WA
COLLEGES: Washington; Montana
POSITION: Offensive tackle
NFL EXPERIENCE: 1972–77
TEAMS: Buffalo Bills (1972–73); Green Bay Packers (1974–75);
St. Louis Cardinals (1976–77); Cleveland Browns (1977)

Steve Okoniewski started out at the University of Washington, but when UM offered him a scholarship, he accepted. At Washington, he had never even considered the prospect of playing professional football. But when he arrived in Montana, that perspective changed. "Around my junior year the NFL scouts were looking at a couple of guys at Montana, and I started to think that if they were looking at them then maybe I did have a shot."

Okoniewski said that he first traveled through Montana with his family when he was seven years old. When he finished high school in Silverdale, Washington, the seventeen-year-old Okoniewski and two of his pals hopped in a 1953 Chevy and headed for Yellowstone for a week.

"I was always just absolutely in love with Montana," said Okoniewski. "In the summer of '67, I fought a fire at Trapper Peak as one of my summer jobs. I knew it would be a change of life from the city of Seattle, but that was in the early '70s, late '60s. Everybody wanted to get back to nature and

In the 1972 NFL draft, Steve Okoniewski was picked by the Atlanta Falcons in the second round (forty-first overall), the Grizzlies' highest-selected player ever in the NFL draft. *Courtesy University of Montana.*

During the NFL strike in 1974, Steve Okoniewski was in Missoula waiting out the negotiations when he found out he'd been traded from Buffalo to Green Bay. *Courtesy Steve Okoniewski.*

whatever. Best move I ever made in my life was the transfer from Seattle out to the University of Montana. I thought it was the perfect mix of [playing] football [and] the great outdoors. It was very, very uncomplicated. That was before Montana had been discovered."

Under coach Jack Swarthout, he had two banner seasons with the Grizzles in 1970 and 1971. Okoniewski's approach to his offensive line work was simple: go out and pound the other guy hard and often. This philosophy is what led to Okoniewski being drafted by the Atlanta Falcons.

In the 1972 NFL draft, Okoniewski, whose playing weight at UM was 240 pounds on his six-foot, three-and-a-half-inch frame, was picked by the Falcons in the second round, the forty-first pick overall. He was the Grizzlies' highest-selected player ever in the NFL draft. Teammate and offensive linemate Willie Postler was selected in the ninth round by the Houston Oilers, but he was released. (The next highest draft pick in Grizzly history was offensive tackle Scott Gragg, also taken in the second round, as the fifty-fourth pick overall in 1995.)

An arch injury in June 1972 wiped out Atlanta's interest in Okoniewski, who wound up being picked up off waivers by Buffalo. "The one thing you learned real quick in the NFL was that you had to stay healthy."

In 1973, Okoniewski was on the roster when the Bills team moved into its new stadium in Orchard Park. (Rich Stadium is now known as New Era Field.) The season was marked by fifth-year running back O.J. Simpson's distinction of becoming the first player in NFL history to rush for 2,000 yards in a season (he did it in fourteen games, no less). Okoniewski started several games on the defensive line that year.

It was a total transformation for the Bills from playing at War Memorial Stadium, where they filmed The Natural, and moving to Rich Stadium, where there was lots of mud and pissed-off fans and coach Lou Saban built the team around Simpson. We went 0-6 in the preseason and there were no expectations for us, and the first game of the year against New England, Simpson went crazy on the ground and he was a phenomenon. Howard Cosell was in the locker room all the time and he gave a lot of exposure to his [Simpson's] performances. The difference in the size of the rosters back then meant something. We had a forty-man active roster, and that number went up in 1973 and after the 1974 players strike. In 1976, they cut back the total.

While he retired as one of the sport's most notable athletes with several rushing records to his credit, Simpson's name is forever associated with a pair of grisly homicides. Simpson was criminally acquitted of the crimes, but many in the public and some legal experts are all but certain he committed the murders. Okoniewski spoke about his former teammate:

One time, Simpson almost killed a guy in practice. It was on a Friday, and he was beat up and we were doing a dry drill and a linebacker smoked Simpson and he wasn't expecting it. Simpson got on top of the guy and he ripped his helmet off and started punching him in the face. Granted, it was a cheap shot. But the fury in the guy [Simpson] was crazy. I have no doubt that if he felt he was slighted he was capable of retribution. As a teammate, Simpson was a great guy and he'd joke and drink beer and wherever he went in a bar there was an automatic party and a good time. Unfortunately, life went the way it went for him.

During the NFL strike in 1974, Okoniewski was in Missoula waiting out the negotiations when he found out he'd been traded from Buffalo to Green Bay. "I was down at the Stockman's at about one or two in the morning and eating a ham and cheese omelet and some guy comes running up to me and says, 'You're going to be a Green Bay Packer.' That was the first I had heard about the trade. I think that 1974 was probably my best year of football. [He started all 14 games.] We weren't that good [finishing 6-8]. The next year, Bart Starr came in and in 1976, I was the last guy cut [from the Packers], then I got picked up by St. Louis."

After one year with St. Louis, Okoniewski wandered up to Cleveland for his sixth year in the league and then north to Winnipeg and the Canadian Football League.

"One thing I think is pretty interesting is all of the coaches I had the chance to be around. I was drafted in Atlanta by Norm Van Brocklin and played under Lou Saban and Jim Ringo and Dan Devine and then Bart Starr and in St. Louis, Dan Coryell, Joe Gibbs and Jim Hanifan. In Cleveland, it was Forrest Gregg. It was interesting to see the contrast and approach each had to managing and organizing players."

Okoniewski said that people wrongly look to the league as if it should have a higher standard than any other industry; most of the players, he said, aren't much different than other blue-collar, hardworking guys who lead a life in the trenches in search of a steady paycheck and concomitant security. "Most of the guys who played in the NFL back then were guys who were just trying to make a living. If you can do it and keep your physical health, it's a great experience. I wanted to become a veteran, because after you hit four years in, you became a vested veteran and you'd get something in retirement."

Post-gridiron, he obtained his master's at Wisconsin-Oshkosh in curriculum and instruction and sports, which set him up to become an athletic director as well as a physical education teacher. He was head football coach at Deer Lodge and also coached track from 1979 through the spring of 1985; in the last three years he also served as the school's athletic director. He accepted a job as a principal in Wibaux (population 589), just a few miles from the North Dakota border.

"Back then in Wibaux it was 2.2 people per square mile and as many rattlesnakes and deer grazing in the town as there were football players on the field," said Okoniewski. "Now it's down to 1.2 per square mile. You had to have a strong like of wilderness and solitude to live in Wibaux, which was twenty-eight miles to the nearest McDonald's. You knew the wind was going to blow, you just didn't know from which direction. There were fifty-five boys in high school and fifty-three went out for the football team."

Okoniewski, sixty-seven, lives in Oconto Falls, Wisconsin, about thirty miles north of Green Bay, and works as the principal at neighboring

Luxemburg-Casco High School. He tries to get back to Montana every year to visit friends, family and former coaches, as well as to "enjoy the beauty of the place."

"There are a lot of commonalities between Wisconsin and Montana, like a love of family and sport. The only difference is that Montana's small towns are forty miles apart and here [in Wisconsin] they are four miles apart. Similar to Wibaux and Deer Lodge, the small towns here are passionate about the performance of their sports teams. In my estimation, nothing can really compare to western Montana. I love the place. It's my first love."

BOB SCHMITZ
BORN: September 10, 1938, Marytown, WI
DIED: June 8, 2004, Glendale, AZ
COLLEGES: Wisconsin; Montana State
POSITION: Linebacker
NFL EXPERIENCE: 1961–66
TEAMS: Pittsburgh Steelers (1961–66); Minnesota Vikings (1966)

Rural Wisconsin native Bob Schmitz graduated from New Holstein High School, a community about forty miles south of Green Bay, in 1956, where he excelled in football and basketball. Logging in at six feet, one inch and 230 pounds, Schmitz played at MSU from 1957 to 1960, where he earned several honors.

He came to Montana State as an agile, fast fullback and finished his career as a Bobcat as a quick interior lineman on his way to what he hoped would be, in his words, a "quiet, unobtrusive" career in the NFL.

Schmitz was bothered by injury in his first two seasons at Montana State, but he "was a late bloomer" said former Bobcat assistant coach Tom Parac. "Bob was a trench guy. He was a big, physical guy for that day and age, six-three plus, 230 pounds or so. He had very good feet, quick, and he was probably among the fastest people on the team. He was a quiet, in-the-trenches, get-the-job done guy."

Schmitz was the linchpin of a line that helped Montana State to an 11-6-1 record in his last two seasons. "Bob was physically very talented," said former teammate and Bobcat legend Sonny Holland. "He was a big, strong, fast kid who ran very well and was very intelligent."

The Steelers selected Schmitz as a fourteenth-round draft choice in 1961, and he played linebacker under coaches Buddy Parker, Mike Nixon and Bill Austin. His career ended in 1966, a season that he split between the Steelers and Minnesota Vikings.

Schmitz was known as "the quiet man" of the Steelers, seldom making the headlines. The Steelers' press book described the linebacker as the "steady, unspectacular type who always is available and who always gives full effort."

He later took up scouting in the NFL, first working for Pittsburgh-based Blesto in 1971 before joining the Steelers as an area scout in 1976. Schmitz's nifty work as a scout surpassed his six seasons as a linebacker with two teams—except for one memorable play. He broke through and tackled future hall of fame running back Jim Brown (1957–65) of the Cleveland Browns for a safety, giving the Steelers a 9–7 victory on November 10, 1963, in Pitt Stadium. "Gee, that's probably the best thing that ever happened to me," Schmitz told the *Pittsburgh Gazette* after he was named NFL Player of the Week for his winning score. "I was lucky to make that tackle, though. We were red-dogging and I went right through their line, hit Brown and then just hung on for dear life."

A profile written about the self-effacing Schmitz after he stuffed Brown for two points appeared in the *Hutchinson News* on November 15, 1963. "Outside of a few thousand folks in New Holstein, Wis., and Bozeman, MT., it's unlikely that many people knew Bob Schmitz played linebacker for the Pittsburgh Steelers the past three years." The accompanying photo shows Schmitz demonstrating on a tackling dummy how he nabbed Brown in the end zone for a safety, giving the Steelers an upset victory.

He worked for the Steelers until 1995, when his former boss with the team, Dick Haley, offered him more money to scout for the New York Jets.

Schmitz was inducted into the Montana State Bobcats Hall of Fame in 2001. He died at age sixty-five at his Arizona home.

JAN STENERUD
BORN: November 26, 1942, Fetsund, Norway
COLLEGE: Montana State
POSITION: Kicker
NFL EXPERIENCE: 1967–85
TEAMS: Kansas City Chiefs (1967–79); Green Bay Packers (1980–83); Minnesota Vikings (1984–85)

Born in Norway, Jan Stenerud didn't play organized football until his senior year of college. Twenty-six years later, he became the first player elected to the Pro Football Hall of Fame as a full-time kicker.

His memorable journey from skier to Super Bowl–winning specialist began when he was invited to Montana State on a ski-jumping scholarship.

"Fetsund is about twenty miles from Oslo, and it has a continuous population of people today," said Stenerud, who's now seventy-three. "After the junior national championship finished in the spring of 1962, I got a letter of invitation from Bob Beck [coach of the Montana State College ski team] in Bozeman. There was a name of a good skier on the letter—Tor Fageraas, a Norwegian Junior National champ—so that meant a lot. Two months later, I had a free education in one of the most interesting countries in the world."

Jan Stenerud's career spanned nineteen seasons and 263 games; he never missed a game because of injury or sickness, and his field-goal percentage actually improved as he got older. *Courtesy Jan Stenerud.*

Expecting a climate similar to that of his home country and eager to participate in the collegiate life, the Norwegian set out for Bozeman, Montana. He wandered around the campus for a couple of days before the dormitories opened and stayed with the parents of Dorothy Bradley, who, beginning in the 1970s, represented Montana in the U.S. House of Representatives for eight terms. When Stenerud arrived at MSU, ski jumping was an NCAA event, and MSU's ski jumpers practiced and competed above Deer Park at Bridger Bowl. The Bobcats won a couple of conference ski titles during Stenerud's period, and he finished fourth at the NCAA meet in 1965, earning All-American status.

"Ski jumping was the main thing," said Stenerud. "It has since been discontinued, in favor of cross-country skiing and the relay. I had to get enough good grades to stay eligible, which was tough because I only had five or six years of English in school. I skied at Bridger Bowl, since Big Sky wasn't open. I skied in McCall, Idaho, Park City, Banff, all over. The western part of Norway has a lot of mountains, but where I lived [Fetsund], it was more like Wisconsin or Minnesota. I liked the climate of Montana and it was a special place to live."

One fall afternoon in 1964, Stenerud stopped to look at an MSU football player practicing extra points; ski team members routinely ran the stairs at the football stadium as part of their offseason training. Stenerud asked if he could boot the ball. He sailed several between the uprights.

In my junior year, I hadn't kicked a soccer ball or any ball for three years. I had round tennis shoes on. I kicked it well. I asked if I could kick with the side of my foot [as a soccer player would do on a corner or penalty kick]. *Dale's* [Dale Jackson, MSU halfback, injured member of the Bobcats squad] *answer was yes. He said that Pete Gogolak* [of the Buffalo Bills] *does it that way.* [MSU basketball coach] *Roger Craft walked across the field and he stood and watched, and he ran over to* [MSU football coach] *Jim Sweeney.*

At least a month or so later, I was running the steps and Sweeney hollered at me, "Get down here, you can kick!" It was the Friday before the last home game in the 1964 season, and he patted me on the back and he said, "What are you doing tomorrow afternoon?" I knew that it was the land of opportunity and that meant to be prepared.

Though he was ineligible to play, Stenerud suited up for the final home game of the 1964 campaign. The next season, he discovered the kicking method he would forever use: standing away from his holder, his first step would be backward. Subsequently, in a 24–7 win against Montana that season, he shocked the Bozeman crowd by nailing a 59-yard field goal on November 6, 1965, at Bozeman's Gatton Field (still the longest field goal in school history).

"I was drafted because I kicked a 59-yarder against the Grizzlies. I got on the radar completely, with what was the longest kick at that time in professional and collegiate football. I got drafted because of that and the scouts came to see. I came to MSU at the right time, when the pro teams started to have a kicker, and at the right time in the evolution of the kicker, the taking off of kicking as a weapon."

Following the 1965 season, Stenerud, who had exhausted his ski eligibility, elected to stay at MSU, and in 1966, he kicked a school-record eighty-two points.

He sustained similar success in the NFL.

In his third professional season, he would kick three field goals to register the first nine points of Super Bowl IV, including a then-record 48-yarder,

Jan Stenerud's memorable journey from skier to Super Bowl–winning specialist began when he was invited to Montana State on a ski-jumping scholarship. *Courtesy Jan Stenerud.*

as the Kansas City Chiefs beat the Minnesota Vikings, 23–10. All in all, Stenerud scored eleven points on three field goals and two point-after kicks, and his successful kickoffs frequently had the Vikings pinned from behind their 20-yard line.

"Every rule change has been done since then to increase the points in an NFL game," said Stenerud. "Back then, you could win with a little scoring and a defense that was dominant. You could win with good defense and a good kicking game. Low-scoring games were common. Now, it is a quarterback and a passing game and more exciting. Back then, if you were the kicker of four field goals, you were the difference maker."

As a pro, Stenerud kicked seventeen field goals over 50 yards, including a 54-yarder in the second quarter of his first regular-season game (September 9, 1967). His personal best was a 55-yarder against Denver in 1970.

I remember my first field goal came against the Houston Oilers in Rice Stadium, a 54-yarder, and we didn't practice with a snapper or holder back then, and the QB was holding. My first attempt, I kicked a low kick [which set a new team record]. *It was a big deal kicking one at 50 and now it's a big deal if you miss at 50.*

"In those years, you had to compete for your job and there were a lot of kickers in camp. It was different. We were just looking at a photo of [Kansas City Chiefs quarterback] *Len Dawson enjoying a smoke in the fresco. There was an astray in every locker room in the mid-1960s. Then, if you did badly in the first two games, you got paid for the two games only and you were gone. There were several hundred kickers in the league in the time I played.*

He kicked for the Chiefs for thirteen years (1967–79); upon retirement, he'd kicked team-record field goals for the Chiefs (55), the Green Bay Packers (53) and the Minnesota Vikings (54). Each mark has since been surpassed. His career spanned nineteen seasons and 263 games; he never missed a game because of injury or sickness, and his field-goal percentage actually improved as he got older.

"I think I may have had twenty tackles in the 260-plus games, and that was me pushing a guy out of bounds near the sidelines. It was a good position. Though, there was an intense pressure to help the team to win games, and if you didn't do well, you got cut."

Eighteen years separate his first and last Pro Bowl appearances (he was honored four times). He retired after the 1985 season, with 1,699 points, second in all-time scoring, and an NFL record 373 field goals (since eclipsed). "I made the Pro Bowl [with the Minnesota Vikings] at age forty-three and when I started my final year I thought I'd be kicking another five years. By my nineteenth year, my back was really bad and I limped through it."

In 1991, Stenerud became the first "pure" placekicker to enter the Pro Football Hall of Fame. He relocated to Kansas City a couple of years ago after living in Colorado Springs for approximately sixteen years. He has returned to Bozeman several times over the past few years to visit friends, play golf and enjoy the memories of a mountain town that transformed the Nordic skier into an NFL original.

"You couldn't predict it—let's put it that way. Another way to look at it is—that it has been an interesting journey."

STEVE SWEENEY
BORN: September 6, 1950, Bozeman, MT
COLLEGE: California
POSITION: Wide receiver
NFL EXPERIENCE: 1973
TEAM: Oakland

Steve Sweeney's first game of the 1970 season against Oregon, the California sophomore from Yakima, Washington, broke free to score a 71-yard touchdown pass from QB Dave Penhall. His career began with a great play, and he continued to make them. He would go on to score twenty-one touchdowns in three years of play, which today places him third among all Cal receivers in scoring. Thirteen of those scores came in his senior year of 1972, along with fifty-two receptions. For his career, Sweeney reeled in 132 passes for 2,043 yards, and he left Cal as the school's all-time leader in receptions and yardage. The dependable receiver was twice named first-team All–Pac 8, and the Bear Backers voted him MVP after his senior season.

Sweeney was selected by the Oakland Raiders in the ninth round of the 1973 NFL draft and played one forgettable year before retiring.

MIKE TILLEMAN
BORN: March 30, 1944, Chinook, MT
COLLEGE: Montana
POSITION: Defensive tackle
NFL EXPERIENCE: 1966–76
TEAMS: Minnesota Vikings (1966); New Orleans Saints (1967–70); Houston Oilers (1971–72); Atlanta Falcons (1973–76).

Born and raised on a sheep and cattle ranch near Zurich, Montana, Mike Tilleman was a prep star at Chinook High School and attended the University of Montana on a full scholarship.

"Mom was an immigrant and dad was the son of an immigrant, and they were Flemish-Germanic who believed that you were born for work," said Tilleman. "As a kid, I baled tens of thousands of hay bales for a dime a bale, with a pitchfork and a truck."

Tilleman played for the Grizzlies from 1963 to 1964, where he was a second team All–Big Sky Conference selection in both seasons. He bypassed his senior season to sign with the Minnesota Vikings, who had selected him with the 163rd pick of the 1965 NFL draft.

"My dad signed my first contract for me when I was 20. There was no TV as far as the draft. In Minnesota, I whipped everybody in training camp and coach Norm Van Brocklin said I had the job. There were thirteen teams, with thirty-two players on each team. I started with the Vikings in 1966 and then got picked off in the Saints expansion draft and then I was traded to Houston. In Houston [in 1971], I made $155,000 and my signing bonus was two cheeseburgers and a six-pack of beer."

Mike Tilleman bypassed his senior season to sign with the Minnesota Vikings, who had selected him with the 163rd pick of the 1965 NFL draft. *Courtesy University of Montana.*

He came to the New Orleans Saints in the 1967 expansion draft and immediately earned starting chores. Tilleman established himself as one of the better young tackles in the NFL, although things didn't go well for the inaugural Saints, finishing 3-11. The offense comprised ragtag veterans such as quarterback Billy Kilmer, running back Jim Taylor and wide receiver John Gilliam. Tilleman, twenty-three, started at left defensive tackle alongside thirty-seven-year-old left defensive end Doug Atkins, a fourteen-year veteran who had started his career with the Cleveland Browns in 1953. The following seasons saw the Saints slightly improve to 4-9-1 (1968) and 5-9 (1969), but the team slipped to 2-11-1 in his final year.

"The original Saints didn't care if you were crazy or not, they just wanted football players: Joe Don Looney, Monty Stickles, Dave Parks and Doug

Atkins. The town embraced us with open arms. Atkins without a doubt was the best defensive player who ever played the game. Atkins controlled the game. I don't know if the elevator upstairs went all the way up or all the way down. One time I saw Atkins twist and toss an offensive tackle by the wrists and take out the quarterback like a boomerang, and take them both out."

On November 8, 1970, Tilleman blocked on Tom Dempsey's NFL record 63-yard field goal as time expired to give the Saints a 19–17 win over the Detroit Lions. "I played in seventy-five percent of the football game, and I was blocking Alex Karras on that play. Karras ended up on Johnny Carson—not me. When we lined up on our own 37-yard line, people thought it was a joke. As a person, Dempsey was a mess and a real screwball, and most kickers aren't wrapped too tight. After he kicked the 63-yarder, people were on the field and stomping their feet. Dempsey would lay in a wheel barrow in practice, looking like an overstuffed sofa."

Tilleman spent two years with the Houston Oilers, marked by two frustratingly bad seasons: 4-9-1 (1971) and 1-13 (1972). He was chosen the NFL's Comeback Player of the Year in 1972, when he led the NFL with fifteen quarterback sacks and in total tackles. He was selected to the NFL's All-Pro team in 1973.

"Losers are harder to play on than winners. But you can't measure heart. But on the Oilers we had both a lousy team and a lousy coach. I really think I represent an era of players and coaches who had no recognition. We didn't win. We weren't on winning teams and we didn't have an opportunity to win."

After his option with the Oilers was bought out, he was traded for a first-round draft choice to the Atlanta Falcons. Tilleman finished his pro career in Atlanta, where he formed a friendship with linebacker Tommy Nobis, the first pick of the expansion Falcons' initial NFL draft in 1966. Nobis was the league's rookie of the year and became the Falcons' first Pro Bowl player. In his eleven seasons, Nobis made five Pro Bowls on teams that went a combined 50-100 and did not appear in the postseason.

Tilleman and Nobis roomed together for several seasons before the latter retired in 1976. As one of the hundreds of former players who filed suit against the NFL claiming the league misled them and hid from them the permanent damage of repeated concussions, Nobis collected from a $765 million settlement in 2012. According to the court filing, Nobis "has experienced cognitive and other difficulties including but not limited to headaches, loss of memory, dementia, depression, fatigue, sleep problems, numbness and tingling in his neck and cervical spine."

"He was absolutely the hardest-hitting Falcon ever. That wasn't only one play, it was every play," said Tilleman. "He's got dementia bad now and I have a lot of friends like that; Nobis, Mick Tinglehoff, guys who have CTE [chronic traumatic encephalopathy] or something of that nature."

An offensive lineman once commented that he would "rather catch javelins for an hour" than to take hard head slaps from Tilleman. Easily the most devastating defensive maneuver in professional football, the NFL outlawed head slaps in the late 1970s.

The first eight or ten plays I would head-slap the guy and it's just playing the piano. I'd hit them hard enough and then they would get apprehensive. In Minnesota, I went up against a guard named Ed White, and we'd be head-slapping each other and at the end of the game we'd go have a beer. Ken Gray from St. Louis was like an octopus, with an arm or leg around you, like a wrestler. Many of the guys with dementia were the centers; my last three years was nose tackle in Atlanta. The center was helpless and most of them [the centers in the 1970s] were undersized like Mick Tinglehoff. He is in an institution. The year after I retired [in 1977] was the last year the head slap was allowed. You'd hurt people that way.

Frequently double-teamed, Tilleman was seldom afforded the luxury of going one-on-one with opposing linemen, but he was nonetheless among the league's top tacklers. Tilleman underwent two abdominal operations prior to the 1969 season, one of many injuries he incurred over the course of many battles.

"I've had forty operations and fifteen ankle operations from football," said Tilleman. "So many of the injuries came from all of the artificial turf we played on, and I've had three artificial ankles. After they changed the bearings in my ankle a few years ago, I developed MRSA [bacteria] in the hospital and my

Mike Tilleman was chosen the NFL's Comeback Player of the Year in 1972, when he led the NFL with fifteen quarterback sacks and in total tackles. *Courtesy Mike Tilleman.*

Mike Tilleman finished his professional career with the Atlanta Falcons in 1976. He played in 149 games over eleven seasons. *Courtesy Mike Tilleman.*

choice was either to die or to lose an ankle. I lost my ankle. At seventy-two, after a life of football, you feel like a dishrag after they have squeezed the water out of you. I've got the mind of a thirty-year-old and the body of a one-hundred-year-old. I've paid more in medical deductibles than I made in my football career."

Mike and his wife, Gloria, live in Havre, where they run Tilleman Motor Company, a local General Motors dealership. Every fall, Tilleman hosts a celebrity pheasant hunt as a fundraiser for the MSU-Northern athletic program, which provides sports scholarships and pays for one full-time coaching position.

"I worked all of the time that I played football and I saved $120,000 from football and I bought my first car dealership with the money. I came back to Havre after football because it's a place of honesty, and good work ethics, and there are opportunities here if you want them."

TUUFULI UPERESA
BORN: January 20, 1948, American Samoa
COLLEGES: Wenatchee Valley; Montana
POSITION: Offensive guard
NFL EXPERIENCE: 1971
TEAM: Philadelphia Eagles

According to the NFL, an all-time high of five Polynesian players were selected in the first sixty-six picks of the 2015 NFL draft. Over seventy players in the NFL are of Polynesian descent. There are thirty players from American Samoa in the NFL and more than two hundred in Division I NCAA football. Samoan-born Tuufuli Uperesa went to high school in Hawaii and transferred to the University of Montana from Wenatchee Valley College.

Uperesa (pronounced Ooo-per-esa) primarily played right tackle for the Grizzlies from 1968 to 1969, establishing himself as a valuable addition on the team's offensive line. He won the team's Paul Weskamp Award (outstanding offensive lineman) and earned first team all-conference honors during his short Griz tenure. He was also a team captain in 1969 for second-year coach Jack Swarthout.

Uperesa was drafted by the Eagles in the sixteenth round of the 1970 NFL draft and appeared in two games in 1971. The team finished third in the NFC East at 6-7-1. "I liked it in Philadelphia, but the only problem was the losing attitude," he said. "They accepted it. I was used to championships."

Securing a spot on the Eagles' offensive line among high draft choices such as Henry Allison (second round, 1971) proved daunting. Frustrated, Uperesa headed north to the Canadian Football League. He played three years with the Winnipeg Blue Bombers and two more with the Ottawa Rough Riders before walking away from the BC Lions midway through the 1978 season.

He returned to Missoula to complete his degree in health and physical education.

Tuufuli Uperesa primarily played right tackle for the Grizzlies from 1968 to 1969, establishing himself as a valuable addition to the Grizzlies' offensive line. *Courtesy University of Montana.*

"I had spent too much time playing Frisbee golf," said Uperesa, who retired in 1997 after working as a teacher and a counselor at the community college and high school level in Pago Pago, American Samoa. "I had a good time in Missoula. I remember meeting a lot of great of people."

RONALD WARZEKA

BORN: December 24, 1935, Great Falls, MT
COLLEGE: Montana State
POSITION: Defensive tackle
NFL EXPERIENCE: 1960
TEAM: Oakland Raiders

Ronald Warzeka is a Montana State product who played one season professionally with the Oakland Raiders. All-conference tackles Warzeka and Ed Ritt of the 1956 Montana State unbeaten football team signed contracts with professional grid teams. The tackles, both 235-pounders, were the mainstays on the Bobcat line and before that at Great Falls, where they starred in high school football. Warzeka, named to the second Little All-America team his senior year, was a four-year football letterman. Ritt lettered three years at MSU.

Ritt was signed by the Chicago Cardinals and reported for training, but he didn't survive the final cut. Warzeka signed with the San Francisco 49ers, but he failed to earn a roster spot. When he was claimed by the Oakland Raiders, the *Oakland Tribune* announced, "George Fields, the 6-foot-3-inch, 245-pound tackle, and his 6-4, 255-pound running mate Ron Warzeka, looms as the blockbusters of the bunch."

Fields's career, however, was over within two years, and Warzeka lasted but one season on a Raiders squad helmed by quarterbacks Tom Flores and Babe Parilli. The team ended with a 6-8 record.

BILL WONDOLOWSKI
BORN: November 29, 1946, Atlantic City, NJ
POSITION: Wide receiver
NFL EXPERIENCE: 1969
TEAM: San Francisco 49ers

Wide receiver Bill Wondolowski, a graduate of Eastern Montana College, played in one game for the San Francisco 49ers in 1969. That team was coached by Dick Dolan and finished with a record of 4-8-2.

KEITH WORTMAN
BORN: July 20, 1950, Billings, MT
COLLEGE: Nebraska
POSITIONS: Offensive guard; offensive tackle; center
NFL EXPERIENCE: 1972–81
TEAMS: Green Bay Packers (1972–75); St. Louis Cardinals (1976–81)

Keith Wortman's mother was born in Billings and his father in Bozeman. Keith's meandering childhood eventually brought him to Billings—at least temporarily.

"My grandfather, Dale Petit, ran ranches for oil tycoon H.L. Hunt in Wyoming and Montana. He was a fascinating man who did cattle drives and rode at his cattle steer ranch six days a week. My dad traveled working

Billings native Keith Wortman
played a total of ninety-seven
games during his NFL career.
Courtesy Keith Wortman.

for Alice Chalmers out of Milwaukee. We'd take summer vacations on the Gallatin River and we bought a lodge with cabins and a trailer park, a grocery store and a gas station, and then eventually he had to get other jobs.

Those other jobs took the Wortman family to Whittier, California, where Keith lettered in football and wrestling at Whittier High School. "I went from being a cowboy to a West Coast hippie. Funny, but my grandfather asked me once what I wanted to be and I said I wanted to be a football player. I'd never played. I had no idea where that came from and the idea stuck in the back of my head."

Disapproval from one of his high school coaches only energized him.

> *My eighth grade coach took the time to tell us on our junior varsity team, "Don't bother!" The guy's name was Mr. Baker. That motivated the hell out of me. That guy tried to crush our dreams. Dave Dalby* [a center who helped the Oakland Raiders win three Super Bowl titles] *and I were both in the eighth grade. Don't ever listen to the naysayers, is what I've learned. Dave and I later had twenty-three years of experience in the NFL, and Coach Baker told us we weren't going to make it. Dave had*

issues associated with CTE and concussions and he is no longer with us.
[Dalby died in a single-car accident on August 30, 2002.]

Wortman was a two-year letterman as an offensive guard on Nebraska's 1970 and 1971 national championship teams. Wortman, who started for hall of fame coach Bob Devaney's Cornhuskers as a senior guard in 1971, never lost a game during his two years at NU after transferring from Rio Hondo Community College. The six-foot, three-inch, 237-pounder helped the Huskers to a 24-0-1 record during his NU career, including a perfect 13-0 season as a starter in 1971.

Following his national championship career at Nebraska, Wortman was chosen in the tenth round of the 1972 NFL Draft by the Green Bay Packers. He spent four seasons with the Packers (1972–75) before spending his final six seasons in the league with the St. Louis Cardinals. He played a total of ninety-seven games during his NFL career.

The versatile Wortman could play any of the five line positions. An extremely aggressive lineman, he played right tackle in three games in 1977 and had a noted debut against Cowboys defensive end Ed Jones. "The offensive line is a different experience. If you stopped to think you would get paralysis through analysis. You need to be ready to react and anticipate what you are going to react to. You have to handle more weight coming at you when they run a stunt. You set up and they fake and if you bite and you are a fool. You get beat once or twice and people think you got your ass kicked! Your mistakes are so visible: the quarterback laying on the ground and they just run those replays."

He was named the Cardinals' most improved player by the St. Louis Quarterback Club in 1978 after starting at right guard for the traded Conrad Dobler. He missed most of the 1980 season because of a knee injury.

Through the majority of Wortman's tenure, the Cardinals boasted one of the stoutest, quickest protective forces in the league at offensive line. "The Cardinals had the best offensive line in the NFL at the time, and my goal was not to be the weak link. Bob Young. Dan Dierdorf. Conrad Dobler. We had an incredible coach in Jim Hanifan, who may be the best line coach ever. He taught us that the methodology was to attack and not to be attacked. You could be the giver and not the taker when it came to hitting people. That doesn't mean there wasn't days you didn't get your ass kicked."

Wortman said that that the model offensive lineman should possess a mixture of brawn and aptitude. "Offensive linemen are smarter than the other guys. In camp every year there were guys who were faster and better athletes than me, and guys who had more God-given ability. But the position to me was about using whatever you had intelligently."

Citing player safety as a major concern, the NFL has legislated much of the surplus violence out of the game, including forearm shots, jarring hits targeting vulnerable positions and devastating elbows delivered to heads.

"Back then, the center would have the ball between his legs, and people would be hitting them in the face with forearms. Dick Butkus would uncork on the center during extra points and field goals. Today, they flag it because the guys are defenseless. The game was played a lot lower then, chop blocking, leg whipping, and between that and the surfaces we played on, those are some of the reasons everyone is so crippled."

Wortman said that he still maintains a friendship with teammate and hall of famer Dan Dierdorf (St. Louis Cardinals, 1971–83, six Pro Bowls).

Sometimes as an offensive lineman you are most likely to injure your own player. You are running stunts and someone gets hit. I destroyed Dierdorf's right leg once. Boom! Unfortunately, he had changed positions from right [tackle] to left [tackle] and that happened. When you get a big injury— you see your present gone, and all of those hours worked, all of the off-season training, and to get a serious injury, it's obviously painful. But the emotional part that you are not going to be able to do what you love doing, that's really emotional stuff. He's still one of my best friends.

Keith Wortman reflected on the sport and its effects:

Personally, I played 18 holes of golf yesterday and I have a nice life. I'm very lucky. I'm mobile and I continue to do the things that I like to do. I had 11 vertebra fused a year ago and [former teammate] Dobler has had the knees and hips replaced, and I feel very fortunate. I'm not a big emotional guy looking back. As far as the NFL, it has agreed to a settlement to compensate former players, and then a couple of other lawsuits tried to make sort of a money grab. But guys are really hurting and the NFL acknowledges it has the funds. Football is a vicious, competitive world, and maybe they shouldn't even play it in high school. You just can't do it without tearing your body up.

3

1980s–1990s

Raúl Allegre

Born: June 15, 1959, in Torreon, Mexico
College: Montana; Texas
Position: Placekicker
NFL Experience: 1983–91
Teams: Baltimore/Indianapolis Colts (1983–85); New York Giants (1986–91); New York Jets (1991)

Mexico-born Raúl Allegre prepped as a foreign exchange student at Shelton, Washington, and received a scholarship to UM as a kicker before transferring to the University of Texas. He spent nine seasons in the NFL and earned two Super Bowl rings with the Giants (XXI and XXV).

The head coach at Shelton had worked with UM assistant coach Pokey Allen and sent a videotape of Allegre to Grizzly head coach Gene Carlson. Allegre earned a full scholarship from the Grizzlies.

"The Grizzlies had just graduated the kicker from the year before," said Allegre. "They didn't have anybody to kick and without seeing me other than the tape and trusting [the Shelton coach], they trusted me. I had no idea what I was getting myself into, what all goes into college football. Even though it [Grizzly football] wasn't as sophisticated as it is now, it was still more than I thought."

Allegre played on UM teams that had losing seasons in 1978 and 1979, but it was his first exposure to the close-knit camaraderie of collegiate life. His learning curve was steep; there was no special teams coach at UM.

"I made some excellent friends that I consider still my friends," said Allegre. "The people there were just wonderful. I have very warm and fond memories of Montana, how beautiful the state is, the city of Missoula and the people there."

After two years at UM, Allegre, son of a civil engineer, transferred to the University of Texas in Austin to study engineering (not offered at UM). "Some people within the state offered to help me transfer to Montana State, but of course I wasn't going to do that."

Though he wasn't selected at the 1983 NFL draft, he signed with the Cowboys and went to training camp to compete against the established Rafael Septien. Allegre performed strongly through training camp, but the Cowboys decided to retain Septien. The Baltimore Colts, however, had watched Allegre kick and

Mexico-born Raúl Allegre prepped as a foreign exchange student at Shelton, Washington, and received a scholarship to UM as a kicker. *Courtesy University of Montana.*

signed him to a contract in 1983 (they became the Indianapolis Colts in 1984). He made three field goals in his first game with the Colts, the second a 52-yarder and the third to push the game into overtime. His first season was his highest-scoring year in the league. He converted thirty field goals and twenty-two extra points for 112 points.

Allegre kicked for the Colts for three years, followed by six with the New York Giants and one with the New York Jets. His first Super Bowl appearance came with the 1987 Giants in a 39–20 win over the Denver Broncos and quarterback John Elway. Allegre kicked four extra points and a 21-yard field goal. His second ring came with the 1991 Giants (who defeated the Buffalo Bills, 20–19) while serving as a backup to starting kicker Matt Bahr.

After his first year in the NFL, he returned to UT to finish engineering classes and graduated in the spring of 1984. After football, Allegre went to graduate school to get a master's in business administration from UT. He ended up as a color commentator for the Dallas Cowboys and later was a color analyst for Fox Sports. He has been employed at ESPN Deportes since 2002 and operates a company called Allegre Sports, which promotes clinics along with sporting events and promotions geared toward Hispanics.

Allegre's last visit to Missoula came in 1991, when he played in the Grizzly Athletic Association fundraising golf tournament. "It was a great time and I treasure my times back then and I'm just happy that I got a start there."

GUY BINGHAM
BORN: February 25, 1958, Koiaumi Gumma Ken, Japan
COLLEGE: Montana
POSITIONS: Center; offensive guard; offensive tackle
NFL EXPERIENCE: 1980–93
TEAMS: New York Jets (1980–88); Atlanta Falcons (1989–91);
Washington Redskins (1992–93)

According to a recent NFL Players Association survey, the average career span of an NFL player is three and a half full seasons. This short length is a result of both injuries and nonstop player transactions.

Looking back on his football career, Guy Bingham, who played center, guard and long snapper in the league for thirteen seasons, is proudest of his longevity. "I was fortunate to be able to play so long. I had a pretty good run. It was great to have the opportunity to be a good teammate, and to be able to contribute," said Bingham, owner of Missoula's Valley Vending, a snack and beverage vending supplier.

Bingham played his college football at the University of Montana and was inducted into the Grizzly Hall of Fame in September 2003. While playing for the Griz, "Bing" was an All–Big Sky Conference pick in 1978 and '79. He also earned UM's Paul Weskamp Award, presented to the team's "Outstanding Offensive Lineman," in 1978–79. Bingham played three different offensive line positions during his UM days.

"I grew up in the state of Washington and I came to visit Missoula on a recruiting trip, and I liked the city because it was a lot like my hometown of Aberdeen," said Bingham.

Although Bingham had hoped to play linebacker at UM, there was an overabundance of talent at that position when he arrived, so he was steered to the offensive line. During this time, Bingham was encouraged by teammate Ron Lebsock to also become a long snapper. "Ron and I snapped the ball back and forth in practice on a daily basis. I learned through repetition. Long snapping is what kept me in the NFL, basically," said Bingham.

In 1980, Bingham, who later graduated from UM with a degree in health and physical education, was drafted in the tenth round by the New

Guy Bingham played college football at the University of Montana and was inducted into the Grizzly Hall of Fame in September 2003. He played center, guard and long snapper in the NFL for thirteen seasons, starting in 1981. *Courtesy University of Montana.*

York Jets. His draft notification came in the form of a phone call from Jets head coach Walt Michaels.

Bingham remembers one of his first preseason games in the NFL, when he was matched up against the legendary "Mean" Joe Greene. Greene's NFL welcoming to Bingham was harsh. "He was in late in the game and we'd been double-teaming him. I thought we were blocking him pretty good. At one point, he snatched me off the ground, hit me in the stomach three times really fast, and then threw me down. I've since forgotten what he said to me."

In his first season as a Jet, Bingham started three games as an offensive lineman. During his career, he played primarily as a long snapper but fulfilled duties as backup guard and center, in short-yardage situations as a tight end and on special teams units as a blocker.

Bingham played on the Jets at a period coinciding with the dawn of the "New York Sack Exchange," the nickname given to the team's indomitable defensive line anchored by ornery ends Mark Gastineau and Joe Klecko.

In 1989, Bingham was traded to the Atlanta Falcons. The season was an unmitigated disaster. Coach Marion Campbell quit after the club started out 3-9. He was replaced by Jim Hanifan, who watched as the team lost its final four games of the year, finishing 3-13. "We had a crummy team. The highlight was that it was the rookie year for Deion Sanders. It was a big media show all the time. He's a nice guy and a media machine."

Bingham played nine years for the Jets, three seasons for the Atlanta Falcons and a final year (1993) with the Washington Redskins. He was one of the most outstanding snappers in pro football, possessing the ability to make his punter and placekicker better. He was also extremely valuable in other areas of special teams play.

"I knew that I couldn't do it forever. I ended up hurting my foot in training camp in a preseason game trying out for the Philadelphia Eagles in 1992. Even though I played that year and the next one, it turned out to be a career-ending injury."

Following the conclusion of his NFL career, Bingham returned to Montana to live and work. Following many years of playing professional football, he found that life after the NFL was a tougher adjustment than he'd ever expected. "Fourteen years, plus college, of being told where to be and when to be there, got to be my life. After I left the game and was free to make my own decisions, it was hard for me to get a grip on things. Making your own schedule was hard for me," said Bingham, who lives in the Grant Creek area of the Garden City with his wife and two children.

When recollecting his life's milestones, Bingham, fifty-eight, sees the past in modest and unassuming terms, free from great pretensions.

"I've been lucky in life with everything. Plus, financially speaking, I've never made any really bad investments. And I've got a great agent who has always given me good advice. No joint replacements yet, either," smiled Bingham.

TONY BODDIE
BORN: November 11, 1960, Everett, WA
COLLEGE: Montana State
POSITION: Running back
NFL EXPERIENCE: 1986–87
TEAM: Denver Broncos

Running back Tony Boddie played five games with the Denver Broncos in 1986 and one more the following season before being released. In his short career, the Montana State product gained 9 yards on four carries and 85 yards in receptions. He also earned one rushing touchdown.

He did, however, earn a Super Bowl in his second season, treating Montanans to the experience of watching a pair of Treasure State athletes in the same Super Bowl: Boddie of Denver met Raul Allegre's Giants (Allegre attended UM) in Super Bowl XXI in 1987.

Similar scenarios included Super Bowl XVII, when the Dolphins and ex-Grizzly Doug Betters played the Redskins, featuring Butte native Pat Ogrin and Bobcat Mark McGrath; Super Bowl XLVIII, as Kalispell's Brock Osweiler and the Denver Broncos went up against Missoula-born Brock Coyle and Seattle; and Super Bowl 50, which featured Columbus's Dwan Edwards, the Carolina Panthers' starting defensive tackle, opposite Osweiler, the backup quarterback for the Broncos.

A few years before he was on a Super Bowl roster, Boddie was part of the promising debut of the Los Angeles Express in the United States Football League. On March 6, 1983, the Express played its inaugural game for the fledgling spring league, defeating the New Jersey Generals, 20–15, before a crowd of 34,002.

Boddie, fresh out of Montana State, stole the headlines from Herschel Walker, the 1982 Heisman Trophy winner and the USFL's first flagship player. Boddie finished with 77 rushing yards to Walker's 66. Boddie also had 49 receiving yards to Walker's 3.

The crowd on that day—the smallest of the four USFL openers— looked sizeable to the kid from the Big Sky, noted the *Los Angeles Times*. "Only three cities in the state of Montana have populations larger than the one that took up temporary residence at the Coliseum Sunday afternoon. And one of those cities isn't Bozeman, where 9,900 of the town's 21,645 residents attend Montana State University. Until a few months ago, Boddie, 22, was one of them—a large talent in a small pond known as the Big Sky Conference."

The *Denver Post*'s coverage of Boddie facetiously referenced his time in Montana. "He didn't come out of nowhere, although Bozeman isn't far from it."

"I think I was really overlooked coming out of high school," Boddie told the *Post*. "I got one letter from Oregon, then they wrote back to tell me there would be no scholarship. Idaho sent me a letter, then they wrote back to tell me the same thing. Montana State just kept sending me letters. They were the only school in the whole nation that offered me a scholarship."

The opener was the largest stage up to that point in Boddie's career. "Except when we played the University of Montana," he pointed out. "Those games were usually sellouts—15,000 people or so."

In three seasons in the USFL (1983–85), all with the Express, Boddie was used primarily as a kick returner.

Referencing the thirtieth anniversary of the USFL's opening weekend, the *New York Times* noted that "Boddie's parents captured the game on a primitive device known as a VHS recorder."

SHANE COLLINS
BORN: April 11, 1969, Roundup, MT
COLLEGE: Arizona State
POSITION: Defensive end
NFL EXPERIENCE: 1992–94
TEAM: Washington Redskins

Shane Collins recovered sufficiently from a knee injury suffered in college in 1990 for the Washington Redskins to make him their second-round draft pick. He tore knee ligaments in his second game but returned as a senior in 1991 to start the final six games and make 42 tackles. At Arizona State, he posted 189 career tackles, including twelve sacks. He started five games as a rookie at right defensive end for the Redskins, recording one sack and 36 tackles.

On December 13, 1992, Collins helped the Washington Redskins come from behind in their thrilling 20–17 victory over the NFC East archrival Dallas Cowboys. "I was just numb," said Collins, who produced a sack on Dallas's last drive that helped thwart a Cowboys threat. "I've never been in a crowd situation like it was at the end of the game. I was getting seasick watching the stands bounce up and down. That's as good as it gets."

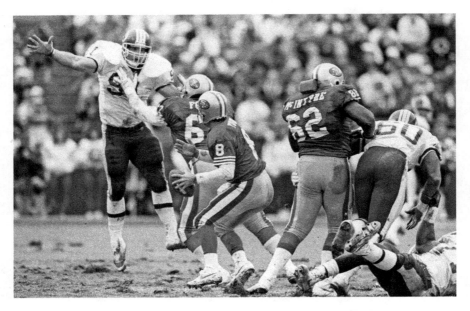

Shane Collins recovered sufficiently from a knee injury suffered in college in 1990 for the Washington Redskins to make him their second-round draft pick. *Courtesy Shane Collins.*

He started five games at right defensive end in 1993. The expectations were that Collins was going to be one of the young players the Redskins hoped would help them through the 1990s. But the oft-injured defensive end never developed: a series of knee injuries limited his quickness and ability to maneuver, and he was unable to penetrate the lineup in 1994. He hadn't played during the regular season following arthroscopic knee surgery in August 1994 and was released in October of that year. (Missoula-born John Friesz started at quarterback in four games for the Redskins, who finished 3-13 that season.)

Collins's release appeared to be a move designed to free up salary-cap room, since Collins was scheduled to make $450,000 that season, and the Redskins were close to the league's $34.608 million ceiling.

After football, Collins entered the construction industry. He has been operating an eponymous business for more than twenty years.

Joe Cummings

Born: June 8, 1974, Missoula, MT
College: University of Wyoming
Position: Linebacker
NFL Experience: 1996–99
Teams: San Diego Chargers (1996); Buffalo Bills (1998–99)

Joe Cummings's story is typical of Montana football players who have made it to the NFL.

"Hard work, good luck, a couple tough breaks," he said.

Football is a family affair: his father, Ed Cummings, played for the Denver Broncos and New York Jets and was inducted into the Stanford Hall of Fame. According to the NFL, there are more than 150 second-generation athletes in the history of the game.

"Myself and my two youngest brothers grew up in the game," said Cummings. "Being raised in an NFL house is hard for a lot of kids, but ours was not a high-pressure house. The mantra from my dad was to show up and work real hard and that what you think of yourself is more important than what anyone else thinks. You decide who you are and that keeps you driving."

Cummings attended high school in Stevensville, Montana, and accepted a scholarship to the University of Wyoming, playing for the Cowboys from 1992 to 1995.

In 1996, Cummings was signed as an undrafted free agent by the Philadelphia Eagles. He was released in preseason, but he played well enough to catch the attention of the San Diego Chargers. "The third week of the season, I got a tryout with four other veteran linebackers and I got the job and made the roster."

In 1997, he was cut in the offseason by the Chargers and couldn't find a home on an NFL roster. However, the following year, he was signed by the

Linebacker Joe Cummings started three games on the 1998 Bills squad, which included notable stalwarts such as Bruce Smith, Doug Flutie, Andre Reed and Thurman Thomas. *Courtesy Joe Cummings.*

Buffalo Bills in the offseason and allocated to the Barcelona Dragons in the now-defunct NFL Europe.

"We lived in a hotel on the beach in the Mediterranean and we traveled over Europe and we were young and when you are some kid from Montana, it's more than you think you'd ever see. At that particular time, the sport showed me things I would've never seen and I probably would never see again. Copenhagen. London."

He started three games on the 1998 Bills squad, which included notable stalwarts such as Bruce Smith, Doug Flutie, Andre Reed and Thurman Thomas. In 1999, Cummings returned to the Bills, starting two games at linebacker in addition to his duties as a special teams player.

> *Buffalo had an awesome team and the city was full of hardworking people and fans. The Bills had an awesome group of hard-core guys who exemplified class in the NFL. In 1997, I was in camp with the Green Bay Packers and I didn't make the final cut, but both teams are markers of small-town football, where people care about football. We [Buffalo] were the number one defense in the NFL that year [1999]. The highlight for me was a game against Brad Johnson's Redskins. I got the start and had my only career sack in a game in which we beat the number one offense in the league.*

The season ended with a heartbreaker to the Tennessee Titans in a game dubbed the "Music City Miracle." The play gave Tennessee a 22–16 victory after Buffalo had taken a 16–15 lead on a field goal. With sixteen seconds remaining in the game, Titans tight end Frank Wycheck threw a lateral pass across the field to Kevin Dyson on the ensuing kickoff return, and Dyson ran 75 yards to score the winning touchdown.

"That very play was the last time I put on the cleats and they beat us fair and square," said Cummings.

> *We knew that we were getting a trick play on the return, and we were expecting to kick a squib kick, and we definitely didn't want to kick it deep. We figured if we pooch-kicked, then that would throw them off.* [A pooch kick is generally high and short, giving the coverage team a chance to mob the person who receives the kick.] *Coach Wade Phillips decided to pooch it, and Titans fullback Lorenzo Neal made an impromptu play to Wycheck and then they scored. The Tennessee special teams coach later said that he had no contingency plans in place for pooching, and that we'd made a good call. On that play, we ran as hard as*

we could under the pooch and tried to be aggressive, and it didn't work. In the NFL of today, that wouldn't have happened, because they've moved the kicking line up 15 yards or so, and we would just boot it into the end zone.

In 2000, Cummings returned to the University of Wyoming and earned an English degree. At the end of the semester, he was drafted by a startup league called the XFL, founded by Vince McMahon, owner of the World Wrestling Federation. "I was at Wyoming finishing up my English degree and I got a phone call from the XFL offering $60K for 12 weeks. I started the first game of the season for the Orlando Rage and injured myself on a tough tackle. I was out of shape. I lost the use of my right arm for three months due to a major neck injury. That was the end of the road, physically, and I transitioned quickly to guiding my home waters in Montana."

Cummings lives in Missoula, but his second home is in the mountains and on the rivers, where he can be found guiding hunting and fishing expeditions. He said that he draws strength from the past and applies it to future goals.

"The game of football teaches a great deal of courage. It's an incredible rush of adrenaline, glory and ego."

SCOTT CURRY

BORN: December 25, 1975, Conrad, MT
COLLEGE: University of Montana
POSITION: Offensive tackle
NFL EXPERIENCE: 1999
TEAM: Green Bay Packers

The six-foot, five-inch Scott Curry played eight-man football in Valier, northwest of Great Falls. He grew into a prototypical Grizzly lineman, a few pounds shy of three hundred pounds but athletic enough to dominate basketball games and return kicks in high school.

Born on Christmas morning in 1975, he attended high school in Valier (population 513 in 2013), graduating with seventeen others as part of the class of 1995. While he doesn't remember many of his days during junior high, he recalls the afternoon Brian Salonen of the Dallas Cowboys visited. Salonen, the former Great Falls High and UM great, enjoyed several years as a tight end with the Cowboys. "When an NFL guy shows up in our little town, it was awesome," said Scott Curry. "I was thinking how cool it would be to play football."

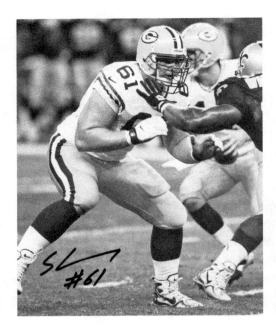

A sixth-round draft choice of the
Green Bay Packers in 1999, Scott
Curry joined a notable list of
Montana-linked Packer alumni.
Courtesy University of Montana.

A sixth-round draft choice of the Green Bay Packers in the 1999 draft,
Curry joined the Montana-linked Packer alumni including Steve Okoniewski
of the Grizzlies and Jan Stenerud and Joey Thomas of Montana State.
Ex-Grizzly Marty Morhinweg and former Montana State assistant John
Rushing coached at one time in Green Bay, and esteemed Packer offensive
lineman Jerry Kramer was born in Jordan.

Curry played in five games for the Packers in 1999. He was active with
the Packers in 2000 but did not play in the regular season. He piled up "the
wreckage" fast, meaning broken bones, torn ligaments and busted joints.
Plagued by a variety of injuries to his neck, knees and shoulders, he retired
after the 2000 season.

While the ride to the NFL was truncated and less glorious than he would
have liked, Curry said that each moment was meaningful, "a dream come true."

"Those days were some of the best times of my life. Green Bay is such a
unique place and there was a good bunch of guys there. There are sure times
when you miss that. It was hard work, but it was worth it."

After football, Scott returned to Valier, where he owns the town's only
grocery store and resides with his wife and two children.

"Those days in Green Bay are memories that are just great," said Curry.
"Now I would say I'm enjoying life in Valier. This is a good place to raise
a family."

RICK DENNISON
BORN: June 22, 1958, Kalispell, MT
COLLEGE: Colorado State
POSITION: Linebacker
NFL EXPERIENCE: 1982–90
TEAM: Denver Broncos

Kalispell native Rick Dennison has appeared in six Super Bowls, three as a coach after three during his playing days. In 2016, Dennison served as offensive coordinator of a Peyton Manning–led Denver Broncos team that defeated the Carolina Panthers 24–10 in Super Bowl 50.

The son of former University of Montana president George Dennison, Rick was born in Kalispell in 1958, but the family moved south to Missoula less than a year later. After George graduated with bachelor's and master's degrees in history from UM, the Dennisons moved to Seattle, where he would earn his PhD.

Rick Dennison, who now lives in Santa Clara, California, said that he still cherishes the memories of the Montana summers of his childhood, the seemingly endless nights, the colorful sunsets, the unlimited world of forests, mountains and exploration. The Dennison family spent the warmer months of the year in the Flathead Valley or the family's property near Lake Inez. "My fondest memories are from spending the summers, just bouncing back between Kila and Whitefish [in the northwest corner] and doing things with cousins," said Dennison. "Fishing, building tree forts and those kind of things."

Rick spent most of his school years in Fort Collins, Colorado, where George taught history at Colorado State University and became associate dean of the College of Arts, Humanities and Social Sciences. (George Dennison, who retired from the University of Montana in 2010 after serving as president for twenty years, died in 2017. He is the school's longest-serving president.)

After graduating from Rocky Mountain High School in 1976, Rick went on to star for the hometown CSU Rams as a tight end. An academic All-American, the young man earned bachelor's and master's degrees in engineering from the school while preparing for his shot in the NFL.

Dennison admits it was exasperating at times being a linebacker for the Denver Broncos. For nine seasons, the six-foot, three-inch, 220-pounder was in a constant fight for playing time. He saw limited time his first two seasons, starting in only one game. After starting in fifteen out of sixteen

Kalispell native Rick Dennison has appeared in six Super Bowls, three as a player and three as a coach. *Courtesy Rick Dennison.*

games in his third season in 1984, he spent another three as a backup to Karl Mecklenburg (linebacker 1983–94), who achieved Pro Bowl status six times in twelve seasons. High performance doesn't always guarantee increased playing time. "It's frustrating," said Dennison. "It's frustrating when you think you're playing well and you don't get a chance to play."

In the summer of 1986, Dennison turned in the best training camp of his five-year career as a Bronco, but unlike 1984 and the early part of 1985, he wasn't considered for starting status. In fact, despite his improved abilities, Dennison was relegated primarily to special teams in 1986 and 1987. Dennison, however, persevered and once again proved that he could still play—and play well. Over the course of the 1988 and 1989 seasons, he started a total of twenty-seven games at right inside linebacker.

After spending the entire 1990 season on the sidelines, he retired at age thirty-two. "All you can do is go home and talk to your wife and come back the next day and try again," said Dennison. "I want to play more but it was not up to me, they told me [when] to play. Once you start, you always want to start."

Dennison's second act as a coach started in 1995 when the Broncos hired him to work under then offensive coordinator Gary Kubiak, a former teammate and roommate in Denver in the 1980s. Dennison was an offensive assistant for two years before serving as special teams coach (1997–2000), offensive line coach (2001–5) and eventually offensive coordinator (2006–8) himself. Dennison joined Kubiak's staff in Houston (2010–13) and in Baltimore (2014), and when Kubiak accepted the Broncos' head position in January 2015, he hired his old friend to coach the offense.

As a player, Dennison's Broncos lost in the title game in the 1986, '87 and '89 seasons. He did, however, pick up a pair of Super Bowl rings during Denver's wins after the 1997 and '98 seasons (he served as special teams coach during those years, the final two of quarterback John Elway's storied career.)

"I lost three as a player, won three as a coach, but that just means I was a better coach than player," said Dennison. "If you ever watched me play, you'd probably say that anyway."

MITCH DONAHUE
BORN: February 4, 1968, Los Angeles, CA
COLLEGE: University of Wyoming
POSITION: Linebacker
NFL EXPERIENCE: 1991–94
TEAMS: San Francisco 49ers (1991–92); Denver Broncos (1993–94)

Mitch Donahue's family moved to Billings from Los Angeles in search of peacefulness and recreational opportunities.

"Back in 1971, we moved to Billings because my dad liked Montana," said Donahue. "He transferred so he could go hunting and fishing and he wanted out of L.A. I grew up on Mitchell Avenue with a bunch of kids who would always have a game of football on somebody's front yard. It was either baseball or football. There was no fear of someone going to kidnap us and we kids always played outside. Though it's a different environment from Billings today, it is still a neat place to grow up, and I moved back after football here to raise my kids."

Donahue's path to the NFL began at Billings West. It was a visit from Brian Salonen—who had already navigated a successful course from Montana to the big stage—that validated his dream.

"When I was in high school, I would not have thought that I would even play pro football. I dreamed about it, but I didn't think it would happen," he said. "Coach Klaboe had [Montana native and former Dallas Cowboy] Brian Salonen come talk to us. Just listening to him talk, and here's a guy that's playing in the Super Bowl, and he's from Montana. The NFL or pro sports—that was something that you could dream about. It didn't seem like it was something that could actually be attained, until I heard Salonen speak. My thinking went from no one in Montana makes it to now it's a possibility and why can't I do it? Then it became a real goal for me."

Donahue excelled at the University of Wyoming, where he was twice chosen Western Athletic Conference defensive player of the year. He was then drafted by the San Francisco 49ers in the fourth round of the 1991 NFL Draft.

"I always liked [Hall of Fame linebacker] Mike Singletary and I didn't know I was going to play middle linebacker. But I loved Singletary and his big eyes and he was always seeing everything on the field. I always followed the Los Angeles Rams growing up and after I was drafted I went to the 49ers and [Denver] Broncos and [Atlanta] Falcons for a bit. Guys from big cities like Chicago and New York had no idea of Montana, thinking we are all a bunch of hicks and ride horses and living by a stream and fetching water."

Donahue said that he felt comfortable in San Francisco, alongside iconic players such as Joe Montana, Jerry Rice and Steve Young, and his being released within two years stung deeply. He was signed by the Denver Broncos in 1993. "Arriving in Denver I was pretty nervous," said Donahue.

I arrived in Denver twenty-four hours before a preseason game and I didn't know the defense and I hadn't practiced and I was nervous in the locker room before game. John Elway really helped make you feel special. Elway had been to Billings a few times and he liked it there and I think he had business partners from Billings. He was the kind of guy who tried to put his team at ease. During games he was always talking, personable, and trying to keep us motivated. He played cards, drank beer, never acted like he was too good for anybody, and always paid for his teammates.

[Tight end] Shannon Sharpe's mouth was always running, always saying stupid stuff against white people. I think he liked to hear himself yap. He is funnier now on television.

By the end of 1995, Donahue's NFL career was over. While he said that he was always leery of the game's exploitative tendencies when he came out of Wyoming, he remains a big fan and defender of the game, warts, blemishes, brutality and all.

Do it over again? You bet. Every year in the NFL they spend a full day telling us the dangers of the game, how to wear equipment properly, how to tackle properly, and they said there was still a chance that, even if you did everything right, you could become seriously injured or die. There is nothing like playing football. Think about 100,000 people screaming or when you a make a play, nothing makes you feel that great. Being introduced at the 49ers stadium and running out of the tunnel—the high-fives, the ovations—that was surreal. I tried to pause and take a mental picture. You can't even explain it.

In the NFL, roster moves aren't always based solely on merit. "What surprised me about the NFL was that it's not fair and there is nothing fair about the NFL," said Donahue. "Sometimes someone will get a favor over others, and you think you should get a fair shake and it's not about that. I really loved special teams and running down on kickoff and knocking people off their feet. The day after my son was born, we [San Francisco 49ers] played the San Diego Chargers, and I was beating up on this one guy pretty good. The last time, he had had enough, and he tried to hit me as hard as I was I hitting him, and I tore ligaments in the knee because of it. We hit a stalemate. I went down."

Memories of the simultaneously jovial and intense camaraderie as well as the unique friendships formed have left the most lasting impressions. "There was a time when a teammate and I put a tailpipe whistle in [San Francisco linebacker] Mike Walter's old Audi, which was the first car he bought with his signing bonus money in the NFL. He was so proud of it. He really thought there was something wrong. He stopped at every intersection, and the whistling stopped. We were following him and just rolling. That part is the part all of us miss more than anything."

Indeed, Donahue said that it was a knotty transition adjusting to life after football. One day he was playing, and the next the clock hit zero, the fans streamed toward the exits and it was over. It took him several years after he retired before he could bring himself to watch football on television. "I missed it for a long time. There are always things that you wish you could do differently. When it's over, it's over. Your life doesn't have to be over. You just have to roll with the punches."

Donahue, forty-eight, owns Donahue's Roofing on the west end of Billings. He opened the business in 1997, two years after he finished his NFL career. His son Dylan plays football at the University of West Georgia and wears the same number as his father: 49.

In the summer of 2016, Mitch Donahue was one of thirteen inductees in the inaugural Montana Football Hall of Fame, in Billings.

"I think it is a big deal because of the level of competition here in the state of Montana in the high school and college levels."

JOHN ELWAY
BORN: June 28, 1960, Port Angeles, WA
COLLEGE: Stanford
POSITION: Quarterback
NFL EXPERIENCE: 1983–98
TEAM: Denver Broncos

John Elway's NFL career is exceptional in the widest sense of the word: he quarterbacked the Denver Broncos to five Super Bowls (1987, '88, '90, '98 and '99), winning the last two. He is the first person to earn a Super Bowl rings as a player and a GM (Broncos, Super Bowl 50).

Elway, who earned nine Pro Bowl selections and was elected to the Pro Football Hall of Fame in 2004, was a star football and baseball player at Granada Hills High School in Los Angeles.

He formed a connection to Big Sky Country early in life. His father, Jack, was an assistant football coach for the Montana Grizzlies for five seasons in the late 1960s and early 1970s. As a youngster, John played Little League baseball, YMCA basketball and Little Grizzly football in Missoula.

"John has great memories of Missoula, and his dad loved Missoula," said Bob Beers, a family friend and Butte native who spent twenty-two years in the National Football League in scouting and personnel. "The family was really happy in Missoula, and I can remember the kids having snowball fights in the house. We'd play baseball at their house. Dad was at third base and I was centerfield. Jack Elway loved Missoula. I never heard him say anything but positive things about Missoula. John's older sister married a guy from Butte."

Jack Elway was on UM football coach Jack Swarthout's staff. They enjoyed unprecedented success in Missoula, including back-to-back 10-0 regular seasons in 1969 and 1970 and Montana's first Big Sky Conference titles.

"As a kid, John was a running back and he was pretty good," said Beers. "The Griz players used to watch John's games on Saturday morning, and we'd be playing our own in the afternoon. Back then, the Little Grizzlies played their games in the Clover Bowl, and they had big crowds. We'd stop and watch them play. John had a quick wit as a kid, just like his old man. He had great one-liners. He was always bugging the college players to stick him in the lockers and he'd pretend to be hot like a mad hornet. He was positive, funny, and he was raised with a twin sister, Jana, who was a great athlete, too."

Jack Elway and family departed Montana in 1971 amid what became known as the "work-study scandal," in which athletes were allegedly paid for work they didn't do. In 1972, a federal grand jury returned a thirty-two-count indictment charging Swarthout and Elway and three other university officials with "conspiring to illegally use federal-aid money" by using some of the funds to pay for "fictitious jobs" for athletes. Though Swarthout was found innocent, the charges blunted recruiting, and the student-body government decided to withdraw financial support for athletic programs.

John Elway, who was in fifth grade at the time, spent the rest of his formative years in Pullman, Washington, where his father joined Washington State coach Jim Sweeney's staff. John played his last three years of high school football in Granada Hills, California, after Jack became head coach at Cal State–Northridge. In 1993, Jack Elway joined Beers's coaching staff at Western Montana in Dillon.

Beers said that John Elway has fond recollections of Montana.

"John has great remembrances of his childhood in Missoula," said Beers. "His idols were Grizzly football players, and they are some of the people whom he respected the most growing up."

MIKE FRIEDE

BORN: September 22, 1957, Havre, MT
COLLEGE: Indiana
POSITION: Wide receiver
NFL EXPERIENCE: 1980–82
TEAMS: Detroit Lions (1980); New York Giants (1980–82)

Born in Havre, Mike Friede's father worked for the Great Western Sugar Company in Billings. While Mike spent most of his youth growing up in northeast Colorado, he spent summers in Chinook.

"My mom used to babysit [Havre-born NFL'er] Mike Tilleman, and he was with the Washington Redskins at the first professional game I ever attended," said Friede. "I remember he was on the New Orleans Saints when they played Denver and I was around eight years old and I stood outside the locker room after the game and Mike was talking to my mom and dad."

Friede led Indiana in receiving with a 24.2 average in 1978. He played in the East-West Shrine and Japan Bowl Games. Possessing good size (six foot, three inches) and excellent speed, he was drafted by the Detroit Lions in 1980. But after starting the first four regular-season games, he was released.

"We were undefeated and I didn't receive any feedback as to why they were releasing me," said Friede. "They were bringing back a veteran named Jesse Thompson [1978–80], and I guess they felt he was more experienced and they'd be better off. I got a phone call [from the Lions] telling me I'd be on the waiver wire and another five minutes later from them asking me if I'd be available and ready to go if someone got hurt. I learnt so much about the business of football then. It hit me squarely in the face.

The Giants picked him up, and within weeks, the rookie had become a crowd favorite. The New York Giants media guide noted that Friede "was one of the Giants' most outstanding rookies of 1980."

Giants owner Wellington Mara was there to welcome me to the Giants. In Detroit I saw [owner William Clay] Ford twice in eight weeks and the third guy I met on the Giants was Mara. It was an incredible family. [Quarterback] Phil Simms was the toughest I've ever played with and he hated to lose. He wasn't someone you'd want to disappoint back in the huddle and I usually caught everything he threw at me. Still, the most exciting part was being introduced before the game and running out on the field for a glorified practice with 80,000 people watching. The only thing that beat that for me was when my two kids were born.

142

The New York Giants media guide noted that Havre-born Mike Friede "was one of the Giants' most outstanding rookies of 1980." The little girl is actually the author's sister, Jennifer D'Ambrosio. As kids, they would visit the Giants' camp. This photo of Mike and Jen is legendary in the author's family. *Courtesy author.*

In his first game, he caught seven passes for 137 yards against the Dallas Cowboys. The following Sunday, he had six receptions for 108 yards against the Green Bay Packers.

Two games later, against the Cardinals, a helmet cracked his right knee. The leg was dislocated, three of the four ligaments were cut, cartilage was damaged and a bone was chipped. The knee had to be surgically reconstructed. For four weeks, Friede wore a cast from hip to toes. He said that for the next five weeks, he wore "one cast from the hip to the top of the knee and another from the ankle to the bottom of the knee." A brace wrapped the knee.

With the fear of further damaging his knee constantly on his mind, Friede played one more season with the Giants and another (1983) with the New Jersey Generals of the United States Football League.

"It was their first year and after they signed Herschel Walker, they went from almost no press to people all over the place and the first owner was Walter Duncan, who was unassuming, and people didn't know who he was. Donald Trump bought the team and as part of the announcement, he gave the players gold-plated luggage, which isn't all that common a sight for someone from Montana. In New York, I remember looking across and seeing the skyline, standing there with my mouth wide open."

Friede lives in Colorado, where he works as a human resource specialist for a food company. He graduated with a college degree at age fifty-seven. "That's my biggest accomplishment—not football."

JOHN FRIESZ
BORN: May 19, 1967, Missoula, MT
COLLEGE: Idaho
POSITION: Quarterback
NFL EXPERIENCE: 1990–2000
TEAMS: San Diego Chargers (1990–93); Washington Redskins (1994); Seattle Seahawks (1995–98); New England Patriots (1999–2000)

John Friesz attended Coeur d'Alene High School and secured his athletic reputation in Moscow, Idaho, rewriting the University of Idaho record book and leading the Vandals to the heights of Division I-AA football world. (From 1978 to 1995, Idaho was a member of Division I-AA.)

"I was born in Missoula and I didn't live there long, for about five years," said John Friesz. "We moved to the Bay Area and then returned to Missoula when I was in the third-grade and stayed about half a year. We moved to Coeur d'Alene, and it's been home ever since."

John's parents, Mel and Mary Jo, were married in Missoula in 1966. The blended family of six (two each from previous relationships and John and his sister) lived in the country, near the Clark Fork River. "John would stand out there by the hour just throwing rocks in the river," said Mel Friesz. "That's probably where he developed the accuracy and his arm."

The Frieszes relocated to Coeur d'Alene, Idaho, in 1975 to run the Greyhound Bus Depot.

Recruited out of CDA High School, Friesz redshirted his freshman season as Idaho won the Big Sky Conference under coach Dennis Erickson. Nicknamed "Deep" and "Sub-Zero," Friesz set records for consecutive 300-yard passing games (10), threw for more than 400 yards six times and finished his career with an average of 305.6 yards a game, or 10,697 yards.

"When I got to the pros there were a lot of people who confused Idaho with Iowa and there were definitely a lot of people who didn't know about the University or the state. But it was fun being from a spot like that, where players coming out of there were few and far between, where you are not another guy from USC or Notre Dame. At Idaho, we threw the ball a lot and we had success, and that makes people look at you. I'm a guy who didn't start my junior year in high school. There were still some small concerns in the NFL that since you were coming from a smaller college that you hadn't competed at the highest level. I always felt that if you were good enough then they'd find you."

Over the course of ten seasons, Missoula-born John Friesz threw forty-five touchdowns and forty-two interceptions and finished with nearly 9,000 career yards with San Diego, Washington, Seattle and New England. *Courtesy John Friesz.*

In 1990, Friesz was a sixth-round draft pick of the San Diego Chargers. In 1991, he started all 16 games for the Chargers, passing for nearly 3,000 yards in a losing season of 4-12. Knee injuries, among other ailments, prevented Friesz from reaching his full potential. Over the course of 10 seasons, Friesz threw 45 touchdowns and 42 interceptions and finished with nearly 9,000 career yards from the Chargers, Washington, Seattle and New England.

"I think the quarterback still gets too much credit for the wins and gets too much blame for the losses," said Friesz. "I think it is easier today to throw for a lot of yards primarily because the defensive back can't touch the wide receiver without being called for pass interference and in my generation it wasn't that way, though they were beginning to tighten up some rules."

Though he couldn't fully wrest the starting QB slot from Rick Mirer, Friesz was impressive in his first starting assignment of 1996, firing touchdown passes of 65, 51 and 80 yards in the Seahawks' come-from-behind victory at Miami.

"I've literally been in every situation, from losing the starting job because of injury to being the backup, and going from backup to the starter because of someone else's injury, and being sat down for poor performance. I've gone through every scenario from changing teams and different systems and having a new coach coming in. I had no expectations going into the league. I just wanted to get a tryout and the last thing I thought would happen would be to have a long career. I tried to focus on the little things in my control. Attitude and effort—you can control those things. I tried to have the same attitude, whether the main guy had just gotten hurt or if I was the veteran bringing along the young guy."

Football is not a contact sport, as it is often described. It's a collision sport, said Friesz. Constant injuries from collisions to his knees and shoulders thwarted his progress. "You can't do anything about the injuries," said Friesz. "But I can't complain. I'm a guy who didn't start my junior year in high school. One thing though is that back then you didn't think about your mind getting hurt, you thought about blowing out fingers, or shoulders, or knees and blowing out your back. I think it is fantastic what the NFL is doing now as far as research and prevention of head injuries and keeping doctors on the sidelines now who are not tied to teams. The league is hiring neutral doctors to be on the field who truly have the best interest of the player."

Friesz finished his career in 2000 as a member of the New England Patriots, on a roster which anomalously carried four quarterbacks: Friesz, Drew Bledsoe, Michael Bishop and Tom Brady (199th pick of the 2000 NFL draft). It was also the first season of head coach Bill Belichick, who entered 2016 tied with Pittsburgh's Chuck Noll for most Super Bowl wins by an NFL head coach.

"I was getting old in football years and Pete Carroll was the head coach and by that time I was tired of moving, of politics, and Carroll was fired, and it was Belichick's first year. Drew was the starter and I was the backup. Brady was fourth in the depth chart, and he never suited up. I can say that there was not a person in the locker room who felt like Belichick was going to be a great leader or great coach, or like Vince Lombardi. It was the opposite. There were concerns about how this dry guy could motivate everyone, and at the time there was not a person in the locker room who felt that Belichick could."

In 2016, Brady became the NFL's all-time winningest quarterback.

I'm one of only three guys who Tom Brady ever backed up. In his first year we played the Jets and both teams were pumped because Belichick left the Jets to coach New England. I remember Monday Night Football and John Madden and Al Michaels and the place was nuts and Brady was next to me in street clothes and I was to be ready there just in case Drew Bledsoe went down. Basically, I was there to show or offer Brady anything that I could. I remember yawning in all of the excitement. Brady asked me what I was doing. I told him that it was November and I wanted to get to Idaho and the whitetail deer, and to be with my boys and my wife. That was a head scratcher for him. But my mindset was that I was super thankful for my career, but I was ready for next chapter.

Friesz, forty-nine, lives a low-key existence in the panhandle of Idaho.

"If there is something going on within 100 miles of me, I do it, whether it's silly and stupid," said Friesz. "If the morels are out, I will go out and look for them. I love all the things that living here brings to the table."

SCOTT GRAGG
BORN: February 28, 1972, Silverton, OR
COLLEGE: Montana
POSITION: Offensive tackle
NFL EXPERIENCE: 1995–2005
TEAMS: New York Giants (1995–99); San Francisco 49ers (2000–04); New York Jets (2005)

After playing high school football at Silverton, Oregon, and college football at Montana, Scott Gragg was selected by the New York Giants in the second round of the 1995 NFL Draft.

Gragg survived eleven seasons in the NFL for the Giants, San Francisco 49ers and New York Jets. During that time, he played in 172 games, including 149 starts.

"My first month of playing with the New York Giants at the Meadowlands was eye-opening," he said. "You just need to get in your own world and not get wrapped up in the media or the size of the city. Jumbo Elliott was in his last year with the Giants in my rookie year and Doug Riesenberg was a highly talented draft pick and we were both new stock. There was a changing of the guard there. Michael Strahan was early in his career and the following year after I arrived they signed Tikki Barber."

At six feet, eight inches and 320 pounds, Gragg clashed in scrimmages with teammate Michael Strahan, a defensive end who spent his entire fifteen-year career with the New York Giants. "All of the battles we had on the practice field, they made me a better player on the field. Off the field, we had different philosophies and personalities and we never invited each other

Scott Gragg survived eleven seasons in the NFL with the Giants, 49ers and Jets. During that time, he played in 172 games, including 149 starts. *Courtesy University of Montana.*

to other's dinner parties. But I helped him be a better player and vice versa. He was highly competitive and that's what football is about. He had power and speed and he could use both to his advantage. He also had a work ethic in practice and he'd run on the treadmill after practice."

Despite starting as the team's right tackle for four straight seasons, Gragg was unceremoniously cut by the Giants at the end of 1999. "When I was released by the Giants five years into my career, I was entering the prime of my career. I was working hard. I felt so much disloyalty when I was released by the Giants. I didn't recognize the different issues that go into the business of the NFL. Loyalty is not a big part of the business of the NFL."

In 2000, Gragg signed with the San Francisco 49ers where he found a home for five seasons. "I came to the team at the twilight of that organization's success and at a time when they were rebuilding that program. I was there under [coach] Steve Mariucci and [quarterback] Steve Young moved on prior to my arrival. Jeff Garcia was there and he struggled. Funny, but the bumps and bruises don't hurt as bad when you are winning and the media is singing your praises."

He finished his eleventh season in the NFL, a one-year stint with the New York Jets, in which where he started seven games. In retrospect, Gragg maintains a mostly positive assessment of his playing days. "I retired healthy," he said.

I had spent a lot of time in the off season getting healthy and it was more and more challenging to do it as I got older. But I made informed decisions myself as to how long to play. One of the biggest misconceptions perpetuated by media and some players is that some way, somehow, ownership was withholding info. The information was always given to me as far as what could happen and what the inherent risks were of taking the anti-inflammatory medicines, and what exercise and lifestyle would help me be successful. Some people perceive the league, the doctors, the coaches or ownership as withholding information and they say that they didn't know there was an inherent physical risk or cognitive risk. From what I recall, it was made obvious or clear what the risks were and we made life choices based on what information was given to us. The risks were made known going in.

That concussions in football have always bothered him comes as little surprise. And yet there's that conflict that additional padding makes certain players even more reckless.

"Today, the more padding guys are using is what is allowing them to use their bodies as human trajectories, because they have the belief that they are being more protected. You should not use your face or facemask to tackle. I think the advancement of training and equipment have made collisions more severe."

After coaching at Silverton High School, Gragg left in 2010 to join Montana's coaching staff as a tight ends coach and recruiting coordinator. He worked his way up to co-offensive coordinator and assistant head coach during his five seasons on the staff. He served as the principal at Fort Benton High School in Montana before returning to the Mid-Valley in Keizer, Oregon, to work as a volunteer assistant lineman coach at McNary High School, where he gets to coach his son, Brian.

"For twenty years I was responsible for getting myself ready to play on a weekly basis. Now, I'm responsible for getting one hundred kids ready. My first week in the NFL, the other offensive linemen and I were watching film, and my position coach was criticizing me a little. He asked me why I played the game. I said, 'Because I love it.' He told me, 'Not anymore. Now it's a job.' I disagree with him. I still feel that way."

MIKE HAGEN

BORN: June 30, 1959, Seattle, WA
DIED: October 11, 2015, Missoula, MT
COLLEGES: Walla Walla; Montana
POSITION: Running back
NFL EXPERIENCE: 1987
TEAM: Seattle Seahawks

Diagnosed with severe Dyslexia as a young boy, Mike Hagen attended Auburn High School in Seattle, where he was an all-state running back. He

Mike Hagen received an opportunity to play for the Seattle Seahawks in 1987 when the twenty-four-day NFL players' strike cost the team one game and forced it to play three others with replacement players. *Courtesy Mark Rodriguez.*

went on to play for the Walla Walla, Washington Warriors and the University of Montana Grizzlies. Mike was named All–Big Sky Conference selection, but that wasn't enough to get him drafted in 1987.

Hagen received an opportunity to play for the Seattle Seahawks in 1987 when the 24-day NFL players' strike cost the team one game and forced it to play three others with replacement players.

Hagen, an active member of Power International, a Bellevue-based ministry, was a gregarious character whose "power trait," according to one friend, "was blowing up a hot-water bottle until it burst." He seemed to correspond well with the peculiar lot who found themselves on the Seahawks replacement roster, including a nightclub bouncer, guard Ron Scoggins; a former Redmond High School and University of Washington lineman, Garth Thomas, whom they tracked down while on a hunting trip in Alaska; and wide receiver, Curtis Pardridge, whom they cajoled away from an interview for a stockbroker job in Florida.

"This is the most trying season I've been through," Seahawks' Chuck Knox told *Inside Sports*. Knox, of course, had an extensive frame of reference, heading into his fifteenth season as a head coach in the NFL, his fifth with the Seahawks. "Because of the strike, it was a very, very trying season."

Hagen played in the first of the Seahawks' three strike games against the Miami Dolphins on October 4, 1987. One week earlier the entire week's schedule had been cancelled, and the replacement players were on the receiving end of insults from regular players, the fans and even the media. One newspaper referred to the team as "the Seattle B-Hawks."

The *Seattle Times* described the zany, tongue-in-cheek mood leading up to the Dolphins game. "While Dave Krieg, Curt Warner and Kenny Easley walked a picket line and Brian Bosworth cracked jokes on the Johnny Carson show, the Pacific Northwest's NFL outpost is at least temporarily home for a group that plays the Dolphins today in what is expected to be about a half-filled Kingdome."

The newspaper described the peculiar assortment of characters masquerading as a major sports franchise, including Hagen, then twenty-eight, a husband, father of three and fullback out of the University of Montana. "Hagen is 6 feet tall and weighs 240 pounds—none of it visible fat. But scars on his forearm are visible."

The Seahawks program provided a mini-biography of Hagen. It said he liked golf, the gospel and weightlifting, as well as blowing up hot water bottles until they exploded and tearing phone books in half barehanded. "I break 10 feet of ice with my head," he offered in his bio. "I can break 3 1/2 feet of concrete with my head." It was written that he was able to bench press as much as five hundred pounds.

In the *Times*, Hagen was referred to as "an Assembly of God ordained minister, who travels with a five-man group performing these feats and preaching." Three of the members of the group known as "John Jacobs and the Power Team" reportedly possessed black belts in Karate, and all supposedly "participated in similar demonstrations." "We do it as a way to draw people in," said Hagen to the *Seattle Times*, "people who wouldn't otherwise go to church." His stunt success ratio, he said, was less than stellar. "I don't always break the bricks," said Hagen. Injuries he'd incurred through his martial arts–infused ministry "include cuts, a burned eye, and burning all the hair off his arms." He was even "rendered unconscious" while doing one show. "We do a thing where I flex my chest and break three two-by-fours," he said. "I was knocked out doing it in Australia."

Following the Seahawks' win over Miami, the replacement players then went to Cincinnati, where they lost to the Bengals. By the time the third and final strike game came around, Hagen, the sports evangelist, was on a bus heading back home to Missoula.

Hagen touched the ball twice in the two games, reaping three yards. He went on to play in the United States Football League as a member of the San Antonio Gunslingers and the 1983 USFL champions Michigan Panthers. After football, he worked as an ordained minister worldwide.

Hagen, a member of the University of Montana Hall of Fame, died at age fifty-six following the complications of a stroke.

SEAN HILL

BORN: August 14, 1971, Dowagiac, MI
COLLEGE: Montana State
POSITION: Defensive back
NFL EXPERIENCE: 1994–96
TEAM: Miami Dolphins

Sean Hill grew up in a small town near the Michigan-Indiana border and attended Montana State. He was a three-time All–Big Sky Conference performer for the Bobcats as a safety and kick returner from 1991 to 1993 and was a first team all-league pick in 1992 and 1993.

A seventh-round draft pick, Hill secured a roster spot on the Miami Dolphins through his hard work as a special teams player. Hill spent his first two seasons (1994–95) as a backup defensive back, recording a total of fifteen tackles.

"I figured when I came there in 1994 to the Dolphins that I probably wouldn't be a starter," said Sean Hill. "That meant excelling on special teams or hitting the waiver wire." He started studying special teams "breakdown films" of Steve Tasker of Buffalo, John Henry Mills of Houston and Mo Douglass of the New York Giants and jotting down notes. "If you want to improve, you watch the best," said Hill.

In 1995, Hill led the Dolphins with seventeen special teams tackles, using his 4.3 40-yard speed to zip down the sideline and get the first shot at the return man.

In 1996, he switched to the free safety position, dressing in twelve contests and starting in five of them as the squad's nickel back. On defense, he recorded twenty-two tackles, one interception and returned a fumble for a touchdown. On September 15, 1996, he had a 12-yard sack on New York Jets quarterback Neil O'Donnell last week and later intercepted O'Donnell. He was tied for third on the team with eight special teams tackles.

Hill's release in the summer of 1997 was considered surprising because he'd signed a two-year contract extension on October 1, 1996. He played in all five of the Dolphins preseason games and led the team in tackles in one of those games.

"Anymore I think you're going to see guys like Sean replaced after three or four years in the league because teams can sign young players for the minimum and then they don't have to worry about paying them a pension," said Cliff Hysell, who coached Hill at Montana State.

JAMES KALAFAT
BORN: February 21, 1962, Great Falls, MT
COLLEGE: Montana State
POSITION: Linebacker
NFL EXPERIENCE: 1987
TEAM: Los Angeles Rams

The name Kalafat holds much recognition and weight in Montana. Perhaps the name Jim Starr is not as familiar.

"I changed it from Kalafat to Starr because I was doing commercials and television and you have to have a stage name, so Jim Starr was a stage name I created for a professional environment for work," said James Kalafat, aka Jim Starr.

James's father, Ron Kalafat, was a Golden Gloves boxer and, during his time at Washington State University, a two-time runner-up to the heavyweight title in the Pacific Coast Championship.

"It kind of bothers me because I'm from Montana and I'm Jim Kalafat, and I don't want to be known as Jim Starr. My dad was a stud as an athlete. My grandfather (Nick) was a national handball champion and he had the biggest set of paws and the people who knew him always talked to about his huge gnarly-looking hands with calluses." (Another Kalafat cousin, Ed Kalafat, was a center in the NBA in the mid-1950s.)

Born in Great Falls, Kalafat starred as a linebacker on the Montana State Bobcats before suiting up in one professional football game as a replacement player for the Los Angeles Rams in 1987.

"I was picked up by the Rams after the Chiefs had cut me in the fourth preseason game after I had a serious ankle injury. It was the strike season but you still had to be one hell of football player to try out and make the team. In my first game I was running down a kickoff at the Superdome and a guy happened to catch me on the blindside and the hit broke my collarbone, broke two ribs, and fractured my scapula. It was something called an impaction fracture, where the end of the scapula had broken off and went in the body, and it punctured the lung. The physician said it was the kind of accident you only see in a car crash. I played the game and afterwards the trainer said, 'oh my god!' The Rams put me on IR for two weeks and then cut me. It was a blindside hit and it all ended abruptly. But due to certain circumstances such as that hit, I ended up in California and part of *American Gladiators* for eight years, and being able to have a great life."

American Gladiators aired weekly from September 1989 to May 1996. The series matched a cast of amateur athletes against one another, as well as against the show's own "gladiators," in contests of strength and agility.

"*American Gladiators* broadcasted 26 shows in the first season and the first 13 of them there was a guy named Malibu, but he wasn't tough enough or mean enough. I got a call from my agent and auditioned and became the longest running of the Gladiators, and I never missed a show in eight years."

Kalafat, who started using the stage name Jim Starr, used the show as a springboard for other financial opportunities. "Once the season ended, you could take the rest of the year and work other screen jobs or do gladiator appearances. A lot of us did trade shows, made extra money signing autographs. For two years I became a celebrity endorser for a supplement company."

He prides himself on never missing a taping, no small feat considering the raw physicality of the competition. "In the seven years I did the show, I had 11 surgeries. Most of them were for shoulder injuries. If you were hurt on that first day of taping, boy, you had to suck it up—buckle your chinstrap and go. The show didn't pay a ton of money ($12,000 total for the first 13-episode season, plus 400 percent in residuals), but still: If you missed an episode, you were going to lose out. To survive, we iced. We took painkillers."

Similar to the bonds formed around football, the crew of *American Gladiators* developed a unique, everlasting kinship. "Years and years later, we have this bond—the kind of thing you only get through athletics, that connection where you get a different sense of self-worth and caring."

Starr, fifty-four, now serves as a product development manager for LifeTime Fitness, a Minnesota-based chain of high-end gyms.

ROCKY KLEVER

BORN: July 10, 1959, Portland, OR
COLLEGE: Montana
POSITIONS: Tight end; running back
NFL EXPERIENCE: 1982–87
TEAM: New York Jets

Back when NFL clubs were allowed a maximum of forty-five players, Rocky Klever was known as the definitive forty-fifth man. In other words, he secured a roster spot through flexibility.

His primary duty with the New York Jets for seven seasons was serving as the second-string tight end, but he could also function as an emergency quarterback, punter, fullback, snapper, field-goal kicker, kickoff man and a coverage performer on special teams.

In fact, playing special teams added stock to Klever's portfolio, and even when he was playing tight end more frequently, he continued his special teams contribution.

Such an NFL career wasn't something Klever had anticipated when he came to UM as a quarterback out of Anchorage, Alaska, in 1977. A former Griz quarterback, Tom Huffer—who had coached at a rival high school in Alaska—was serving as a UM graduate assistant coach the year before Klever was a high school senior. Huffer informed coach Gene Carlson and his staff about Klever and suggested they should recruit him.

Once in Missoula, the coaching staff switched him to running back, and he hustled for a school-record 2,228 yards in his career. The New York Jets drafted him as a runner in the ninth round in 1982, an intended counterpart to UCLA product Freeman McNeil. He showed some impressive skills during rookie training camp in 1982 but fractured a finger and a shoulder and spent the year injured on the sidelines. "My first couple of years, nothing was guaranteed, and I was lucky to hang on. It worked out well because Tom Coombs [a tight end drafted in 1982 from Idaho] couldn't play special teams. He got hurt once and I kind

Rock Klever's primary duty with the New York Jets for seven seasons was as the second-string tight end, but he could also function at several other positions.
Courtesy University of Montana.

of filled in, and before you know it, they liked me at tight end. That's half the battle if the coaches kind of like you. "

Klever experienced a lockout (1982) and a strike (1987) during his NFL career. His most memorable year was in 1985 when the Jets finished the campaign a stout 11-5 and in week eleven (November 17, 1985) scored the most points in club history in trouncing Tampa Bay, 62–28. The hometown offense racked up 581 yards of offense, with Ken O'Brien tossing five touchdown passes, three to tight end Mickey Shuler.

Klever's NFL career ended after he was on injured reserve for his entire last season with a back injury and then was cut by the Jets because he couldn't pass his physical.

His fondest memory of playing in the NFL was having Griz teammate Guy Bingham, who was already with the Jets when he arrived as a rookie, as a friend and teammate. "'Bing' knew all the guys, and they accepted me quicker because of him. There was a little bit of a hazing going on with rookies. It wasn't anything brutal, so Bing always told me what to do, and how to do it, and when to do it, and before you knew it, you fit right in and you were one of the guys."

After leaving the Jets, Klever owned a Gold's Gym in New Jersey and coached football at Northern Arizona and Carroll College in Helena, and he tried his hand at the bar, liquor store and restaurant businesses.

RYAN LEAF

BORN: May 15, 1976, Great Falls, MT
COLLEGE: Washington State
POSITION: Quarterback
NFL EXPERIENCE: 1998; 2000–01
TEAMS: San Diego Chargers (1998, 2000); Dallas Cowboys (2001)

Sadly, Ryan Leaf's name in NFL circles is synonymous with blunder, cockiness and disappointment. Marked by immaturity, injuries, alcohol and prescription drug problems—and, eventually, prison time—his name has become an infamous footnote of Montana sports history.

Leaf is routinely listed near the top of the "Biggest Draft Busts Ever" list, which is a sharp contrast to the expectations attached to a quarterback drafted behind Peyton Manning, at no. 2, in 1998.

Leaf's meteoric rise, and his precipitous unraveling, still troubles the people of the Treasure State. For Montanans, his fall is a complicated component of the state's football identity, a personal affront more than simply another tale of a draft pick gone awry. Outside Montana, Leaf's name and memory still represents Montana football and Big Sky athletes. In spite of everything, of the thousands of kids to play four years of high school football in Montana, only two have ever started an NFL game at quarterback (Leaf and Brock Osweiler).

The San Diego Chargers selected Leaf with the second overall pick in the 1998 NFL draft. But unpredictability, rashness, a volcanic temper and substance abuse led to his steep decline. San Diego went 1-15 during Leaf's final season with the team in 2000. He retired from the NFL after three seasons, during which he threw fourteen touchdowns and thirty-six interceptions and completed 48.4 percent of his passes. By 2012, Leaf was back home in Montana. Growing desperate, he schemed to acquire drugs.

On April Fools' Day in 2012, members of the Central Montana Drug Task Force closed in on Leaf, tracking his cash-on-delivery payments to pain killers he ordered over the Internet from New York and Florida. He was already on probation for stealing his injured players' pills while serving as an assistant football coach at West Texas A&M in Canyon, Texas. He later served thirty-two months in prison for burglary convictions that Leaf said stemmed from his addiction to painkillers. He was released from prison in December 2014.

After professional failure, drug abuse, suicide attempt and prison, one of the NFL's biggest draft busts, age forty, is reported to be turning his life around.

"I'm grateful for how it's turned out," said Leaf to *Sports Illustrated* in April 2017. "The biggest thing is for my family, what they've had to go through. But the pleasure they live in now, or at least for the last 2½ years, is immeasurable."

BLAINE MCELMURRY
BORN: October 23, 1973, Helena, MT
POSITION: Defensive back
COLLEGE: Montana
NFL EXPERIENCE: 1997–99
TEAMS: Green Bay Packers (1997); Jacksonville Jaguars (1998–99)

Blaine McElmurry prepped at Class C Troy High School. Perhaps no other NFL player outside of Montana derived from such a sparse population.

"I came from a tiny high school in Troy," he said.

Troy had no stoplight. It had a movie theatre that barely ran. You would drive down and wave to every car, because you knew every car. It always felt a little bit invisible, and in Montana you can feel invisible anyway. My dad was a football coach in Troy since I was in the second grade and babysitting was going to practice. But Troy is a united town and everyone follows sports and sports are big and it feels extra special to come from there and play in the NFL. I think that once you realize that we're all just people and we're all trying to struggle through life that it makes things a lot less overwhelming, and you realize that you can pretty much do whatever you want to do.

After a successful collegiate career at Montana, the six-foot, 190-pound undrafted McElmurry made it to the final cut with the Tennessee Titans in 1997 and then went to the Philadelphia Eagles, who kept him for about a week. Two days later, the Green Bay Packers signed him, and he was activated late in the 1997 season.

"My dad grew up in Wisconsin and I grew up loving the Packers. It's very similar to Missoula, a small town, and in Green Bay it was amazing how close the fans felt to the players and the organization did a good job connecting fans to players. It's an extra special connection and the players are so accessible. Reggie White. Brett Favre. I remember coming into a team meeting and looking around and seeing the guys I had seen on TV and thinking it was a dream or it wasn't right."

Even today, his memories of the 1998 Super Bowl feel surreal (though on the Packers roster, he was listed as inactive). (The Packers lost Super Bowl XXXII to the Denver Broncos, 31–24.) "Less than a year earlier I was playing for the Grizzlies and then I was in the middle of a bunch of cops clearing traffic and was being escorted all over and hopping on to buses. John Elway won his first Super Bowl and Denver was the underdog and expectations were that we were going to win. The Packers had a party planned and it was hard to celebrate a loss."

McElmurry was injured in training camp in 1998 and wound up going back to the Titans where he made the practice squad. He was picked up by the Jacksonville Jaguars, where he was on their active roster for about three years.

In Jacksonville, I came later in the season before Christmas and it was still 90 degrees at practice. I was there for five days and I was playing in a

Born in Helena, Blaine McElmurry prepped at class C Troy High School. Perhaps no other NFL player outside of Montana came from such a sparse population. *Courtesy University of Montana.*

Sunday Night Football against the Pittsburgh Steelers after the safety went down and they put me in the game. I still didn't know where the bathroom was after five days. I didn't know what the heck was going on defensively. I played half the game at safety and my teammate, he'd have to tell me every play, shouting out generic names: Cover 2, Man 3. In the NFL there are so many adjustments and formations and a lot of mental checking and mental stuff. I got to be in on a tackle of Steelers running back Jerome Bettis and I had a couple of passes broken up. At the press conference after game coach Tom Coughlin said, "I don't know how to say his last name, but he had a great game!"

He was close to another Super Bowl in 1999 as a member of the Jacksonville Jaguars, losing the AFC Championship game to the Tennessee Titans. "In Jacksonville, we were on pace to beat the all-time lowing scoring output for a defense. We were coming after people and people weren't scoring against us. I played forty snaps against the San Francisco 49ers on defense [for the Jaguars], against Terrell Owens and Jerry Rice and Steve Young."

In three seasons at safety with Green Bay and Jacksonville, McElmurry made nineteen solo tackles, six assists and intercepted one pass. The hurts piled up during two stints with NFL Europe, including a hernia and a pair of shoulder and knee surgeries, which ultimately pushed him into retirement.

"They sent me to NFL Europe to get more playing time. I threw the guy out of bounds and I ended up with a hernia in Jacksonville. In Europe, I suffered a torn shoulder. It wasn't from a big hit or because some guy crushed me, but just fluke injuries. I knew I belonged there and I had higher hopes for staying long. Some days I miss it a lot. But now that I've been out of it for awhile I don't miss it as much because I know I can't play anymore. I guess it was at the point when I still thought I could play that I missed it more."

Now a resident of Missoula, McElmurry builds single- and multi-family homes and apartments and helps his wife raise three daughters. He said he keeps tabs on the current class of Montana-raised NFL products.

"I'm always keeping track, either reading about them in the paper or Googling them. A state like California has so many guys that you and don't think about it, where here it is easy to hone in on them and take a little pride."

Mark McGrath

Born: December 17, 1957, San Diego, CA
College: Montana State
Position: Wide receiver
NFL Experience: 1981; 1983–85
Teams: Seattle Seahawks (1981); Washington Redskins (1983–85)

After a stellar prep career in the Seattle area, McGrath, a five-foot, eleven-inch, 175-pound wide receiver, attended Montana State and later earned a Super Bowl ring for the Redskins' 27–17 win over the Dolphins in 1983.

McGrath played four seasons in the NFL, with the Seahawks (1981) and Redskins (1983–85), compiling fifteen career catches for 181 yards and one touchdown.

"I was not citified and that was the beauty of attending Montana State. Winning the national championship, lettering, and playing on national television, was all great exposure my first year. I've always wanted to be a Husky and it turned out I worked out in Seattle, with Warren Moon. I almost switched. I was homesick. But I stayed at Montana State and I couldn't have enjoyed it any more."

Bobcat Mark McGrath played four seasons in the NFL with the Seahawks (1981) and Redskins (1983–85), compiling fifteen career catches for 181 yards and one touchdown. *Courtesy Mark McGrath.*

The Seattle Seahawks formed in 1976, and when McGrath signed with the team as a free agent in 1980, the team was still cultivating its fan base in the community and earning its respect in the league.

"The draft now is a big ordeal. It's on ESPN. Back then interested teams said to stay home and answer if the phone rings. You didn't know when it was over, and no there were no cell phones." He continued: "I ran across my contract with the Seahawks and including every single incentive I could've reached, I would have made $126,000 over three years. My rookie salary was $30,000. The next year $35,0000 and next $45,000. Today, the minimum is $450K. I think the signing bonus was a little over $2,200 dollars. [Seattle] quarterback Dave Krieg signing's bonus was $500 and he made $25,000 a year.

"Seattle didn't even have a minicamp. The Redskins had a four-day minicamp and training camp in July. You had an old, storied franchise in Washington. In Seattle at the time, the crowd was a wine and cheese tailgate crowd, dressed up, sweaters around the shoulders. Today, they are animals, and crazed and loud."

On January 30, 1983, Super Bowl XVII was held at the Rose Bowl in Pasadena, California, in front of 103,667. The Washington Redskins triumph over the Miami Dolphins 27–17 on the strength of an iconic 43-yard touchdown run by John Riggins.

"We had a one week break and we practiced all week in Washington," said McGrath.

> *By Wednesday, it seemed like every player wanted to play it in the airport parking lot and get it over with. Even though it was 3:00 a.m., in the hotel there were 500 people in the lobby. Players left rooms through their hotel windows. If you had a dinner reservation or wanted to see your family, it took 90 minutes to exit the building, so guys were sneaking out of windows and back doors even then.*
>
> *I wish I could go back and take everything in and enjoy it again. Especially the camaraderie and going out of the tunnel at the beginning of the game with 80,000 people screaming. At Montana State, half the time we had 7,000 people in the stands. But it's still the greatest place in the world in my mind.*

McGrath is the last Bobcat wide receiver to play in the NFL. Mike Jefferson was drafted by the Dallas Cowboys in 2008, but he never played in a regular season game and was released at the end of the season.

MIKE MCLEOD

BORN: May 4, 1958, Bozeman, MT
COLLEGE: Montana State
POSITION: Defensive back
NFL EXPERIENCE: 1984–85
TEAM: Green Bay Packers

Mike McLeod's reputation as a person exceeds his sterling reputation as a football player.

"Mike was not just a good player," said Sonny Lubick, former MSU head football coach. "He was a great player. I can remember when he came to Montana State, that right away you knew he was something special. He worked hard, he was a pleasure to have in the program, and he was a great person."

At MSU, McLeod was known as a crafty defensive back with a knack for intuiting what direction the ball and play were headed. Of his five career interceptions at MSU, none was more memorable than the pick he made against Idaho State in 1979. With MSU up 7–0 early in the second quarter, McLeod intercepted a pass from Dirk Koetter and returned it 89 yards for

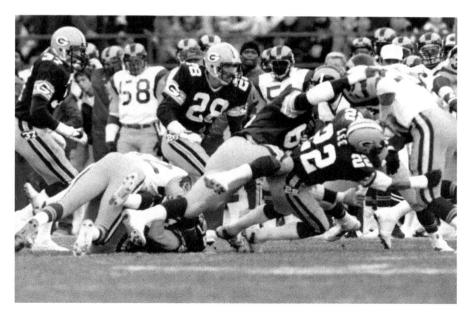

Following his days as a Bobcat, Mike McLeod (no. 28) signed with the Green Bay Packers, where he stayed on the roster for the 1984 and 1985 seasons. *Courtesy Mike McLeod.*

a touchdown. The run back set a school record for longest interception return, eclipsing the twenty-year-old record held by his father, Jim.

Following his days as a Bobcat, McLeod signed with the Green Bay Packers where he stayed on the roster for 1984 and 1985 seasons, primarily as Tom Flynn's backup. He later headed north to the Canadian Football League and the Edmonton Oilers.

Though a big city, Edmonton was a football culture similar to Green Bay in that is was community-owned team, and we won the Grey Cup for first three years I was there and they won five total in a row. Warren Moon was the quarterback and when he went down to the NFL the team rapidly declined. At one point, Tom Wilkinson, a short, pot-bellied guy from Greybull, Wyoming, was the starter.

Both of my years in Green Bay we went 8-8, and I'd never been on a losing team ever until then. The coaches were way more intense. The athletes were bigger, stronger, and faster and I was way undersized. I was overwhelmed in the NFL. In the NFL on special teams there can be guys 50 pounds heavier and 6 inches taller and that's humbling quickly. When you get annihilated by these great athletes, well, that is quite eye-opening. Canada had more quickness, finesse and athleticism and not much size, more of a grind it out type game.

McLeod said that the coaches on the Packers often incited hatred for other players and teams and cultivate a war-like mentality. "Violence in the NFL was encouraged. We were encouraged to go after people and go for heads and things like that. I remember kickoff coverage team in my first game [against the Tampa Bay Buccaneers], I was running crossways and a guy blindsided me, forearmed me, and dislocated my jaw, and I didn't see him coming. He was probably a linebacker. Guys in film room watched the clip and say, "Welcome to the NFL."

"One time when both Mark Murphy and Tom Flynn were both hurt, I was going to start against the Bears and I had been practicing with a taxi squad guy, who had a 15-inch cast on his forearm. I intercepted a ball and while I was still in the air, he got me in the ribs with the forearm cast. I cracked two ribs and had a lacerated kidney and spent a week in the hospital urinating blood, and I missed the final eight weeks. Games were violent and the practices were violent too."

Forrest Gregg, a hall of fame tackle, was the Green Bay Packers' special teams, and his seriousness and intense professionalism ensured his squad

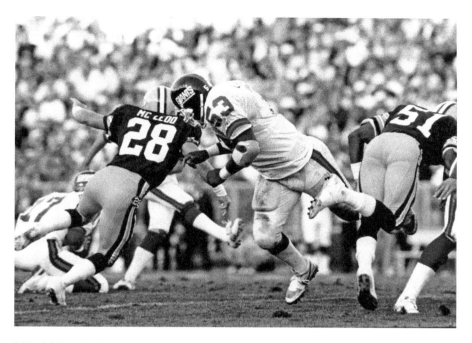

Mike McLeod said that the coaches on the Packers often incited hatred for other players and teams and cultivate a war-like mentality. *Courtesy Mike McLeod.*

the honor of being the best kickoff coverage team in the NFL. "We'd have an onside kick in games and these little fast guys, kind of the kamikaze guys, would go after a person's knees and take him out. [Gregg] was one intense, intimidating tough man who had soft side when he wasn't coaching or playing. Vince Lombardi called Gregg the best player he ever coached."

Another special for memory for McLeod was traveling with the Packers to Denver to face the Broncos on October 15, 1984. "I grew up in Cheyenne, and our family had season tickets to see the Broncos. They kicked the ball off and we fumbled it and they scored. We down 14–0 on returned fumbles right from the start. Our field goal kicker had the chance to tie it late, but he missed and Gregg cut him on the spot. Guys were always coming and going on the roster. Guys were gone the next day, or even the same day. There'd be a handful of new guys coming in every week."

After two seasons in the NFL in which he dressed for twenty games, started in one and had an interception, McLeod left to obtain law degrees from the University of Alberta and the University of Wisconsin. He works and lives in Bozeman.

THOMAS NEVILLE
BORN: September 4, 1961, Great Falls, MT
DIED: May 9, 1998, Fresno, CA
COLLEGES: Weber State; Fresno State
POSITIONS: Offensive guard; offensive tackle
NFL EXPERIENCE: 1986–92
TEAMS: Green Bay Packers (1986–88; 1992); San Francisco 49ers (1991)

Born in Great Falls, Thomas Neville grew up in Fresno, California. An offensive lineman, he attended Weber State in Utah before transferring to Fresno State. He played three seasons for the Green Bay Packers, took a couple of years off from football and returned to play one year with the San Francisco 49ers before rejoining the Packers for one more season.

In 1998, Neville's life turned for the worse, and he began to engage in behavior his family members described as "bizarre."

Neville lived a seemingly normal life in Fairbanks, Alaska, where he worked managing real estate and coaching high school football teams. The married father of one, described as "a big, gentle bear," had been visiting Fresno when he was picked up at a Fresno hotel by police after menacing strangers with a hunting rifle. He was transported by ambulance to a hospital and later was transferred to Cedar Vista Hospital Fresno, a private psychiatric center. Two days later, he assaulted another patient and rammed through a locked steel door.

The six-foot, five-inch, 350-pound former lineman was shot dead by police after he barricaded himself in an apartment complex across the street and violently refused to surrender. After being caught hiding in a supply closet, he was confronted by Fresno police and after throwing "two to three officers into a wall" received about a dozen gunshot wounds. He was thirty-six. "It's a complete shock to everybody," his stepsister, Sherell Neville, told the *Fresno Bee*. "This was not at all like how he would normally behave. He was a completely rational and calm person. I have no idea what the events were that led up to this."

Former Fresno State football coach Jim Sweeney, who coached Neville from 1982 to 1984, called him "a gentle giant."

Neville's death was one of the factors that motivated his former Green Bay Packers teammate Ken Ruettgers to establish Games Over, a foundation which assists professional athletes' adjustment from sports to retirement. (The suicide rate among retired NFL players is nearly six times the national average of 12.1 per 100,000.)

Since 2001, Games Over has grown to include about eighty consultants, most former football players but also college and career professionals, marriage and family counselors and transition counselors.

Challenges are daunting. "Almost eighty percent of NFL players are either bankrupt, divorced or unemployed two years after leaving the game," said Ruettgers. "Many suffer from effects of denial, drinking and drugs, lack of purpose, depression, anger and bitterness, loss of structure and isolation."

"Having been there myself, I can speak the language. For these guys, they've lived a whole life of entitlement. Everything has been given to them and done for them. They don't know any other way. Now, nobody is calling them, nobody is giving them anything. The first step is giving them an orientation into real life. Our goal is to help guys accomplish more with the rest of their life than they ever did as a pro athlete."

PAT OGRIN

BORN: February 10, 1958, Butte, MT
COLLEGE: Wyoming
POSITION: Defensive tackle
NFL EXPERIENCE: 1981–82
TEAM: Washington Redskins

Pat Ogrin's earliest childhood memories involve neighborhood football games and small-town athletics.

"Though I was born in Butte, my dad worked for Montana Power Company and we lived in Cut Bank out on the middle nowhere until I was in seventh grade. My dad transferred back to Butte and I always heard stories about Butte, even as a kid, things like how you'd get beat up every day and what a rough town it was. That's not how it was. I have good memories of Butte."

Following an all-state prep career for the Butte High Bulldogs (graduating in 1976), Ogrin gridded collegiately for the Wyoming Cowboys, where he garnered a pair of all-conference selections.

"My first year [1976] we went to the Fiesta Bowl and we got killed by Oklahoma 41–7. We ran a four man front. We had mediocre seasons the rest of way out and that was a little disappointing."

Ogrin, a six-foot, five-inch, 265-pound defensive tackle, played two seasons with the Washington Redskins, in 1981–82. "The sports magazine had me projected to be a fourth-round pick but three-fourths into my final [college] season I hurt my knee and that changed that."

Ogrin's first season he played with members of the Over-the-Hill Gang, a GeorgeAllen–coached Redskins team of the early 1970s, named due to the large number of veterans on the team, many of whom also played with Allen when he coached the Los Angeles Rams from 1966 to 1970. (The average age of the starters was thirty-one.)

Allen's guys were so old-looking, guys like Diron Talbert, Coy Bacon, and Paul Smith. Coach Joe Gibbs came in my second year and he had different philosophy. I hadn't one-hundred percent recovered from my knee injury so I was placed on injured reserve. The older guys didn't like seeing a rookie on IR, figuring the team was wasting their time on a guy who hadn't played. My second year I lived there (in Washington) in the offseason and the minicamps went well and when I got into the training camp, I felt good about it. I got released as a late cut and since I knew the system I was brought back part way through the season.

Butte's Pat Ogrin, a six-foot, five-inch, 265-pound defensive tackle, played two seasons with the Washington Redskins (1981 and 1982). *Courtesy Pat Ogrin.*

Ogrin saw action in the last six games of the season as a backup defensive tackle. "One of the thrills was playing in Dallas and being in Dallas Stadium and awe of that and playing against [running back] Tony Dorsett. I remember trying to tackle Dorsett and I don't think I did and also playing against Pat Donovan, of Helena. My second year in training camp I went against [Hall of Fame offensive guard] Conrad Dobler, and all the stories had been floating around about how dirty a player he was. He was a tough guy."

He was a member of the team in Super Bowl XVII when the Redskins beat the Dolphins, 27–17, in the Rose Bowl. Washington running back John Riggins was named the MVP, finishing the game with two Super Bowl records: the most rushing yards in a game (166) and the most rushing attempts (38). On fourth down and 1 yard to go, Riggins broke free on a 43-yard touchdown run.

"It was a media circus and Coach Gibbs tried to keep us isolated from that. Of course, I remember John Riggins running around. That run iced it for us. I believe he held out most of my rookie year and he was one of those guys who just did whatever he wanted to do. He wore his old farm boots to practice and rode his pickup truck and was a down-to-earth guy."

Ogrin never played in another regular-season game in the NFL. He spent two seasons in the USFL, with the Denver Gold (1983–84) and a stint in the Arena Football League with the Pittsburgh Gladiators (1988).

Since then, Ogrin, who was inducted into the Butte Sports Hall of Fame in 1997, completed pharmacy school in North Carolina and re-located to his current home in Louisiana.

"Sometimes you appreciate the things that you've done only after you been out of them for a while. Still, when you hear the name of someone who is from Montana and playing football, you pay attention and you watch and you look for them."

BRENT PEASE

BORN: October 8, 1964, Moscow, ID
COLLEGES: Walla Walla; Montana
POSITION: Quarterback
NFL EXPERIENCE: 1987–90
TEAMS: Minnesota Vikings (1987); Houston Oilers (1987–88);
Miami Dolphins (1989); Chicago Bears (1990)

Brent Pease graduated from high school in Mountain Home, Idaho, in 1983. He played quarterback at Walla Community College from 1983 to 1984 and at Montana from 1985 to 1986.

Pease passed for 3,056 yards and thirty touchdowns in ten games as a senior at Montana in 1986. He ranked ninth at Montana in both single-season and career passing. Years later, while he was offensive coordinator and quarterbacks coach, the team compiled records of 14-1 (1996), 8-4 (1997) and 8-4 (1998). During Brent Pease's tenure, the Montana Grizzlies finished with ten or more wins four times in eight years.

"What I liked most about playing in college was just being a leader and trying to lead everybody on the team and I always enjoyed the adrenaline that comes with that," said Brent Pease. "Montana defined me, built my character, it's where I met my wife, and it's where both of my kids were born, and I have such a strong affiliation for Missoula and what it did for me. I feel strong roots there."

Pease was drafted by the Vikings in 1987 and was later released and picked up by the Houston Oilers. (His Griz teammate Mike Rice was also drafted in the eighth round by the New York Jets in 1987. But Rice didn't survive the final cuts in the preseason.)

Former Griz quarterback Brent Pease was a backup for Warren Moon and the Houston Oilers in 1987 and 1988. *Courtesy University of Montana.*

"[Vikings quarterback] Tommy Kramer was in rehab and they had Wade Wilson, and myself, and they traded for Rich Gannon, and that's when I got released. I have good memories of the experience and appreciate the opportunity to play at that level and how difficult it is."

Pease started three games with Houston during the strike-shortened season in 1987. For some strike replacement players, most realized their first NFL game would be their last game. As the man who replaced quarterback Warren Moon, Pease said he tried to concentrate on practice. "I knew when [the strike] was over, the situation would probably be over. I think I did a good job. I thought I made a good enough impression to stay. I was humble about being there."

Pease was a backup for Warren Moon and Cody Carlson during the 1988 campaign. On October 9, he threw three pass interceptions and was booed by his own fans, but he didn't let it get him down. After replacing Carlson, who broke his thumb in the first quarter, Pease overcame the gaffes and ran four yards for the only touchdown late in the third quarter, and the Oilers got past the Kansas City Chiefs, 7–6.

The Oilers had such an identity with the House of Pain at the time and a prolific offense and I played with played with Mike Rozier, Alonzo Highsmith, Allen Pinkett. Guys like Mike Munchak were great to be around and to see how they acted as professionals. Coach Jerry Glanville was so good at telling jokes and one liners, and had such a sense of humor that he left tickets for Elvis Presley and James Dean impersonators. But you never wanted to be in his dog house.

He graduated from Montana in 1990 with a degree in health and human performance with an emphasis in social science. In 1991, he was the first quarterback selected in the World League of American Football, the no. 1 selection of the Birmingham Fire. He is currently the offensive coordinator at the University of El Paso.

"I still have a passion for the state [Montana] and the school [UM] there. I played there, got my education there, coached there, and I would head over when I had time off to the in-laws' ranch in Fort Benton. It's part of the fabric of what I am."

LARRY RUBENS

BORN: January 25, 1959, Spokane, WA
COLLEGE: Montana State
POSITION: Center
NFL EXPERIENCE: 1982–83; 1986
TEAMS: Green Bay Packers (1982–83); Chicago Bears (1986)

Montana State graduate Larry Rubens played center in the NFL for two seasons with the Green Bay Packers in 1982 and 1983. A fifty-seven-day strike by the NFL players shortened the 1982 season to nine games. The NFL players' union called for a strike immediately following the Packers' Monday night win over the New York Giants on September 20, 1982. At that point, Green Bay was 2-0, having opened the season with a record-setting come-from-behind win. Trailing the Rams 23–0 at the half, the Packers scored 35 unanswered points to win.

At the end of the abbreviated season, Green Bay rolled into the playoffs with a 5-3-1 record, good enough for third in the NFC, their first playoff berth since 1972. In the playoffs, Green Bay would crush St. Louis, only to lose a heartbreaker to Dallas in the NFC semifinals.

Rubens snapped punts both years for the Packers.

Rubens played in the USFL for the Memphis Showboats as their starting center and returned to the NFL with the Chicago Bears in 1986 and 1987. He dressed in forty-one regular season games in his professional career.

Brian Salonen
Born: July 29, 1961, Glasgow, MT
College: Montana
Positions: Linebacker; tight end
NFL Experience: 1984–85
Team: Dallas Cowboys

The fierce sport at first seemed unnatural to Brian Salonen, the son of a high school football coach. Though he romanticized the game as a kid, once he was in the midst of its crushed bodies and broken bones, he wasn't sure if he was cut out for its violence. Then sometime in his junior year at Great Falls High School, "the switch turned on."

"Gosh, you would get on the bus and travel four or six hours for a game and some people never imagine that," said Brian Salonen. "Growing up in Great Falls I remember always wanting to be a Bison and putting on the silver shiny helmets, and it was a great culture back then. I never liked football that much, the contact, being sore and getting hurt and getting hit, and I didn't care for it. It's not human nature to go out with helmets and pad and whack one another. But when I was junior in high school in Great Falls High, I was one of the shiny helmets of the Bison running out under the lights, and I didn't enjoy it that much until that switch turned on."

The six-foot, three-inch, 229-pounder broke into the lineup as a true freshman in 1980. By 1981, Montana had its first winning record in six seasons, including a 27–17 win over Montana State. By 1982, the Griz had a winning streak over the Bobcats and a Big Sky banner to hang. Salonen's 150 catches and 1,882 yards are the most by a Grizzly tight end, and each total ranks in the top twenty in school history.

When Salonen joined the Cowboys in 1984, Dallas was in the midst of a run that included seventeen playoff appearances in eighteen seasons. Dallas had won the NFC five times since 1970, including claiming Super Bowl titles in 1971 and 1977. Salonen, who grew up idolizing the Pittsburgh Steelers and linebacker Jack Lambert, had talked with the Chicago Bears before the draft, and coach Mike Ditka expressed interest

Brian Salonen's 150 catches and 1,882 yards are the most by a Grizzly tight end; each total ranks in the top twenty in school history. *Courtesy Brian Salonen.*

in signing the Montana product. He had no gripes when that didn't pan out as promised.

> *I was supposed to be on the Bears team. But the Cowboys drafted me and when I arrived, wow, just look at the names: Tom Landry, Tony Dorsett, Randy White, Ed Jones, Everson Walls, Herschel Walker, Tony Hill. It's amazing to look at the power and talent we had assembled. The marketing and promotion of that goofy star on the side of the helmet is one of the greatest marketing or advertising things America has ever seen. The America's team brand, to the cheerleaders, to Tom Landry, to the wins to the respect and discipline they embodied, there's nothing like it. Whether they love you or hate you at Dallas, everyone is interested in you.*
>
> *There were forty-nine guys on the roster back, and now you've got a practice squad and a fifty-three-man roster. There were only twenty-eight teams then—four less than there are today. So (adding in the practice squad of ten players) that's about fourteen less guys per team back then. It's hard to make a team now, and those were not great numbers to make a team back then.*

In Salonen's first year, he was inserted into situational offensive formats, though he contributed primarily on special teams.

I have a singular memory of Jack Lambert, one of the biggest bad asses in the history of the league. He was not huge. But there was no one tougher. As a rookie I remember trying to block him and I literally cut up field and had that guy a foot away, and I put my head down and I was barreling though, I hit the line and hit something. I thought that I pancaked him. But in a split second, I turned around and I got up and Jack Lambert was laying on top of (teammate running back) Ron Springs. I had missed him completely—at full speed. He dodged me and he crushed Ron Springs. I had hit the Pittsburgh safety behind me. Tom Landry later said, "all you rookies missed him completely! Are all of you rookies blind?"

He started his second season as a reserve tight end. Tight end Doug Cosby was ahead of Salonen on the depth chart, which severely diminished his prospects of participating as a starter. While he had experience as a backup kicker and snapper, he had not played at outside linebacker since high school, and he did not play on special teams in college. But he knew that diversity as a utility man would strengthen his chances of sticking around.

I went in to see Tom Landry the January before the [1985] season because I knew I was going to be the odd man out. I said, "Hey, how about I play at outside linebacker as a backup and as an extra tight end and I play on all special teams?" I'm sure Landry was wondering, who is this crazy guy from Montana who hasn't played linebacker since high school? I heard nothing from him. He was terrible at communication and he didn't converse with you. We went through minicamps and I was still listed as tight end. I show up one day for training camp in July and the offensive coordination said he switched me to defense. Even though I'd asked for it, my first thought was that they were going to try me, cut, and I'd be done playing. I was actually crushed.

Few players in the modern era of the National Football League have competed in positions both offensively and defensively. Chuck Bednarik, a stalwart at both linebacker and center for the 1960 NFL champion Philadelphia Eagles, is considered the last full-time two-way player in the National Football League.

"I'm not sure how many guys can say they had a chance to play on both sides of the ball in the NFL," said Salonen, who works as a financial advisor in Missoula. "I made the team that second year and handled that adversity. That story to me is a life story to me. You face rejection and you handle things and even when things don't go your way, you react appropriately. Work ethic, discipline, respect and the ability to adapt to change, these are things that have stuck with me my entire life."

Indeed, Salonen competed in the National Football League at a time when Montana-born players were a rarity on the league rosters.

"It was a tremendous feeling being in Dallas where many guys on the team had never even heard of Montana. But Montana had the reputation of toughness and respect and discipline. I felt like since I was from Montana I was going to give them hell, and I loved that. Few from Montana then had the opportunity to go to do that. It [representing Montana] was always something on the back on my mind."

KIRK SCRAFFORD
BORN: March 15, 1967, Morristown, NJ; raised: Billings, MT
COLLEGE: Montana
POSITIONS: Tackle; guard
NFL EXPERIENCE: 1990–98
TEAMS: Cincinnati Bengals (1990–92); Denver Broncos (1993–94);
San Francisco 49ers (1995–98)

Kirk Scrafford's father was a Fish, Wildlife and Parks service agent who relocated to Billings, Montana, when he was in the eighth grade.

"He was a petrol agent in charge of the region and he traveled a bit," said Scrafford. "I grew up hunting and fishing. I remember watching Monday Night Football on the two TV channels available back then and seeing the Miami Dolphins' Larry Csonka and Bob Griese. I played hockey [years earlier, when we lived] in North Dakota and started playing football in eighth grade as a wide receiver. I was skinny and tall and I couldn't catch the ball. I was moved to the offensive line and I played there for 19 years."

Scrafford was a 210-pound offensive lineman when he graduated from Billings West High School, and throughout his NFL career, his weight rarely surpassed 275 pounds. He played for nine seasons with the Cincinnati Bengals, the Denver Broncos and the San Francisco 49ers. His teammates included Steve Young, Jerry Rice and Terrell Owens.

Kirk Scrafford
played nine
seasons with
the Cincinnati
Bengals, Denver
Broncos and San
Francisco 49ers.
*Courtesy University
of Montana.*

I credit Rob Lebsock, the offensive coach [at Montana], *who taught me good technique and quickness, and I was tall, probably six-six my senior year and probably 195 pounds. I put on weight to 225 by freshman year in college. Even in the NFL, I was skinny, and the heaviest I ever played was at 275. Reggie White was huge and he was a big man and still quick. I ended up having to play against him quite a few times when I was in San Francisco in the playoffs. The first time was my second year in Cincinnati and I was 255 pounds and Joe Walter, our right tackle had a heart problem, and all of a sudden I was playing against Reggie in Veteran's Stadium. He had a reputation for being intimidating. They had a name for it, "White Fright." I played well the first half. But in the second, he figured he could bum rush me and he threw me into* [Bengals quarterback] *Boomer Esiason several times. He picked me up off the ground, and after the game it was the first time I ever felt completely rag dolled.*

During his rookie year with the Bengals in 1990, his first professional start came on the road against the Los Angeles Raiders' defensive end Howie Long, a future hall of famer. "I remember Howie said to me, 'Shouldn't you be playing baseball instead?'" said Scrafford. "Los Angeles was an intimidating scene in those days. Everyone in the stands looked like they'd just gotten a ticket out of jail. There were more fights in the stands than there were on the field."

The Bengals ended up making the playoffs that season, even winning a playoff game in January 1991, something they have yet to do since then.

> *The attitude in Cincy was a far cry for the 49ers. [Owner] Mike Brown once said it didn't matter if the team made it to the Super Bowl or if they 8-8, he had one obligation and that was but fill up the stands. I think the last time they won a playoff game was my rookie year January 1991 we beat the Houston Oilers and lost to the [Oakland] Raiders. Cincy cut costs wherever they could. [Coach] Sam Wyche had a lot of players from the 1988 Super Bowl team and playoffs when I got there my rookie year. But the second year was rough. Dave Shula was coach my third year and I was trying to play on one leg and he lost confidence in me.*

He spent two seasons with the Denver Broncos, primarily in special teams situations.

"I didn't enjoy the kickoff coverage in Denver," said Scrafford. "The wedge was the worst job in the NFL and there were too many injuries. It would've added years to my career if I'd not done it. I think Cincy cut me a couple of times. Denver cut me and I had a change to go to the 49ers, to a team that had won the Super Bowl the year before and was a first-class organization. As a player you don't want to leave any bad performances on film, because that's your future, and you can tell when players quit. To me, score and the records didn't matter, and I tried to play the best I could, I guess."

Scrafford said that he liked the fact that he never witnessed individual players being valued above their teams. He also enjoyed the mental preparation of football. "You would study your next opponent and you knew who they were before you played against them. The first time we'd play somebody you knew them from film and you would get butterflies during the warm-ups. But once the game started you were settled down, and then fired up. I loved football. I loved being part of the team and contributing and when you played, you got instant feedback on whether or not you were improving every day."

Persistent pain from a neck injury forced Scrafford into retirement after the 1997 season with San Francisco, but midway through 1998, his 49er teammates cajoled him into returning for one more playoff run. In the 1998 NFC Wild Card game Steve Young threw a game-ending touchdown pass to Terrell Owens, lifting the 49ers over the Green Bay Packers in the 30–27 thriller. On that final play, Scrafford's blocking assignment was archrival Reggie White. At the end of the 1998 season, Scrafford elected to hang up his cleats.

"I was happy to have played as long as I did. You'd always like to play a few more years, but everybody runs out of gas eventually. I got out of it and can still do some of the things I enjoy doing."

Scrafford splits his time between Costa Rica and an eighty-five-acre piece of land nestled in the Bitterroot Valley between Lolo and Florence. He said that football is like riding a motorcycle—there's only so much a helmet can do. He points out that more and more NFL players are being diagnosed with some form of chronic traumatic encephalopathy, a traumatic brain disease linked to repeated hits to the head. CTE has been linked to repeated brain trauma and diagnosed in hundreds of former football players. It can also cause symptoms of Lou Gehrig's disease (amyotrophic lateral sclerosis). He said he will undergo a battery of tests in the future.

"CTE appears to be more at your frontal lobe and middle lobe and affecting how you control of emotions, and when you look at the head studies in retired football players, and see how it affects behavior things, and depression, and memory. If I had sons I would not urge them to play football."

MICKEY SUTTON

BORN: August 28, 1960, Greenville, MS
COLLEGE: Montana
POSITIONS: Defensive back; punt returner
NFL EXPERIENCE: 1986–90
TEAMS: Los Angeles Rams (1986–88; 1990); Green Bay Packers (1989); Buffalo Bills (1989)

One of the outstanding players in the Big Sky in the early 1980s, Mickey Sutton always seemed to be where the ball was. "Whenever a big play was made, it seemed that Mickey was making it or forcing it so someone else could make the play," said Larry Donovan, the Montana Grizzlies head coach from 1980 to 1985.

Left: In five seasons with three NFL teams, former Griz Mickey Sutton returned seventy-six punts for 695 yards and ended up with five interceptions. *Courtesy University of Montana.*

Right: Rams Coach John Robinson compared Sutton with the mythical baseball player Shoeless Joe Hardy. "He just kind of came out of nowhere," Robinson told the *Los Angeles Times. Courtesy University of Montana.*

After Sutton played at Montana, he played for the Hamilton Tigercats in the Canadian Football League and the Pittsburgh Maulers of the USFL. When that franchise folded a year later, he was picked up by the Birmingham Stallions for the 1985 season before becoming a free agent.

In the summer of 1986, Sutton arrived in Los Angeles so late that the Rams didn't even have time to insert his name or mug shot in the media guide. One day he wasn't there and the next he was starting right cornerback. Rams coach John Robinson compared Sutton with the mythical baseball player Shoeless Joe Hardy. "He just kind of came out of nowhere," Robinson told the *Los Angeles Times*. He did anything he could to secure playing time, including grabbing punts and playing defensive back for passing downs. In his first preseason game against the Houston Oilers, he ran back the opening kickoff 34 yards, scooped a fumble to set up a touchdown and returned another kick 55 yards to set up another.

Inside Sports wrote that Mickey Sutton "has become a curiosity piece for several reasons." The piece continued: "First is his size, or lack of it. Generously listed as five feet, nine inches and 172 pounds, Sutton looks more like the poor kid who gets stopped a few steps away from the roller-coaster ride. You half expect to find bits and pieces of Sutton's little body strewn across the playing field after a game. But short doesn't necessarily mean weak. You get hit by Sutton and somehow you know it."

"The size has never bothered me," he told *Inside Sports* in 1987. "I've always been the smallest since I started playing."

While Sutton's NFL career had been as a reserve, he had a knack of working his way into lineups at critical times. He substituted when the Rams' Henry Ellard was unavailable for punt returns and Ron Brown's injury forced the teams to look for a new kick returner late that same season. When Pro Bowler Leroy Irvin was in the midst of his 1987 contract dispute, Sutton started at right cornerback for three games.

In five seasons with three teams, he returned seventy-six punts for 695 yards and ended up with five interceptions. "When my number was called, I just went in and tried to do the job," said Sutton.

KEVIN SWEENEY
BORN: November 16, 1963, Bozeman, MT
COLLEGE: Fresno
POSITION: Quarterback
NFL EXPERIENCE: 1987–88
TEAM: Dallas Cowboys

The ninth and youngest child of Montana State football coach Jim Sweeney, Kevin attended Bullard High School in Fresno and Fresno State University.

Jim Sweeney's dad was a hard-rock miner and Irish immigrant who worked in the mines of Butte for thirty-five years. A native of Butte who was born in 1929, Jim may be best remembered as the man who guided the Flathead Braves to a pair of state football championships during a five-year reign in the late 1950s. At the time he left in 1960, his teams had strung together eighteen straight wins over his final two seasons.

Jim Sweeney coached at Montana State University (1963–67) and Washington State University and spent time as an assistant coach with the NFL's Oakland Raiders and St. Louis Cardinals. He coached Fresno State's football team for nineteen seasons and retired with a school-record 144 victories. He died in 2013 at the age of eighty-three.

Kevin Sweeney was selected by the Dallas Cowboys in the seventh round (180th overall) of the 1987 NFL draft. He was waived on September 7, 1987, but re-signed after the players went on a strike on the third week of the 1987 season. As part of a replacement team given the mock name "Rhinestone Cowboys" by the media, he became the fourth rookie quarterback to start for the Cowboys, joining Don Meredith (1960), Roger Staubach (1969) and Dak Prescott (2016).

The Dallas Cowboys closed out the third week of strike-replacement football with a loss to the Washington Redskins. In that contest, regular Dallas quarterback Danny White returned to action. According to the *Dallas Morning News* recap, White and running back Tony Dorsett received "a hostile greeting from the crowd before the game," and each "was hassled" every time they touched the ball. When White didn't play well, the crowd chanted, "We Want Sweeney, We Want Sweeney."

Sweeney was kept on the Cowboys roster for two seasons. He retired in 1989 after failing to earn a spot with Dallas or any other team.

KIRK TIMMER

BORN: December 18, 1963, Butte, MT
COLLEGE: Montana State
POSITION: Linebacker
NFL EXPERIENCE: 1987
TEAM: Dallas Cowboys

Butte native Kirk Timmer played middle linebacker for Montana State from 1982 to 1986. He was chosen by the New York Jets in the tenth round of the 1987 draft. The NFL players' union went on strike midway through the 1987 season to lobby for a collective bargaining agreement, leaving many teams without complete rosters.

Owners hastily gathered replacement players—derisively referred to as a "scabs"—to fill the void, one such player being Sean Payton, a reserve quarterback for the Chicago "Spare Bears." Though he completed just eight of twenty-three pass attempts during his transitory stint in the league, Payton later succeeded in the NFL, coaching the New Orleans Saints to a Super Bowl XLIV championship. Playing among the mostly obscure replacement players, Timmer dressed for one game with the Dallas Cowboys.

Corey Widmer

Born: December 25, 1968, Alexandria, VA
College: Montana State
Positions: Defensive tackle; linebacker
NFL Experience: 1992–99
Team: New York Giants

After high school football practice, Cory Widmer would head outdoors, select a massive tree trunk and run with it up the hill behind the house he shared with his mother, stepfather and two older siblings.

Following graduation from Bozeman High School, Widmer had two options: MSU or the U.S. Army. He chose the former and was an anchor on Montana State's defense from 1987 to 1991, earning two-time second-team All-America (1990–91) honors as a defensive tackle and Big Sky Defensive Player of the Year in 1990. Widmer played in the Blue-Gray, Hula and Senior Bowls and was a seventh-round draft pick by New York Giants in 1992. At the time, the Giants were searching for a successor to the exceptional Lawrence Taylor, who anchored the team on defense for thirteen seasons (1981–93).

The six-foot, three-inch, 256-pound Widmer played eight seasons at middle linebacker for Giants, the last four as a starter. "I just wanted to get drafted, and then I got drafted," said Widmer. "Then, I just wanted to make the team, and I made the team. Then I wanted to be the special teams' MVP and I won that. Then, I wanted to be a starter. I had my sights set on being the Giants' defensive MVP."

He was released after the 1999 season following a back injury. Widmer, according to NFL statistics, tallied 271 career solo tackles and 113 assisted tackles. "Middle linebackers typically aren't covered, so you've got to go over the guard who tends to be a pretty big guy. The impacts are a lot more than any other position except for fullback."

Football is the most violent sport in the world, and Widmer said that he has no one to blame or point fingers but himself for the decision he made to participate. He expected contact on every play, injury as an occupational hazard. Yet, he can rattle off a multitude of situations when he was brutally "dinged around." "My rookie year at Montana State, I hit a guy from Kansas State and we both got knocked out. We were sitting there staring at each other and waiting to see who could get up first. When I hit [in professional football], I hit leading with my face, and I would literally bend the steel face mask every game. Sometimes it would pancake the whole helmet."

Widmer said that cold weather games compounded the brutality of routine football contact. "My helmet had this plastic liner that was hard as a brick in the cold weather games that were common in college in Montana and while in New York. When the turf froze in Giants Stadium, and the helmet smacked the ground, your brain took another beating."

Widmer once sustained a concussion so wicked that the coaches yanked him out of the game and sent him to medical specialists for a battery of tests. Fearful of losing his job and paycheck, "he stormed out of the doctor's office," he said. Subsequently, he found himself in the middle of an altercation on the practice field with a teammate. It was at that period that he noticed shifts in his attitude and behavior.

"I felt more aggravated at times. It was then that I became a complete believer that concussions can change personalities."

Following his retirement, Widmer said that he tried to fill the excitement void through extreme sports. In November 2007, he was injured in a paragliding accident in the Chilean Andes. The injury didn't cause any paralysis. However, the then thirty-eight-year-old Widmer severely fractured a vertebrae, which required the removal of two ribs to stabilize his back.

He lives in Manhattan, Montana, not far from his alma mater. At age forty-nine, he said he is grateful for the opportunity that football provided him to grow from a young man into a man. But the chronic pain and persistent concern over head trauma has left him ambivalent about the experience.

"The worst thing about the NFL is that you look down the road and see what it does to your body," said Widmer. "You trade fame for pain. I made that commitment a long time ago."

2000s–PRESENT

KEN AMATO
BORN: May 18, 1977, Puerto Rico
COLLEGE: Montana State
POSITION: Long snapper
NFL EXPERIENCE: 2003–11
TEAM: Tennessee Titans

Ken Amato was exposed to every sport as a kid in Miami, Florida, from tennis to volleyball to football.

"I started playing football in the fourth grade," he said. "My dad said I had so much energy and I needed to always be doing something."

Amato earned all-state and all-conference honors as a linebacker at Moorpark High School and received a scholarship offer from the Bobcats in the summer of 1997. He arrived in Montana without visiting, stepping off the airplane sight unseen, unprepared for the elements. "When I first got there," said Amato, "I remember it was already getting cold, and sometime around September, and I had no winter coat. My mom had to mail me one."

Once MSU coaches noticed that he had the experience as a long snapper that the team needed, they encouraged him to develop in that role.

I wasn't really looking to long snap. I was more focused on playing linebacker. I had long snapped at Moorpark. But once [the coaches] *asked, I wouldn't say no. I didn't mind it. It's what got me in the NFL*

Bobcat Ken Amato spent nine years and 125 games with the Titans, serving as the long snapper for both field goals and punts. He was a member of the special teams coverage unit. *Courtesy University of Montana.*

and gave me an opportunity. In the pros, I wanted to do everything I could to help the team, but it is risky business if you lose a long snapper, and they don't want you to get hurt. A change in the long snapper could hurt important aspects of the game, and the long snapper can be the difference between winning and losing, a missed PAT, or even a poor punt.

In addition to long snapping, Amato recorded eighty-nine career tackles, five and a half sacks and one fumble recovery on defense during his two seasons with the Bobcats.

"I stayed all of the summers I could. I didn't go home and I went to Yellowstone and I worked at a fly shop for my wife's stepfather in Cooke City. But I saw how things worked coming out of a smaller school. You don't get the same look."

After he graduated from MSU with a bachelor of science degree in sociology, he returned to Miami, where he worked with juvenile offenders. A friend suggested that Amato give pro football one more attempt, and the two went out to a park and filmed Amato's long-snapping abilities. He then mailed the tape to a number of NFL teams.

"Few people can work at it and get better at it and do it consistently," said Amato. "The coaches and staff in the NFL, they can tell right away if you have that instinct, that quick twitch, or if you can move laterally."

He was one of four long snappers to attend a tryout with the Tennessee Titans in 2003. When the top man on the depth chart struggled in the first exhibition game, the Titans asked Amato to step in. "When I came in, teams wanted only guys who did that [long snap]. Now, a lot of teams want guys who can play another position. "

He spent nine years and played 125 games with the Titans, serving as the long snapper for both field goals and punts. He was also a member of the special teams coverage unit. He contributed to Rob Bironas's development as a Pro Bowl kicker and was the long snapper when Bironas set an NFL record with eight field goals in a game during a 38–36 win at the Houston Texans on October 21, 2007. The record kick came as time expired following a 63-yard drive in the final minute led by Titans quarterback Kerry Collins.

"That was awesome. We didn't realize how many field goals he had hit until afterwards. The eighth kick was a game-winning kick, and that was the most exciting of them all."

After the NFL, Amato spent three years coaching at Brentwood High School in Brentwood, Tennessee. While at Brentwood, Amato completed two Bill Walsh NFL Minority Coaching Fellowships with the Green Bay Packers (2014) and the Cleveland Browns (2015). Amato joined the Limestone College Saints in 2016 as the special teams coordinator and the outside linebacker coach.

He said he holds a soft spot for his alma mater, which presented him the opportunity to lead a life of football.

"I'll go to an appearance or to sign autographs, and I will run into someone from Montana State," said Amato. "They know I'm an ex-Bobcat, and they want to let me know. That's great, because I'm a big Montana State guy."

COLT ANDERSON
BORN: October 25, 1985, Butte, MT
POSITION: Defensive back
COLLEGE: Montana
NFL EXPERIENCE: 2010–present
TEAMS: Philadelphia Eagles (2010–13); Indianapolis Colts (2014–15); Buffalo Bills (2016)

When Colt Anderson charged onto the field at Washington-Grizzly Stadium, his unwavering work ethic and nose-to-the-grindstone intensity stood out. He figured that he was going to "go big or go home." Coaches were quickly impressed with the level of his devotion.

"In Montana, we don't have a professional sports team," said Anderson, a native of Butte.

We don't have an FBS program [Football Bowl Subdivision, formerly known as Division I-A, the top level of college football]. *The University of Montana is our kind of professional team and the one*

Colt Anderson of Butte started a career-high four games at free safety for the Eagles in 2012, registering thirty tackles on the season. *Courtesy University of Montana.*

that everyone watches. Coming out of high school, I wasn't really offered anything but that walk-on spot. I didn't want to have the regret of having never given it a chance. So, from the get-go, I just wanted to be a guy who worked hard, and when my time came, I'd be ready. I started out on special teams, but I had an assistant coach, Tim Hauck, who really believed in me. I just kept moving my way up the depth chart and I ended up starting three years there.

Anderson helped guide the Grizzlies to the national championship game in 2008 and determinedly spent the spring and summer prepping for an NFL career. Undrafted, he headed into minicamp motivated by a sense that he belonged.

Initially, Anderson inked a three-year deal with the Minnesota Vikings and since then has logged several seasons with the Philadelphia Eagles (2010–13) and two with the Indianapolis Colts (2014–15) and is currently on the roster of the Buffalo Bills. He started a career-high four games at free safety for the Eagles in 2012, registering thirty tackles in the season.

In the off-seasons, Anderson returns to Butte and enjoys the company of college buddies in Missoula. Many of his summer days are spent on float trips along the Blackfoot and Clark Fork Rivers, and he can frequently be found working behind the bar at the Missoula Club, which he co-owns with his brother Beau.

The siblings purchased the Missoula Club on July 6, 2016, adding a new chapter in the Missoula landmark's history and continuing its close connection to Griz football. The Mo Club, as it is affectionately called, first opened in 1890 and has operated in its current space at 139 West Main

Street since 1926. Well known for its no-frills beer and hamburgers, the bar's local lore is such that Bill Clinton opted to pay a visit in 2008 when he was in Missoula to campaign for his wife, Hillary, in the Democratic presidential primary election.

"What I love most about Montana are the people," said Anderson. "It's just a family-oriented, community-oriented state. There might be fewer than one million people in the state. And that's even though it's the fourth largest state in the country. Everywhere you go, you know somebody and they treat you like family. I just really appreciate that and I love going home. There's a reason my wife and I have a house back in Butte, because they're blue-collar people who treat you right and know how to have fun."

The most ruthless weekend of the NFL season—the final roster cut in September from seventy-five players to the fifty-three allowed during the regular season—wasn't sympathetic to former Montana Grizzlies in 2016. Seven Montana products were among the hundreds of players cut, including Marc Mariani (cut from Chicago but later signed by Tennessee). Anderson said that he always keeps his fingers crossed that his "band of brothers" can endure the last trim.

"That's kind of one of the things I learned talking to guys in the NFL," said Anderson. "Montana is a little different from other schools. It's kind of a big band of brothers. We're able to talk to one another, root for one another, and that's what I'll always cherish about my time there."

In 2010, he and another brother, Luke, launched a clothing company called UPTOP that includes Griz- and Montana-themed apparel. "UPTOP was a term coined by Luke representing the celebration of two guys jumping up and colliding in mid-air," said Anderson. "Everything we did usually ended with an UPTOP celebration."

Luke works full time at the company, and Anderson plays a part forming brand strategy, marketing and publicity tactics.

"It started back in college as a joke, really," said Anderson. "My brother worked in the retail industry and we just started out making a couple T-shirts and the popularity just kept growing. Friends started wearing it and people from my hometown and then the whole state kind of caught on. We started taking it more serious. In the offseason, in my spare time, I like to dabble in fashion."

Kroy Biermann
Born: September 12, 1985, Hardin, MT
College: Montana
Position: Defensive end
NFL Experience: 2008–15
Team: Atlanta Falcons

Kroy Biermann grew up as a typical rural Montana kid. He played and explored in the dirt, mud and snow under the vastness of a seemingly endless sky. He was raised on a passion for sports, the outdoors and hobbies such as tinkering with the engines of old trucks.

"Pretty much the only thing to do [in Hardin] was sports and work," said Biermann. "That's what I was raised on—sports and working hard and trying to do everything to achieve my goals. All the stuff you grow up in Montana doing."

Biermann spent his early years in Fort Smith, Montana, a village in Big Horn County of about 150 people near the Bighorn Canyon National Recreation Area where his father was employed as an engineer. When Biermann, the youngest and the only son of the three Biermann children, was in middle school, his family moved forty-five miles northeast to Hardin.

As a Falcon, Kroy Biermann of Hardin started 37 of the 114 games he dressed in, tallying twenty-three and a half sacks, including a career high of five in 2009. *Courtesy University of Montana.*

Biermann elevated his game from that of a standard rural high school football player to the recipient of the Buck Buchannan Award, an honor given to the best Division I-AA defensive player. He loved what high school football meant to his small community, how the lessons doled out on the field taught boys to become men. In college, he stood out for his quickness and discipline.

On April 27, 2008—NFL draft day at Radio City Music Hall in New York City—Biermann received the phone call that he, his family and practically the whole town of Hardin (in southeastern Montana, population approximately 3,700) had been hankering for. He had become the first Hardin High School graduate to be drafted into the NFL. In celebration, Biermann was named mayor of Hardin for a week and received the key to the city. "When he started talking to [Falcons' coach] Mike Smith and the general manager, we knew it was good news," said Keith Biermann, Kroy's father. "Then it popped up on the TV that he'd been drafted by the Falcons."

As a Falcon, Biermann started 37 of the 114 games he dressed in, tallying twenty-three and a half sacks, including a career high of five in 2009. In his spare time, Biermann enjoyed the frequent sojourns back to the Montana of his youth, where the way of life he remembered as a kid remained unchanged. "The kids in Hardin need a role model and need somebody they can see that has come from the same place they have, and that they can achieve whatever they dream. It's a good thing and I'm happy to represent Montana and Hardin."

Off the field, Biermann garnered reality-star status when he married Kim Zolciak in November 2011. Zolciak had previous appeared as a member of the cast of *The Real Housewives of Atlanta*. Zolciak and Biermann parlayed their relationship into a series called *Don't Be Tardy*.

As of November 2016, the show, which features the day-to-day routine of the couple and their blended family of six, was airing its fifth season. In September 2016, Biermann became a free agent following his release from the Buffalo Bills. He said that he is enjoying time away from the game and that if his NFL career is over, he has fully enjoyed the experience.

"This year was the first year the boys started school," said Biermann. "It's exciting to take them to school and pick them up and see the excitement in their eyes and do their homework with them. Had I been somewhere else, I would have missed out on a lot of that stuff. There are no definitive answers to where this thing will end up, but it's definitely been a fun journey. I love my family and I feel like it is second nature to me to be a father and a husband."

Dan Carpenter

Born: November 25, 1985, Omaha, NE
College: Montana
Position: Kicker
NFL Experience: 2008–present
Teams: Miami Dolphins (2008–12); Buffalo Bills (2013–16)

Dan Carpenter attended Helena High School, where he was a member of the National Honor Society and maintained a 3.7 grade point average. As a football player at Helena, Carpenter was a two-time all-state and a two-time all-league selection as a kicker and punter. In his senior season, he converted twenty-six of twenty-nine point-after attempts and converted five field goals, with a long of 53 yards.

Additionally, he was a first team all-conference and second team all-state selection as a wide receiver, notching school records with 931 receiving yards and thirteen touchdowns.

"He has always been an amazingly hard worker and a great competitor, and that work ethic and competitiveness have carried over into his college and the NFL," said Helena football coach Tony Arnston. "He is basically self-taught. He learned how to kick without attending any of those expensive kicking schools."

Carpenter enrolled at the University of Montana (where he met his future wife) and became the placekicker for the Grizzlies as a true freshman in 2004. In his four years at Montana, Carpenter, a two-time All-American, converted on fifty-four of seventy-five field goals (72.8 percent) and punted seventy-one times for a 41.8-yard average.

After going undrafted in the 2008 NFL draft, Carpenter, who majored in chemistry, signed a two-year contract with the Miami Dolphins, becoming the fifth Helenan to play in either the AFL or NFL. Those preceding him were the following: John Dolan, who played

Dan Carpenter has kicked for several NFL teams, and as of 2016, his nearly one thousand points scored ranked thirteenth among active players. His field goal success rate of 84.307 percent ranks him thirteenth all-time. *Courtesy University of Montana.*

for the Kenosha Cardinals (1940) and Buffalo Lions (1941) in the Midwest Football League, a minor professional football league that existed from 1935 to 1940; Earle "Pruney" Parsons of the San Francisco 49ers (1945–46); Bob "Spud" McCullough of the Denver Broncos (1962–65); and Pat Donovan, a member of the Dallas Cowboys (1974–83).

Carpenter tallied twenty-one field goals and 103 total points in his first season, becoming only the second rookie in NFL history to make fourteen consecutive field goals, equaling the mark of New York Giant Ali Haji-Sheikh in 1983. On December 5, 2010, Carpenter made a 60-yard field goal in a home game against the Cleveland Browns, the fifth-longest in NFL history.

Carpenter has kicked for several NFL teams. As of 2016, his nearly one thousand points scored ranked thirteenth among active players. His field goal success rate of 84.307 percent ranks thirteen all-time.

BROCK COYLE
BORN: October 12, 1990, Bozeman, MT
COLLEGE: Montana
POSITION: Linebacker
NFL EXPERIENCE: 2014–present
TEAM: Seattle Seahawks

The University of Montana has a lengthy history of having players chosen in the NFL draft. On eleven occasions, the Grizzlies have had two or more players selected in a single draft year. The highest selection in school history was in 1938, when the Chicago Cardinals made fullback Milt Popovich the no. 15 overall pick. Likewise, the Grizzlies have a history of successful NFL walk-ons.

Brock Coyle went undrafted in 2014 but was signed shortly after by the Seattle Seahawks. With ample natural-born ability and some timely coaching, he has been able to reach a talent level people simply couldn't ignore. Coach Pete Carroll intended to keep Coyle around as a reserve, but on October 31, 2016, Coyle made his first start as strong-side linebacker.

Ironically, Coyle and Seahawks linebacker Jordan Tripp played together at Montana. Not only were they in the same class, but they also started together at linebacker and were team captains together as seniors. In 2016, they had adjacent lockers in the Seahawks dressing room.

"We're so focused on this season and the team and winning games that we don't really realize how special it is," Coyle told the *Seattle Times* in November

2016. "It is pretty special that we came into Montana together, graduated together, were team captains together our senior year, and now we're on the same team in the NFL. It's pretty special."

Dave Dickenson
Born: January 11, 1973, Great Falls, MT
College: Montana
Position: Quarterback
NFL Experience: 2001–02
Teams: San Diego Chargers (2001); Seattle Seahawks (2002);
Miami Dolphins (2002); Detroit Lions (2002)

Dave Dickenson didn't grow up wishing he could play quarterback as a professional. His earliest memories, he said, included dreams of becoming a successful athlete at Charlie Russell High School.

"My father and brother coached football and it was a rite of passage to make the high school football team and to be a part of that," he said. "The cross-city game in high school was the biggest game of my life."

Dickenson played quarterback at the University of Montana, where he led the Grizzlies to the 1995 NCAA I-AA championship. In Dickenson's first year as a starter, in 1993, Montana won its first Big Sky championship since 1982, the fourth league title in UM history. In 1995, Dickenson threw for 5,676 yards and fifty-one touchdowns (including in the playoffs) in leading the Grizzlies to their first national championship in school history. In his three years as a starter, Dickenson piled up thirty-three wins in forty starts.

"The Big Sky Conference has risen to become one of the premier conferences in the West, and much of that has to do with the rise of Dave Dickenson and the Montana Grizzlies," said Mike Kramer, currently the head coach at Idaho State. Kramer was the head coach at Eastern Washington during Dickenson's playing days in the mid-1990s. "When Montana won the national championship [in 1995], it thrust the Griz into the stratosphere, and the rest of the league has been chasing them ever since."

Dickenson spent the entire 2001 season as the third-string quarterback for the San Diego Chargers. Following training camp in 2002, he was released by San Diego. He was signed by the Seattle Seahawks, where he served as their third quarterback for three games and then served as the third backup for eight weeks with the Miami Dolphins, before wrapping up the season third on the depth chart for the Detroit Lions.

*When I signed in San Diego it was the day they released Ryan Leaf,
and we both played in Great Falls. Ryan had a reputation and when I
walked in I didn't look the same part. I was more into competing more than
talking. There was a little bit of a wall up there after Ryan's situation.
They had Junior Seau and Rodney Harrison, Drew Brees and LaDainian
Tomlinson. But I was never able to crack it in San Diego.*

*In Seattle I was playing with Trent Dilfer and Matt Hasselback and
Shaun Alexander. Miami had Ricky Williams when I was there and
several hall of famers. When I got to Detroit I saw the other side, a team
with little talent. They maybe won two games the whole season and there
was a reason for it. I wanted to play the game and if Detroit would have
offered me a contract I would have kept playing. You don't make memories
by sitting on the bench.*

Dickenson more than compensated in the Canadian Football League for
what he couldn't muster in the NFL, throwing for 22,913 yards with 154
touchdowns and fifty interceptions and retiring as the CFL's all-time leader
in passing efficiency (110.4). He's been the Calgary Stampeders' offensive
coordinator since 2011 and took over as the head coach before the 2016
season. Dickenson retains some of the old-time tough-guy coaching ethos.

"I fear failure," said Dickenson. "It's something I can't have associated
with the last name Dickenson. When you do something and you are a part
of it and you are associated with it, I want it to be successful."

He keeps tabs on the crop of Montana products currently fighting for
places on NFL rosters.

*Back then Division I-AA had a reputation of being bumbling. But now the
scouts know that our guys are big, fast, and have the look. Jordan Tripp is
as athletically gifted as anybody. When we won [the championship in
1995] we proved people wrong. Marshall was acting cocky and we were
being made fun of, and I was happy to stick it to them and win. The win
helped put our state on the map. In my opinion, it's still a little underrated
conference because you can watch a game and see great plays and great fans
and it's a perfectly sized stadium. The state supports it [Division I-AA
football] like no other.*

Dickenson said that there is nothing unobtainable about a dream, no
matter where the dreamer resides, and that if football is used in a strategic
way, it can change lives, families and whole communities.

"In today's world, more guys can dream and follow the tradition of the CM Russell quarterbacks," said Dickenson. "We in Montana are proud when one of our own has success and everyone kind of roots for each other. It doesn't matter if you went to Butte or Capital High [and continued to the NFL], you are rooting for the Montana kid to make good. Growing up in Great Falls, I didn't have a good sense of the world and we weren't wealthy. It was football that allowed me to see the world nationally. It's all positive for me."

TRAVIS DORSCH

BORN: September 4, 1979, Bozeman, MT
COLLEGE: Purdue
POSITION: Punter
NFL EXPERIENCE: 2002; 2004
TEAMS: Cincinnati Bengals (2002); Green Bay Packers (2004)

Travis Dorsch's NFL career was an act of serendipity, not strictly pre-planned. Dorsch attended Bozeman High School and was a letterman in high school football, basketball and track and field for the Bozeman Hawks.

"Well into my junior year in high school, I never thought about playing football in college or the pros," he said. "My first passion was baseball. If I could take on the whole world all over again, I'd be a baseball player, honestly. It wasn't until the fall of 1997, when I figured that this [a football scholarship] was something that could provide an education and that I should give it a serious look."

Similar to other athletes with Montana roots who have attained careers in the NFL, Dorsch excelled in several sports. Dorsch dislikes that third-graders practice in full pads, and he dislikes how today's kids specialize in one sport before they hit puberty.

"Montana is so encouraging, and we don't have the idea of specialization like they do in bigger cities or states," said Dorsch.

In Montana, you do not have to pick just one sport and play it year round. It's good to be encouraged to switch from football to basketball and to get better doing all of these things. Multisport athletes have a history of doing well in Bozeman.

One of the coolest things for me about high school athletes in Montana is that those seven-hour road trips toward the Dakotas forge relationships,

Travis Dorsch of Bozeman was drafted in the fourth round (111th overall pick) in the 2002 NFL draft by the Cincinnati Bengals. *Courtesy Travis Dorsch.*

forge friendships in a special way. Maybe in Los Angeles, your longest road trip is fifteen minutes. But you never forget that five-hour road trip to western Montana or eight hours to Salmon, Idaho, and the feeling of being on the bus, singing, yelling and hollering after a win.

Dorsch carried the Montana label on his sleeve, even if it didn't always show.

Montana really does have an "it-takes-a-village" mentality. When a player is from Montana, he represents not only himself, but his family, his high school, his city and his whole state. The difference in Montana is that everyone who goes out from here, everyone knows him, and everyone claims him and says, "It's our guy!" There are not a lot of guys in raw number to have had made it from here to the big time. Montana has a strong pride mentality, maybe like guys from Atlanta do. Similar to when a guy makes it there to the NFL, you follow that guy. Atlanta maybe has more people than in Montana as a whole. But it's the same concept: he is one of us and we are going to follow that guy.

Dorsch played football for Purdue University and was recognized as a consensus All-American. While attending Purdue (1998–2001), Dorsch set several records, including career scoring (355 points), career field goals (sixty-nine) and career punting average (48.4). He is the only athlete in Purdue history to have kicked a field goal and thrown a touchdown in football and hit a home run and recorded a win as a pitcher in baseball.

"One of my teammates, he was from Georgia, and he thought Montana was a Canadian province," said Dorsch. "At Purdue, I probably played in about fifty games and my parents were at every single one of them—home and on the road. When you think about the amount of time, money and energy, I realize how fortunate enough I was to have that. To me, I think about the relationship between family and sport and everything crystallizes. It's the genesis of what I am doing now [at the University of Utah]."

As a professional football player, Dorsch was drafted in the fourth round (111th overall pick) in 2002 by the Cincinnati Bengals. His only NFL regular-season experience came with the Bengals in 2002. He had five punts, averaging 32.4 yards, as an injury replacement for starter Nick Harris. His net average of 1.8 yards per kick remains the lowest in NFL history (five-kick minimum).

"There are not a lot of guys in raw number to have had made it from here [Montana] to the big time. My teammate on Cincinnati was Thatcher Szalay, and there we were, two guys on a fifty-three-man roster from Montana, and what a great story that is."

Dorsch was on the 2004 Green Bay Packers playoff roster and was a practice squad member with the Minnesota Vikings in 2004. "My time with the Packers was short, very short. I was signed on Friday, January 9, before our Sunday, January 11 divisional playoff game at Philly. I was on the active fifty-three but did not play. The plan was to punt and kickoff the next week had we won. We did not win. This was the infamous fourth and 26 game." (The Eagles defeated the Packers, 20–17, following an improbable fourth-down pass completion by Eagles quarterback Donovan McNabb.)

After a stint in NFL Europe the following year, Dorsch exited the game. He is currently an assistant professor at Utah State University in Logan, Utah, and completed his doctorate at Purdue in sports and exercise psychology in 2013.

"I think so much of my life is about being in the moment and open myself up to new experiences," said Dorsch, a veteran of eight Ironman triathlons. "When it was time for it [football] to be done, I was happy with that. I was ready for something new and I knew I had a lot more to give the world."

Dwan Edwards
Born: May 16, 1981, Billings, MT
College: Oregon State
Position: Defensive tackle
NFL Experience: 2004–15
Teams: Baltimore Ravens (2004–9); Buffalo Bills (2010–11); Carolina Panthers (2012–15)

Dwan Edwards, a graduate of Columbus High School (a town with a population of 1,893 in the 2010 census), spent twelve seasons in the NFL. He was selected in the second round (fifty-first overall pick) by the Ravens in the 2004 NFL draft out of Oregon State.

Edwards spent several seasons with Baltimore and a pair with Buffalo before landing with the Carolina Panthers in 2012.

In 2015, he played in fourteen games for the Panthers, finishing with one sack. Led offensively by slick-footed quarterback and league MVP Cam Newton, the Panthers went 15-1 during the regular season, advancing to the Super Bowl with a 49–15 victory over the Arizona Cardinals.

The final game of Edwards's career came in the Panthers' Super Bowl loss on February 7, 2016, to the Denver Broncos. Denver's linebacker Von Miller—the game's MVP—helped topple the Panthers, 24–10. It was also the final game in the storied career of Broncos quarterback Peyton Manning.

Edwards was released by the Panthers in March 2016, less than a month after the Super Bowl. He had signed a two-year contract extension worth $4 million just one year earlier. The six-foot, three-inch, 305-pound defensive lineman had nineteen and a half sacks in his career, fourteen coming during his four seasons in Carolina. Edwards said the bitterness of loss stuck with him for some time but that he has dealt with it and can now frame the loss positively.

"Time passes and you get the time to reflect and you think about what the Panthers were able to accomplish and see it as an amazing season," he said. "We came up a little short, but that doesn't take away from it. There are no bad feelings about it now. After twelve years, you think you'll never get that opportunity. I played twelve years and the average is about three. To get to play that long was a blessing."

Two days before the Super Bowl, the town of Columbus, Montana, celebrated Dwan Edwards Day. The Columbus PTA sold nearly one thousand custom Panthers blue-and-black Dwan Edwards T-shirts. Tosha Vavak, president of the Columbus PTA, told the *Charlotte Observer*, "It's because he gives back." "He has stayed humble. He never forgot where he came from," she said. "Any chance he gets, he'll stop by and say hi. These guys need to know with hard work they can grow up to be successful like he is."

In the summer of 2016, Edwards was in Billings putting on a youth camp at Wendy's Field at Daylis Stadium for boys and girls going into fifth through eighth grades. It marked the seventh year of the Dwan Edwards Elite Football Camp. "It's always great to be back, a great reflection of where I come from," he said. "There's no way

Dwan Edwards, a graduate of Columbus High School (in a town with a population of 1,893 in 2010), spent twelve seasons in the NFL. *Courtesy Montana Football Hall of Fame.*

I thought at their age I'd be playing in the NFL. You can't put limitations on yourself. You cannot put ceilings on yourself. I encourage them to dream big and go after it."

Edwards said that at age thirty-five he plans to take a deep breath, spend more time with his wife and children and accept and enjoy whatever the universe deems appropriate for his future.

"For the most part, I'm pretty excited about hanging it up and seeing what's next. I've had an amazing journey and the people in Montana have been amazing."

JIMMY FARRIS

BORN: April 13, 1978, Lewiston, ID
COLLEGE: Montana
POSITION: Wide receiver
NFL EXPERIENCE: 2003–7
TEAMS: New England Patriots (2001); Atlanta Falcons (2003–4); Washington Redskins (2005; 2007)

When Jimmy Farris was in the fifth grade in the mill town of Lewiston, which has a population of about thirty-two thousand strung along a stretch of Snake River slack water, his teacher provided each student with a sheet of paper displaying an empty picture frame. The kids were instructed to envision and illustrate their future within it.

"I drew a stick figure of a football player," he said. "I believe it was Lawrence Taylor. I believed that in ten or fifteen years, I would be a linebacker for the New York Giants. So when I look back, I say, 'Wow, this was a lifelong dream.'"

He accepted a scholarship offer to the University of Montana and became a Division I-AA All-American, playing wide receiver. In 2001, he was invited to attend the San Francisco 49ers' preseason camp for the longest of shots of making the roster of an NFL team. His stay was brief. But being released by the 49ers turned into a stroke of good fortune: during the playoffs a few months later, he signed with the Tom Brady–led 2001 New England Patriots, and his rookie campaign ended with a Super Bowl XXXVI championship ring. (Brady himself was the unexpected product of being at the right place at the right time. A sixth-round draft choice in 2000, the backup QB stepped in when Drew Bledsoe was injured and never relinquished the position. He has guided the Patriots to seven Super Bowls, winning five of them.)

Farris said that the Patriots' 20–17 victory over the St. Louis Rams in the 2002 Super Bowl happened so fast that it was all a bit of a haze. On February 3 that year, he stood on the sidelines of the New Orleans Superdome field, part of a dynasty-to-be, full of emotion as he watched the lovely Mariah Carey sing the national anthem. "We didn't have the two weeks off before the Super Bowl that year," he recalled. "I didn't have time to do much of anything. I changed voice mail to something like, 'If you are calling to say congrats on the Super Bowl, and if you are not a blood relative, and are calling for tickets, they are fifteen hundred bucks.' I barely had time to talk to my parents."

He spent six seasons in the NFL, including three with the Atlanta Falcons and two with the Washington Redskins. His family kept close tabs on his career. His mother, Sharon, once called Atlanta Falcons head coach Jim L. Mora and pleaded with him to give her son more playing time.

His career wasn't extravagant—Jimmy played in thirty-six games and caught seven passes, two of which were touchdowns—but coaches appreciated that he treated practices like playoff games. When the Redskins had to open a roster spot during the 2005 season, coach Joe Gibbs decided he had no choice but to say goodbye to Farris. It was a reluctant decision for Gibbs, who once labeled Farris a "Little ol' guy who fights his guts out."

The Redskins re-signed Farris for two games in 2007. When his playing career ended in 2009, he was only thirty. "Things went by so fast, and there was always a constant struggle between enjoying the moment of living the dream and struggling with the thought that I could be out of here tomorrow. I couldn't stop to smell the roses."

In October 2011, Farris challenged for Idaho's First District seat in the U.S. House of Representatives, losing to Republican incumbent Raúl Labrador.

CASEY FITZSIMMONS

BORN: October 10, 1980, Wolf Point, MT
COLLEGE: Carroll College
POSITION: Tight end
NFL EXPERIENCE: 2003–9
TEAM: Detroit Lions

The lingering ill effects of concussions forced Casey Fitzsimmons out of football at age twenty-nine. He had sustained seven documented concussions during his seven-year career, including one on December 6, 2009, against the Cincinnati Bengals that caused him to end the season on the injured reserve list.

"This has been a very difficult decision," Fitzsimmons said in a statement released by his agent. "I feel like 2009 was one of the best seasons of my career, because I was so consistent and was able to contribute in a variety of ways. If it wasn't for the concussions, I would not be retiring."

"It's frustrating because the rest of my body is still capable of playing at a high level in the NFL," he said at the time of his retirement. "However, given the seriousness of the risk associated with continuing to play, I have to listen to the advice the team has given me."

Following an evaluation by team doctors, Fitzsimmons was advised by the Lions to retire. At the time, his doctor said that he had still been feeling

Chester High School and Carroll College graduate Casey Fitzsimmons played seven seasons (2003–9) with the Detroit Lions at tight end. *Courtesy of Casey Fitzsimmons.*

the effects of his latest concussion; some of the symptoms Fitzsimmons was experiencing included memory loss, confusion, blurred vision and headaches. Several years removed from the sport, Fitzsimmons finds simple tasks such as driving and reading, memorization and recalling faces or names challenging.

"Football gave me everything that I have," said Fitzsimmons. "But it has taken mental toughness to get past the dark days and places, and it is disheartening to see the big hits on the news channel. Those big hits are what people pay premium price to see. It's the modern-day gladiators and they bust each other up. If it were a pillow fight, nobody would care."

He entered the NFL in April 2003 as an undrafted free agent after earning NAIA (National Association of Intercollegiate Athletics Football) All-America honors at Carroll College in Helena. Fitzsimmons started eleven games as a rookie and played a total of ninety-nine career games in the NFL. He had eighty-eight catches for 677 yards and five touchdowns. In his final three seasons, he returned seven kickoffs for 113 yards and a score.

The Chester High School graduate was a key component for Carroll during his time there (2000–3), using his six-foot, four-inch, 250-pound frame to tally 244 receptions for 2,698 yards and twenty-one touchdowns. He was a four-time All-Frontier Conference selection and a two-time All-American. He went undrafted in 2003. According to Lions president Tom Lewand, Fitzsimmons was brought to the Lions "strictly as a camp body." However, the Fighting Saints product not only made the team but also started in eleven games, caught 23 passes and hauled in two touchdowns. Fitzsimmons was a member of the winless 2008 Detroit Lions, perhaps the worst team in the history of any sport.

> *My rookie year, I was the second youngest guy on the team, and I'd only flown on an airplane a handful of times before that. People would tell you how crappy it was there in Detroit. But I would say that the people are not different from Montana. I couldn't have ended up at a better place. It's a blue-collar city of working-class people who busted their ass to go to one or two games a year. That was the worst part about being on a shitty team. I'd think of all the folks who were sacrificing hard to be there, and what it took for them to be able to go watch a home game. But not to produce—it was hard on me and hard on the other guys on the team.*

Fitzsimmons and his wife, Allison, have three children. They have a ranch near Helena. Fitzsimmons said that ranching is the medicine his soul and spirit require.

"I run cows and grow hay to feed and sell," he said. "I don't want to talk about football with people. I'm more interested in finding a herd of cows that breed up well and perform exceptionally well in the feedlot. Every day is an all-day deal. I played football to be able to ranch and I saved all of my money for the opportunity to buy a small beginning herd of thirty. I'm intrigued by ranching. There is a learning curve, and I like the lifestyle of being outside and in the woods and in nature. That's what drew me in the most."

Fitzsimmons is one of only two NFL players to come out of Carroll College. (Pocatello, Idaho native and Carroll graduate Dave Romasko was a tight end on the Cincinnati Bengals for all three of the 1987 strike games stocked with mostly replacement players.) Fitzsimmons, who said that he is frequently asked why he chose to return to Montana instead of "riding off into the sunset," said that he has always lived mindfully of his heritage.

"In Montana it's easy to see the way people love football and I'm proud of where I'm from. My work ethic was instilled in me from my mom and dad and the folks of Montana, and every time I put my jersey on it wasn't just for myself, but my family, and my state, my college. I never wanted to disrespect the name or colors on the jersey or disrespect my college or state by doing something stupid."

DANE FLETCHER
BORN: September 14, 1986, Bozeman, MT
COLLEGE: Montana State
POSITION: Linebacker
NFL EXPERIENCE: 2010–14
TEAMS: New England Patriots (2010–13); Tampa Bay Buccaneers (2014)

The highlight of Dane Fletcher's six professional seasons came in Super Bowl XLVI, when he recorded one tackle for the New England Patriots in their loss to the New York Giants, 21–17.

Fletcher, a reserve linebacker and core contributor on special teams, injured his ACL for a third time late in the 2014 season while playing for the Tampa Bay Buccaneers. He failed at a comeback bid with the Patriots in 2015.

Ready to transition to another phase in life, Fletcher decided that he would study "the human body and its kinetic rehabilitation." He focused his studies on the physical recovery of the human body and how preventive training and maintenance, if any, could avert or minimize injuries like his own ACL issues.

In 2015, the Bozeman native and Montana State graduate opened the Pitt, a training facility in his hometown, where he advises and customizes health, fitness and holistic classes to developing athletes who aspire to succeed at collegiate or professional levels.

"They're not just here to train and get better but also to learn and learn why they're getting better," he said. "They know why this is doing what it is and how they can improve if they have a deficit somewhere. We want to be knowledgeable outlets for these kids. We provide them with a legitimate feeling that this building was built specifically for a training facility, a place where you can run into professionals of all different ages and sports."

Dane Fletcher said that playing for the Bobcats and in the NFL supplied him with the experience he needed to become a leader and mentor and that he selected the most beneficial tips and traits from other training programs, including that of the New England Patriots, and brought them back to Montana.

"What sets us aside from the competition here in Montana is that we're completely different," said Fletcher. "My coaches and I are very familiar with training athletes and training adults as well. We are different. We have an indoor sandpit. We have all this technology to replay what kids are doing and show them on the charts just how they are doing in their class compared to everyone else in the country."

JUSTIN GREEN
BORN: April 30, 1982, San Diego, CA
COLLEGE: University of Montana
POSITION: Fullback
NFL EXPERIENCE: 2005–7
TEAM: Baltimore Ravens

Raised in a single-family home by his dad, who coached football, Justin Green played two years at Montana and was chosen 2003 Big Sky Newcomer of the Year. Green had a skill set that blended fullback and halfback positions and was a solid inside runner for several years as a Baltimore Raven.

Born in San Diego, Green said that he was struck by Montana's large expanses of land and the generally friendly demeanor of its residents. "The

Justin Green had a skill set that blended fullback and halfback positions and was a solid inside runner for several years as a Baltimore Raven. *Courtesy University of Montana.*

major difference for me was that the people that I first met here, they talked to you and greeted you and were interested in you," said Green, who has been working with the UM Grizzles as a staff member since 2012. "People here say hello or ask you how you are."

Coming to Missoula from the eighth-largest city in the United States (San Diego County is home to more than three million residents) was like a breath of clean mountain air to Green. "I remember my first day off of the plane—it was eye-opening. It was like the [1998 fantasy-comedy] movie *Pleasantville*, where it starts out in black and white and then it turns to color. It seemed perfect. The neighbors knew who everyone else was and the neighbors seemed to look for everybody. It represented the true meaning of being able to borrow a cup of sugar."

Green said he was also struck by the pride and seriousness of the Montana Grizzlies organization.

"People identify themselves with it as a source of pride and success. Every game matters, and you've got a high-velocity crowd that expects you to win. Expectations are high to produce on the field, and there is a certain respect that guys understand from day one. They are representing themselves, their teammates, their friends and their family, Missoula and the area, and the state."

Drafted by the Baltimore Ravens in 2005, Green's honeymoon in the NFL was short-lived; the reality of the sport's survivalist drama sunk in fast.

"In the NFL, there is no time to figure things out. The team has fifty-three players, and you are taking someone's job. You need to make sure you are doing your job. If things are not good, you need to be adding the things to make it good. If the team is winning, you don't want to be the reason that failure happened."

There was no shortage of legends or unforgettable characters on the Baltimore Ravens roster during Green's tenure.

That surreal feeling of seeing [teammate] *Deion Sanders—everyone wanted to be him. I remember thinking it was pretty remarkable to be in the huddle with Jamal Lewis, and the first time I blocked Ray Lewis in practice, Ray gave me a quick spur move and I fell on my face. I have a picture of me in the huddle with Jonathan Ogden and Jamal Lewis and Kyle Boller, and I'm there in the middle.*

On the field and off the field, Ed Reed was the same, an awesome dude to be around. When he was the punt returner, you wanted to make sure you blocked well for him. Another thing was how kicker Matt Stover took care of his body, physically. He was a kicker but he was so diligent about taking care of his core and being effective in his job.

In 2009, Green was let go by the Ravens after three seasons and thirty-nine games logged.

TUFF HARRIS
BORN: January 23, 1983, Crow Agency, MT
COLLEGE: Montana
POSITION: Defensive back
NFL EXPERIENCE: 2007–8
TEAMS: Miami Dolphins (2007); Tennessee Titans (2008)

Born in Crow Agency, Chester David Harris earned his nickname by surviving a winter bout with pneumonia that nearly killed him as an infant. In the biting winter of 1983, doctors in Billings fought to keep him alive. Only after hours of sustained resuscitation did his condition stabilize and did he begin breathing unassisted. Touched by the boy's willingness to fight and endure, his grandmother christened him with the nickname "Tuff."

Harris decided sometime around the fifth grade that he would play in the NFL. He and his brother Jay would collect and trade football cards

Born in Crow Agency, Tuff Harris decided sometime around the fifth grade that he would play in the NFL. *Courtesy University of Montana.*

and spend hours tossing around the football in front of his grandparents' house. He always liked the physical contact of football, as well as the game's pageantry, such as the halftime show and the hoopla.

"My friends laughed at me and thought I was crazy," said Harris, a mix of Crow, Cheyenne and Bulgarian decent. "I was from the reservation. We grew up in a town of about thirty people, so there were no neighborhood kids to play with us. I'd snap the ball and run, and he'd throw it to me, then we'd line up and do it again."

During his freshman and junior years at Lodge Grass High School, Harris excelled at basketball. He transferred to Colstrip High School and ran the fastest 100 meters in the history of the state (10.77 seconds). Harris led Colstrip to two state titles in track, which earned him a scholarship to Montana as a sprinter.

Harris walked on to coach Joe Glenn's Grizzly football team in 2002 and redshirted. He earned a starting spot at cornerback and shattered the Big Sky Conference records with his punt returning abilities. Harris assumed return duties in his junior season. In his first game fielding kicks, he returned a punt 74 yards for a touchdown in a UM win over Portland State.

At age twenty-four, Harris, who graduated from Montana with a bachelor's degree in sociology (3.87 GPA), signed with the Miami Dolphins as an undrafted free agent in 2007. As a professional, Harris struggled for playing time; he said that the politics of the game often decides who sits and who starts. "If a guy is getting paid, he's going to play. It's a business. It's not always the coach's decision whether you're on the field or not. Even if you're playing well and working hard, you never know how they're crunching numbers in the front office."

When the Dolphins cut Harris, he had a short stay with the New Orleans Saints before getting cut again and signing with the Tennessee Titans. He made it on the active roster and even earned playing time in the team's 2008 AFC divisional playoff game against the Baltimore Ravens. He failed to earn a roster spot in the NFL in the next season.

Post-football, Harris returned to eastern Montana, where he started One Heart, a nonprofit organization developing leadership qualities and improving the quality of life on the Crow reservation. (He has also recently been involved with Christian charity work in Latin America.) "To my knowledge, there's never been a Crow or Cheyenne who has played in the NFL. I don't really think about it until I come home, and then people are constantly coming up to me, saying, 'Talk to my son. Tell him what you've done.' On the reservation, there are a lot of issues that need to be changed and that's the process I've been given to try and figure out."

He said that even though athletics can greatly enhance one's self-esteem and self-worth, the glory days and successes derived from athletics aren't enough to sustain a full, healthy life. He knows that on the Crow Agency the violence, the poverty, the fight for resources—it never ends. Hope is what Harris has to provide.

"Where I come from, all people care about is basketball. And it's kind of sad in a way, but for some people, the biggest accomplishment in their life was winning a state championship. That's the pinnacle of their vision. They could do that, and their lives would be complete. I'm trying to show that there is more than that."

On August 12, 2016, Harris was one of the thirteen inaugural inductees of the newly formed Montana Football Hall of Fame in Billings.

TIMOTHY HAUCK
BORN: December 20, 1966, Butte, MT
COLLEGE: Pacific; Montana
POSITION: Defensive back
NFL EXPERIENCE: 1990–2002
TEAMS: New England Patriots (1990); Green Bay Packers (1991–94);
Denver Broncos (1995–96); Seattle Seahawks (1997); Indianapolis
Colts (1998); Philadelphia Eagles (1999–2001);
San Francisco 49ers (2002)

Tim Hauck played fourteen seasons, totaling 183 games for seven different franchises (Patriots, Packers, Broncos, Seahawks, Colts, Eagles and 49ers). He served as a starting strong safety for the Philadelphia Eagles in 1999, coach Andy Reid's first season.

"Growing up, I was an Oakland Raiders fan and I liked their style, physical and hard-nosed, and I grew up idolizing guys like [hall of fame center] Jim Otto. My mom and dad were raised in Butte, and my dad was a coach with thirty years' experience. I was raised in Big Timber, in a high school with under two hundred kids, and a town of under two thousand. I grew up hunting and fishing and playing sports year-round. Baseball. Track. Football. That was a great way to live in a small town in Montana."

Timothy Hauck is currently the safeties coach for the Philadelphia Eagles. *Courtesy Philadelphia Eagles.*

A two-time first team All-American (1988–89), Hauck played safety at Montana for three seasons after starting his college career at Pacific University in Oregon. He was voted the Big Sky Conference's defensive MVP as both a junior and a senior.

> *My brother* [Bobby] *and I went to UM, and I think that when I was playing we had about ten cousins going there at the same time. It was my first choice coming out of high school and later in the NFL I was undrafted and brought into camp as just another body. But what I learned at Montana allowed me to make a statement and become known in the NFL. Everything about it was what helped me achieve what I did in my career and put my nose to the grindstone, work every day, accept every opportunity and make plays, and it was nice to hear people say he's not what we thought he was, or he's faster or he's more physical. Coming from Montana, you make your owns breaks.*
>
> *When I got into the NFL, I would hear comments all the time about Montana, like, "Do you still ride horses out there?" and people half-joking, "Is it up in Canada?" But I've always identified myself with it* [Montana]. *And then, of course, you'd get all of the questions about the Unabomber and the Freemen* [militia].

Hauck's first regular-season game came at age twenty-four as a member of the New England Patriots. "I was put in and played against the Bills. It was in the first quarter, and we were in a two-deep defense. I cruised into my drop position and a moment later [wide receiver] James Lofton is about 10 yards behind me. Thank god the QB—I believe it was Jim Kelley—didn't find him. My career could have been over before it ever started."

Hauck's reputation as a vicious hitter only intensified after his crunching collision on October 10, 1999, with Dallas Cowboys wide receiver Michael Irvin ended the hall of famer's career. "It's strange, because the city of Philadelphia put me on a pedestal for that hit," said Hauck.

> *Irvin was not a liked person around here. He was playing at a high level at that point in his career and you never want to see someone done for life. Football is a violent game played by big, fast, physical people and rules have changed in the past ten, twenty years regulating what you can do and what you can't do. But my intent was never to hurt him. I saw him run a slant route, and when I went to tackle him, he actually ducked under me and I saw his head go into the turf. I barely got a piece of him. And the league never once fined me for that hit on him.*

Hauck said it was a clean, textbook tackle, "fast and physical." He has not seen Irvin in person since.

The play Michael Irvin got hurt on was a very basic pass route. He was running a shallow slant route, and I got a great break on the ball. I got such a good break, I thought I was going to end up with a huge hit, but he knew I was coming, too. He tried to go down and go under the blow. Instead of a huge hit, I just ended up with a glancing blow that knocked his head into the Vet [Veterans Stadium] turf. The next thing you know, he was not getting up. You don't expect any play to be career ending, and you hate to see players get hurt. I don't feel bad about the play. I was just playing football the way it is supposed to be played.

Hauck recorded 236 career tackles, forced five fumbles and recovered six. Many of his favorite moments took place in 1999–2000 with the Eagles. In those years, he started eighteen games, hauled in his only career interception and pounced on a crucial onside kick recovery.

Coach Reid and the Eagles made me a nice contract offer and the promise to be able to compete for a starting job. This was the best decision I made in my NFL career. I loved Philadelphia and the fans treated me very well. I think they could relate to a blue-collar player like myself.

There was a playoff game versus the Bears [2001] where I had a great hit on a kick-off early in the fourth quarter. It created a fumble, we recovered it and this sealed our victory and a spot in the NFC championship game. Another play which stands out was against the Saints in 2001 or 2002. It was my first start of that season. [Saints wide receiver] Joe Horn didn't warm up with his teammates—he followed me around the whole pregame and talked more trash than any one human can talk. Early in the first half, I got one of my best hits of my career on him. He did not play much the rest of the game.

Hauck retired after his 2003 season with the 49ers. He then joined his brother Bobby on the coaching staff at the University of Montana. He spent four years at his alma mater, overseeing the entire secondary in 2007 after three years working with the safeties (2004–6). During Hauck's tenure, a number of Grizzlies heard their names called in the NFL draft, including safety Colt Anderson, running back Chase Reynolds, wide receiver Marc Mariani, defensive end Kroy Biermann and cornerback Trumaine Johnson, all still active in the league as of 2016.

"In general, there aren't all that many of us who play at the NFL level from Montana," said Hauck. "We all come from unique situations and we all share a lot of similarities and even now I keep track of the University of Montana guys and Montana guys who are out there fighting, and I enjoy seeing them grow and achieve the things that they've achieved."

Hauck coached safeties at UCLA for a squad that ranked second in the Pac-10 Conference in pass defense in 2008. He spent the 2009–10 seasons as assistant secondary coach for the Tennessee Titans and the 2012 season as an assistant coach for the Cleveland Browns, overseeing the defensive backs.

He is currently the safeties coach of the Philadelphia Eagles.

KRIS HEPPNER
BORN: January 18, 1977, Great Falls, MT
COLLEGE: Montana
POSITION: Kicker
NFL EXPERIENCE: 2000
TEAMS: Seattle Seahawks (2000); Washington Redskins (2000)

When Seattle Seahawks coach Paul Holmgren signed UM star kicker Kris Heppner to a free agent contract in 2000, he brought the young man in to motivate and pressure the other kickers.

"I wasn't supposed to make the team and he intended to bring me in as filler," said Heppner. "A lot of teams will bring in a rookie to compete with the veteran, and I was a long shot. Holmgren's notorious for having competition among kickers, while some of the old coaches are not too keen on kicking or the kicking profession. In practice and preseason, you kick and kick and kick. But the wily veterans, they are only kicking ten or twenty footballs a day, and there are the rookies showing up and kicking nonstop."

Encouraged by a single mother, Carol Heppner-Dawson—whom Kris credits for nurturing his athletic ability and

Born in Great Falls, Kris Heppner kicked in the NFL for two separate teams in the 2000 season. *Courtesy Kris Heppner.*

"The NFL kicker is brought in with 80,000 screaming and the only thing I can compare it to is a relief pitcher in baseball or a professional golfer dealing with a ball and a skill," said Kris Heppner. *Courtesy Kris Heppner.*

providing material and emotional support—Heppner appeared in eight games in 2000, four for the Seattle Seahawks and then another four for the Washington Redskins. "I'm proud to have made it that far as a long shot," he said. "I had a bone spur under the kneecap in my kicking leg and at times during games I couldn't even lock my knee up. I was getting injections. But during training camp I was still kicking the ball in the back of the end zone."

Heppner was on the Seahawks roster for five weeks, rooming with running back Shaun Alexander. "After five weeks, Seattle released me, and I was whitetail deer hunting in Missoula, and the Redskins called, wanting to bring me in with five other veteran kickers. I wore my hunting clothes to the plane and landed in D.C. and ended up winning the competition."

In his first appearance as a Redskin, he went three for three in the first half against the Cardinals but missed one 52-yarder that snuck to the left of the goalpost in the second half. He missed another with five minutes remaining, a 37-yarder that leaned too far left.

After his team imploded, Redskins owner Daniel Snyder responded by publicly haranguing and (eventually firing) coach Norv Turner as well as releasing Heppner.

"I think I finished at 57 percent field goal accuracy in the NFL," said Heppner. "The NFL kicker is brought in with eighty thousand screaming fans, and the only thing I can compare it to is a relief pitcher in baseball or a professional golfer dealing with a ball and a skill. You are disposable as a placekicker."

Heppner said that even though his premature exit from the game gnaws at him from time to time, he enjoyed the ambassadorship as a Treasure State representative.

> *Looking back, it was a fun time for football in Montana.* [Great Falls product] *Ryan Leaf was on the cover of all of the newspapers, and it seemed like either Ryan or Dallas Neil or I were in the Great Falls Tribune every other day. Neil and I are probably the only two past NFL'ers in Montana history to grow up together, go to the same Great Falls High School, graduate together* [class of 1995], *both get scholarships to the Grizzlies as a kicker and punter, and somehow we both get into the NFL.*
>
> *We are a small state and we are not in the big city or into a big, fast lifestyle here. We have family values and we do take football serious and our community gets around their NFL players and can relate to them more. Everybody knows everyone in Montana. You are only a couple of people away from knowing someone that knows you.*

Heppner, a married father of three, lives in the Flathead Valley.

LEX HILLIARD

BORN: July 30, 1984, Kalispell, MT
COLLEGE: Montana
POSITION: Running back
NFL EXPERIENCE: 2009–12
TEAMS: Miami Dolphins (2009–11); New England Patriots (2012); New York Jets (2012)

Growing up in Montana taught Lex Hilliard lessons about perseverance and teamwork—working together to achieve something bigger than yourself. Applying these tenets, Hilliard totaled eight letters at Flathead High School in Kalispell and completed a unique double of 100 meters and shot put on the three-time state champion track team. He was selected first team All–Big Sky in 2004 and 2005 and won the 2005 Walter Payton Award. His hard work at UM impressed his coaches and endeared him to the fans.

Drafted in the sixth round by the Miami Dolphins in 2008, Hilliard as a rookie rushed for 89 yards and amassed 158 yards in receiving. He slashed

Plagued by a fractured shoulder blade, running back Lex Hilliard lost his NFL job in the summer of 2013. At age thirty-two, he struggles with the effects of concussions from football. *Courtesy University of Montana.*

hard to gain inside yards and ripped through unsound tackle attempts. He was known to "play to the whistle" and run "with great energy."

He spent time in the Minnesota Vikings camp in 2012 and played with the New England Patriots before landing with the New York Jets as the starting fullback. Plagued by a fractured shoulder blade, Hilliard lost his NFL job in the summer of 2013.

"The first year or so after surgery, I worked hard and I thought I'd be coming back. Everything seemed to be going in place," he said. "Then I got my first x-ray and things weren't healing right and the doctors told me to give it more time. I go for a second x-ray a couple months later and things still weren't looking right. Then it's almost at a year and six months and I go for another checkup and things still aren't looking right. I've had problems with my pituitary gland after breaking my scapula, and the pituitary gland affects hormone levels. The gland was not producing the hormones needed to seal the bone, and the bone was not healing."

In 2015, he moved back to Kalispell with his wife and their four homeschooled kids. An electrical fire burned their home to the ground several months after their return. The community organized a fundraiser on the family's behalf, and friends such as Griz alumnus Doug Betters gave emotional support. The NFL supplied financial assistance, allowing Hilliard to cash in his 401k to help fund a new home, approximately a mile from their old one.

Hilliard purchased several pieces of heavy machinery, including diggers and tractors, in hopes of starting a business leasing such equipment. However, he recently returned for a forty-day stay at the After the Impact program, a neuro-rehabilitation facility based in Ann Arbor, Michigan. The specialized program offers education and care for individuals with health and behavioral issues from post-concussion syndrome, post-traumatic stress, traumatic brain injury (TBI) and other similar diagnoses.

"I've been struggling with some of the concussion stuff from playing football," said Hilliard.

It was something I had been hiding from my family and wife. I am just trying to live life normally and dealing with all the pain from playing. It's an intensive help program and I'm still battling it. My ears are always ringing. I have that underwater feeling as if I'm going underwater. I see things that aren't there and I hear voices and hear things. I've had changes in my vision and damage from whipping my head around trying to catch passes out of the flat.

*I don't remember taking medications and what the doctor recommends.
I'm a candidate for a service dog because I have balance issues. I have
ups and downs for my moods. CTE can't diagnose you until you are dead
and gone. At After the Impact, I was with other guys who had symptoms
of TBI, and they put you in a group talking with other guys and in the
atmosphere where the guys understand. Beyond the glory, there is a backlash
and the mending, the surgeries and now the mental part. I hope I can raise
awareness of what soldiers and football players are going through.*

Hilliard said that he sustained one diagnosed concussion as a member
of the Dolphins and more likely sustained several more undiagnosed ones
throughout his college and professional career.

*The problem with the concussion diagnosis system in the NFL is that if
I get one as a pro football player then the workload goes up for everyone
else, and we protect each other and we keep each other playing. There are
precautions for spotting concussion symptoms, but guys are hiding it. I
remember puking after a big hit and still playing and the coach was stuck in
the dilemma of winning games and balancing the player's well-being. But
for the coach it comes down to winning games and not getting fired and it
puts them in a bad position. When I got my concussion in Miami, I still
played four or five plays after that.*

Retiring from professional football at age twenty-eight was a bitter pill to
swallow, conceded Hilliard. He planned on sticking around longer and had
been physically and mentally prepared for a long haul. He tried satisfying his
taste for the sport as assistant coach for the Kalispell Flathead football team.
But after he was diagnosed with an enlarged aortic valve, he stepped down
out of concern for his health.

Adversity is no unfamiliar terrain to Hilliard, who defied the odds and
managed to exceed the average career length in the NFL, surviving four
seasons as a fullback, a reduced position that most current teams seldom
incorporate into their lineups. Despite the concussions and physical ailments,
Hilliard isn't embittered as to the experience of football.

"The relationships and the camaraderie were wonderful. I've learned a
lot of life lessons, like how hard work pays off and that work ethic carries
over. I tried to be the first one to work and last one to leave. I learned
that when you stamp your name to something, you stamp your pride to
it, whether you are painting a picture or tying on your shoes, you are

stamping your name to it. Football teaches you to prepare, perform and educate yourself and take pride in what you do."

Still, Hilliard, a father of five, including three boys, is understandably ambivalent about his sons' dreams to one day play professional football.

> *It's beautiful to see the joy they get for the game and to see them share their joy on the sidelines with their teammates. My son's ultimate dream is to play in the NFL, one of them, and that's all he talks about. How do I tell him not to do what I did and what I had success at? You can see the broken leg. You can see the wheelchair. Mental illness you can't see. For a ten-year-old hitting another his age or a twelve-year-old hitting another his age, the impact is the same as an adult hitting an adult. It's scary for a parent to know their kid is playing football.*

TYRONE HOLMES

BORN: September 10, 1993, Eagle Point, OR
COLLEGE: Montana
POSITION: Outside linebacker
NFL EXPERIENCE: 2016–present
TEAM: Cleveland Browns

Tyrone Holmes attended Eagle Point High School in Oregon. He passed on a Division I scholarship at Portland State to attend the University of Montana. "It was just cool because [Missoula] was an actual college town," Holmes told Cleveland.com in September 2016. "Football is life out there. If you've ever heard about Montana football, in that town and that area and for the state it's just as big as any other program. So to go out there and get a big-time football experience was really fun."

The Jacksonville Jaguars selected the Montana edge rusher and winner of the 2015 FCS Defensive Player of the Year Award, in the sixth round of the 2016 NFL draft. Holmes registered twenty-five and a half sacks for Montana over his final two years and earned an abundance of accolades. As part of the recruiting process, Holmes visited with the Jaguars six times to discuss defensive schemes and fits and to assess his physical conditioning.

"The sixth visit was actually a special one, because of Jordan Tripp, who was a good buddy of mine in college," said Holmes. "I went out to dinner with him when I was there and he really got me excited about the team and got me excited about the organization and coaches. Having Tripp would have been a big help and I felt really excited about it. The Jaguars were an up-and-coming team and I was excited."

Holmes was one of six defensive players drafted by the Jaguars, but he was vulnerable to the team's roster cuts. After failing to make the Jaguars, he was claimed by the Cleveland Browns. He registered one sack in limited backup duty. Holmes, however, said that he is determined to increase his playing time in the future. He has no doubt that he has the physical tools (six feet, two inches, 253-pounds) and mental grit to make a career in the NFL. He is expected to be a youthful and energetic part of the Brown's defensive rotation in the future.

"I am a tough player," said Holmes to Jaguars.com in August 2016. "I'm relentless. I'm never going to give up. I'm going to go 100 miles per hour, and I'm going to give one-hundred percent effort. There isn't a specific quarterback I want to sack. I want to sack them all."

Chris Horn
Born: July 13, 1977, Caldwell, ID
College: Rocky Mountain College
Position: Wide receiver
NFL Experience: 2004–5
Team: Kansas City Chiefs

Montana's first institute of higher learning, Rocky Mountain College (RMC), has a football history that dates as far back as 1931 with the hiring of Herb Klindt, who instituted football and several other sports.

Located in Billings, the NAIA school, which has a student body of approximately one thousand, has sent one player to the National Football League: Chris Horn. "My older brother and my best friend were at RMC a year in front and the coaching staff had a pipeline to me," said Horn, who was inducted into the RMC Hall of Fame in 2009.

I came from a small town [Caldwell, Idaho], and I was used to the small atmosphere and feel very comfortable there [in Billings], and it was a perfect fit. When you grow up in a small town you are overlooked. The big towns and big schools in Idaho have a mentality of overlooking small schools on smaller levels. I think the attitude is that the competition is not as good. I went to high school thirty minutes for Boise State University and they didn't even offer me a walk-on.

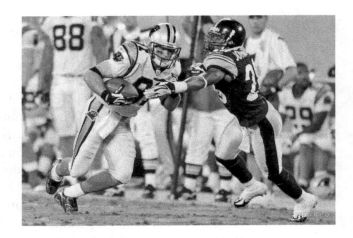

Chris Horn, a wide receiver with the Kansas City Chiefs in 2004 and 2005, is the only professional player to come from Rocky Mountain College in Billings. *Courtesy Chris Horn.*

> *I ran in toward that same experience again in Rocky to get to the next level. But I believed I was good enough to play the game in the NFL. The doors opened at the right time and when they opened, I took the opportunity. I also saw it as God's glory through my play, my action and my words. You can come from the smallest town in Idaho or Montana, or the smallest college in Montana, and if God wants you to go to the NFL, then nothing is beyond God's grace.*

As a walk-on, Horn earned a position on the practice squad of the 2003 Kansas City Chiefs (who allocated him to the Amsterdam Admirals of NFL Europe.) The following year, Horn cracked the roster as one of five receivers out of a field of thirteen contestants.

Horn said that professional football is a balance of sanctioned violence and absolute restraint and that enshrined throughout its rules is a mortal danger that requires players to remain in control during the commission of their violent acts.

> *You need to reach a threshold of playing at a point that is close to being reckless, but very under control. You play on that threshold. You have to have the courage to walk on that fine, fine line and the courage to play the game with no fear. Sometimes when you see a player lose control or throw his helmet—he is not an idiot—it's just that the game of football requires that you play it with courage, speed and perfect balance of reckless and all-out playing, yet under control. What you are seeing is a player falling off of that cliff or slipping down that slide. It is a microcosm of life.*

His first career touchdown came on September 26, 2004, against the Houston Texans.

"When you come from a small cornfield town in Idaho or Montana, you don't experience many moments like that. It was my first NFL game, and it was a home game against the Texans. During my first time in the huddle and a TV timeout, [hall of fame tight end] Tony Gonzalez welcomed me and said congratulations on being here. A few plays later, I caught my first pass. A few plays later, my first NFL touchdown."

His first career start (one of three starts) came in the 2005 season on October 13 against the San Diego Chargers. That season, he led the Chiefs in special teams tackles and was one of the special teams captions.

The NFL continues to tinker with the kickoff rules, and there are rumblings that, for safety reasons, kickoffs could someday be eliminated altogether. Horn came to appreciate the full-throttle spectacle of the most dramatic start to any sport.

> *Dante Hall* [Chiefs teammate] *was one of the most electric kick returners in NFL history, and all you had to do was to create a little bit of a hole and he'd take it when returning. We'd do the wedge coverage and they don't do it anymore. Smaller guys would get to wedge first. You would run full speed and bust a wedge open and take out the blocker, and whoever was behind would make a tackle on the ball player. It was absolutely the highest impacted collision of anything throughout the game—two full-speed collisions in the middle of the field. Anyone who has played football for a long period, especially beyond college, has sore knees, hips or shoulders or ailments from the game. My shoulder and knee reminds me that I played and was a part of a violent, high-speed and high-impact game.*

In 2006, Horn was released by the Chiefs. After being released from the trainings camps of the New Orleans Saints (2006) and the Carolina Panthers (2007), his journey in the NFL was over.

Now living in Arizona, Horn received an honorary doctorate degree and a master's degree, both obtained while playing professional football.

LEVI HORN

BORN: October 2, 1986, Spokane, WA
COLLEGES: Oregon; Montana
POSITION: Offensive tackle
NFL EXPERIENCE: 2011–12
TEAMS: Chicago Bears (2010–11); Minnesota Vikings (2012)

Born in Spokane, Levi Horn traces his Northern Cheyenne roots to the Lame Deer area of Montana. Born and raised in Spokane, he weighed nearly twelve pounds at birth, was eating solid food at one month and dwarfed the teaching tables at kindergarten (he sat at his own desk). In sixth grade, he was six feet tall; in eighth grade, he was six feet, four inches tall and weighed 240 pounds.

High school football provided Horn with a focus for his mind and a worthwhile activity for his enormous size. Horn, all-state in class 4A at tight end, was about to become John R. Rogers High School's first Division I scholarship athlete in twenty-five years. He would take that scholarship from Oregon of the Pac-10. He felt comfortable transferring to the University of Montana, which provided him with the feelings of returning home.

"It was an easy transition," said Horn. "In Oregon, nothing worked out for me. I saw more Natives there than at other colleges and it was a big family. I love Montana and it made me the man that I am. [Coach] Bobby Hauck and staff made sure we were humble and humble players from Montana."

Undrafted in 2010, Horn, an aggressive offensive lineman with a propensity to run on sheer emotion, spent 2010 and 2011 as a member of the Chicago Bears practice squad. He was cut by the Minnesota Vikings before the start of the 2012 season.

"They talk about God-given talent, and I can say I didn't have that," said Horn. "But the work instilled in me at Montana through Bobby Hauck and others, that's what it was. I had passion, I worked really hard, and when I lined up at the line I knew that the guy in front of me wasn't going to try harder. I didn't see a regular-season game and it wasn't for lack of trying. On the practice squad, I was there to make guys better, and I was blessed to have been there for two years."

TRUMAINE JOHNSON
BORN: January 1, 1990, Stockton, CA
POSITION: Cornerback
NFL EXPERIENCE: 2012–present
TEAM: St. Louis Rams / Los Angeles Rams

As a senior quarterback, Trumaine Johnson passed for 1,800 yards, rushed for 500 yards, scored twenty-two total touchdowns and was named first team all-league on offense and defense. He was voted to Stockton High School's football "Hall of Fame" at defensive back.

Johnson was an atypical true freshman starter, tying for the team lead with four interceptions and earning Big Sky honorable mention selection at cornerback. He started in the first eleven games but suffered an injury against Idaho State and missed UM's last five games. Johnson was a four-year starter for the Griz. He finished his career at UM with fifteen interceptions and was first team All–Big Sky Conference three times.

In December 2011, Johnson put the Grizzlies on the front page of the local news in a negative way when he pleaded no contest to disorderly conduct charges in Missoula stemming from a loud party two months earlier. He was fined and sentenced to ten days in jail, with that time suspended under conditions that included an order not to commit any other offenses for six months. Johnson was tased during the incident after he resisted officers' attempts to subdue him. An internal investigation by the Missoula Police Department showed that officers were justified in their use of force.

Despite the incident, he was still considered one of the best cornerback prospects for the 2012 NFL draft and was selected by the Rams in the third round. He finished his rookie season with two interceptions and thirty-five tackles. Rams' defensive backs coach Brandon Fisher—the son of head

The Los Angeles Rams placed a franchise tag on Trumaine Johnson (no. 22) in the off-season before 2016, retaining him for more than $13 million. *Courtesy University of Montana.*

coach Jeff Fisher—was Johnson's teammate at Montana. When the Rams decided to draft Johnson in the third round, the younger Fisher was the one who made the first phone call.

In 2013, Johnson was arrested in Missoula and charged with drunk driving. Police officers stopped his car around 2:00 a.m. near the corner of Front and Owen Streets because Johnson was driving without headlights.

Johnson recorded his best career statistics in 2015, registering seventy-one total tackles and seven interceptions. The Rams placed a franchise tag on Johnson in the off-season, retaining him for more than $13 million.

Marc Mariani
Born: May 2, 1987, Havre, MT
College: Montana
Positions: Wide receiver; kick returner
NFL Experience: 2010–16
Teams: Tennessee Titans (2010–14; 2016); Chicago Bears (2015)

Following a splendid career with the Grizzlies—which included a dizzyingly acrobatic catch in the 2008 Football Championship Subdivision title game against Richmond—Marc Mariani (pronounced MARY-annie) was picked by the Tennessee Titans in the seventh round of the 2010 NFL draft.

He made the Pro Bowl as a rookie return specialist with the Titans in 2010 and has overcome several major injuries to become a productive asset. Mariani suffered a badly broken leg during the preseason in 2012 and missed the entire season. In 2015, he signed with the Chicago Bears. In addition to amassing 610 yards in return duties, he made twenty-two pass receptions for 300 yards.

Mariani returns to Montana in the off-season. In the summer of 2015, he organized a camp at Pepin Park in Havre for kids in grades kindergarten through eight. The camp was part of the NFL's Play 60, a campaign that encourages youth activity in order to battle the trend of childhood obesity.

"It is so special and gratifying for me to be able to bring something like that to my home state," Mariani said. "It's special to return to the community that raised me and has supported me along the way. It is really an awesome day out there with the kids."

Mariani, who has three career returns for touchdowns (two punts, one kick), said that not committing turnovers and keeping possession of the football is nearly as important for a kick returner as gaining positive yards.

Above: Following a splendid career with the Montana Grizzlies, Marc Mariani was drafted by the Tennessee Titans in the seventh round of the 2010 NFL draft. *Courtesy University of Montana.*

Right: Marc Mariani made the Pro Bowl as a rookie return specialist with the Titans in 2010 and has overcome several major injuries to become a productive asset. *Courtesy University of Montana.*

Mariani started the 2016 season with the Bears. In October 2016, the Titans welcomed him back to Nashville after he was released by Chicago. The organization decided to re-sign the twenty-nine-year-old as a veteran upgrade over the young, untested players they were planning to use on punt and kick returns.

"Ball security and decision making is just so important," Mariani told ESPN. "For both sides [in the Texans' September 22, 2016 loss to the Patriots on *Thursday Night Football*] there were balls on the ground. It happens every week. I take pride in that, and I want to be the guy that people count on back there to do the right thing and give the ball back to the offense in the best field position possible."

DYLAN MCFARLAND
BORN: July 11, 1980, Kalispell, MT
COLLEGE: Montana
POSITION: Offensive tackle
NFL EXPERIENCE: 2004–5
TEAM: Buffalo Bills

Dylan McFarland sees himself as a kid from the Flathead who lived the NFL dream. For every star, there are five hundred NFL hopefuls like McFarland, on the fringe of professional football.

In high school, McFarland was recruited by bigger schools such as Oregon, Washington and Harvard. But during his senior year, he broke his foot, and interest waned. That injury, he said, helped direct him to the University of Montana. At UM, he won a national championship and earned two All-American selections with the Grizzlies between 1999 and 2003

McFarland was drafted by the Buffalo Bills in the seventh round in 2004. For the next three years, the six-foot, five-inch, 300-pound offensive tackle bounced around on the Bills' practice squads and game roster and as part of NFL Europe allocation (Hamburg Sea Devils).

"A lot of what got me there was learning that what you need to do when you have adversary is that you bounce back. Being a Montanan, I grew up around farming and ranching communities and the expectation was that you always work hard. I don't consider myself a farm and ranch kid, but Montana is part of that culture where there is never a sense of entitlement, and for me that attitude spilled over to the pros."

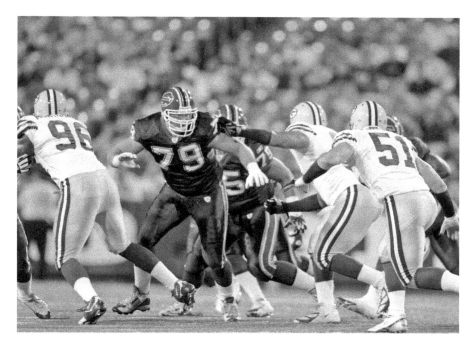

Montana native Dylan McFarland was drafted by the Buffalo Bills in the seventh round of the 2004 NFL draft. *Courtesy University of Montana.*

At an off-season scrimmage at Lambeau Field in Green Bay, he found himself jogging out onto the Frozen Tundra with Brett Favre standing on the opposite sidelines. He also met NFL icons such as Jerry Rice and Emmitt Smith. In addition, his job was protecting quarterback Drew Bledsoe, the Bills' starter at the time.

> *Guys like Bledsoe you've watched for so long, and now you're sitting in a locker room with him. I remember sitting at the team meeting in Buffalo and there's Bledsoe and Takeo Spikes sitting in front of me, and that was pretty surreal. Spikes must have had the biggest neck I've ever seen. Drew had been to a Super Bowl with the Patriots, and we'd spent a lot of time together, in meeting rooms, dinner and going to the bar, and on the buses. I was in shock and awe that these were regular guys who were doing the same thing I was doing.*

McFarland saw limited regular-season action for the Bills.

I had the confidence that I could play and I was happy to get the opportunity. But you are not the starter for a reason and much of the talk is about the skill level. There are probably ten percent of guys in the NFL who are that much better than anyone else. There are 80 percent of players who are pretty close, with just a few degrees of separation. Then there are the 10 percent who are down at the bottom. After all, [Super Bowl–winning quarterback] Kurt Warner was once stacking groceries, which shows that you are only a few opportunities away.

McFarland said that the Montana guy in him felt a certain kinship to blue-collar Buffalo. "Buffalo reminded me a lot of Butte," said McFarland. "It was a giant steel and shipping city in the 1950s and 1960s, and the industries died. It had a great base of people who grew up knowing what it was, and what it could again be. They have good fans. Win or lose, they don't tell you how shitty you are. They are engaged, and they care a lot about the success of their team. It felt like a small town to me."

Despite the city's string of four consecutive bitterly disappointing Super Bowl losses 1990 to 1993, the Bills organization and the fans have remained resilient. "It was a huge disappointed for the city and the players involved, but the guys who were involved and who were always around—Jim Kelly, Thurman Thomas, Darryl Talley and coach Marv Levy—they looked at it as a success. Buffalo welcomed them back and didn't get hung up on the losses, and that speaks well to the city. In Buffalo, there were not guys who were flashy or acted entitled."

During a game in NFL Europe, McFarland tore the cartilage in his left knee. He continued to play seven more games before undergoing micro-fracture surgery.

"In Germany, I had long weekends to explore and it was great to be a Kalispell kid in Hamburg trying to figure things out. What's strange there is that in American football, when you are home and the offense has the ball, everyone is quiet. In Europe, they screamed, yelled and chanted the whole time, like an entire party. They showed great support, thought they didn't necessarily know what was going on all of the time."

After surgery, McFarland said he returned to the football field before his knee was healed and ended up needing a second surgery in December 2006 to repair a torn meniscus. When he showed up for tryouts a few months later for Carolina and Oakland, he failed his physicals.

"I don't believe I'll ever be 100 percent again," said McFarland. "But that was part of my decision to play football. Physically, I want to be able to go fishing, hiking and enjoy Montana and to be able to teach my kids how to play basketball. One thing I don't miss is the instability of playing football—the week-to-week, day-to-day pressures with your body and not knowing if you're going to make the cut. There is always a new crop of guys going to take your job."

McFarland, who lives in Missoula, said that he always had a strategy after football; he started a law practice after its conclusion.

"In the NFL, guys are wrapping up their careers at thirty-one and they don't have a plan. Some of them fall into depression circles or even take their own lives. I like the law and I've been interested in it since a young age. I intend to be a lifetime learner."

ZACH MINTER

BORN: November 6, 1990, Glendale, AR
COLLEGE: Montana State
POSITION: Defensive tackle
NFL EXPERIENCE: 2013
TEAM: Chicago Bears

Zack Minter attended Cactus High School in Glendale, Arizona. As a defensive tackle, he was selected to the All–West Valley Region and was named a first team all-state player. He also was selected as the West Valley Defensive Player of the Year.

Minter dominated at times during an All-America junior season that saw him earn unanimous first team All–Big Sky Conference recognition. He notched seven and a half sacks and eleven tackles for losses. But a nagging hamstring injury slowed his progress his senior season. Minter, however, signed a contract with the Chicago Bears as an undrafted free agent. Minter made his NFL debut in week six of the 2013 season, rotating in the lineup against the New York Giants. On November 5, 2013, Minter was waived, and after unsuccessful tryouts with the Dallas Cowboys and Cincinnati Bengals in 2014, he joined the British Columbia Lions and later the Saskatchewan Roughriders of the Canadian Football League. He spent 2016 with the Calgary Stampeders and re-signed with the Saskatchewan Roughriders as a defensive lineman in February 2017.

Dallas Neil
Born: September 30, 1976, Great Falls, MT
College: Montana
Positions: Punter; tight end; halfback
NFL Experience: 2000–2
Team: Atlanta Falcons

When not a single professional team showed interest in Dallas Neil as a punter after he finished playing for the Montana Grizzlies in 1999, he used his creativity and sense of humor to get noticed.

Neil purchased a four-foot-wide mannequin leg from Dillard's in Missoula, packaged it up and sent it off to Frank Gansz Jr., the special teams coach of the St. Louis Rams, with a letter reading, "I'd give my right leg to play for the Rams."

"I had sent out audition tapes and I had not gotten one single call," said Neil. "No combine invites, no calls at all, no calls for workouts. Nothing. So, a friend and I decided that we'd get a mannequin leg and attached a note and send it to the St. Louis Rams, a team that had the worst punter in the NFL. When Frank called me, he was laughing hard on the phone. He hadn't even looked at the audition tape. Finally, days later, when he was finished laughing, he said, 'I looked at the tape and you look pretty good!'"

The coach told *USA Today* about the incident, resulting in some attention for Neil. While Neil didn't end up with the Rams, the effort generated some interest from Green Bay, Atlanta and Denver. The Falcons signed him as a punter.

"In 2000, there were some games all I did was hold coach Dan Reeves's headset chord for him," said Neil. But he quickly earned a name in training camp as someone who was willing to fill other positions. During the tryouts in 2001 he also ran pass routes and scrimmaged as a tight end on the scout team.

"When I was in third grade in Great Falls, I would pick up a football and kick it a mile. It was definitely a gift. I had punted in high school and I punted at Montana. I would play at other positions to help and I played tight end in college. In the NFL, I started to grow up and get stronger and even though I went to camp solely as a punter, if they needed someone to run routes in practice, I'd do it."

At the start of the 2001 preseason, Neil, who weighed only 215 pounds, was steered toward positions requiring bigger, bulkier bodies. During an exhibition game in Tokyo against the Dallas Cowboys, coach Reeves yanked

Over the course of three seasons with the Atlanta Falcons, Great Falls native Dallas Neil played several positions, including halfback. *Courtesy Dallas Neil.*

Neil by the facemask and threw him into the game as a halfback. Neil caught the ball in the flat and scampered 25 yards. He played the rest of the game.

> *Reeves was a walk-on for the Dallas Cowboys* [as a player]. *Reeves pulled me aside one day and said, "You know, Dallas, I don't think you've dropped a ball in three months* [in practice]. *I want to see you*

put some pads on you and see what you can do." You are not going to say no. Let me put it this way: I was the hit of the day for four consecutive days on the news outlets. It was not a fun experience to start—getting hit from 255- to 290-pound guys. Thankfully, in practice, there were no hits below the waist.

I needed to add a pound a week until I got to 245 pounds, and I was told that if I showed up a single pound under I would lose money. I've heard of fines for guys for being too heavy, but I don't think there has ever been someone who was threatened in the reverse, fined for being too light. I started drinking gallons of orange juice, eating two breakfasts in the morning, and eating mac and cheese at midnight.

Teammates on the Falcons began to call him "Rudy," after the movie that told the story of the former Notre Dame walk-on who defied the odds to play for the Fighting Irish. Neil had several catches for the Falcons during the preseason, including one on national television when the announcers talked about his "Rudy" nickname. He had gone from nearly being cut to making the team as the third halfback and third tight end.

Neil did well enough in games to stick around for almost three years, playing mostly special teams but also some halfback while serving as the backup punter.

"I had a blast. There are fifty-three guys on a team, and I was somewhere between player number fifty and number fifty-three. I played in all three preseason games every year, as the backup punter, on special teams or as the second or third halfback or tight end."

Neil said that he upheld the reputation of Montana footballers as players who will supply an abundance of energy and passion for the price.

When I got to the NFL, Montana guys had already had a definite reputation for working hard, paying attention and following through in every way. I guess the water, the parents and the grandparents out there must have done something right. I think it was one of the reasons that I was selected as a free agent was because guys from Montana had gone before and it was worth it to coaches to take a risk on a Montana guy as free agent because they won't embarrass you.

One thing I will always remember was walking through the locker room and seeing Patrick Kearney with his shirt off. The guy looked like Hercules, and I was convinced that I might die when tackled by him, and secondly, it looked like every one of these guys was on steroids. But I was wrong. I hung

*out with them for four years and none of them were. They were just genetic
freaks. I never met anyone who violated the substance abuse policy at all.
Over the course of a year or two, you become that* [an NFL player], *and
your body adapts. You become that* [size] *or you get creamed.*

A left ankle injury during his third year forced a year off and finally his
release by the Falcons. Neil led the NFL in punting during the preseason
that year, but he never again settled in with a pro team. Coach Reeves hadn't
given up on Neil. Hours after he released him, Reeves had him on a flight to
visit with the New York Jets (who soon released him).

In 2002, the Falcons brought in [tight end] *Algee Crumpler, and I
figured I'd wrap up my cleats and be done. But Reeves tried to give me
another chance. In fact, he fired me at nine in the morning and he had me
on a plane to play for the Jets at noon. He was a fatherly figure, who would
invite the players to his home to go on turkey hunts.*

Once you get to that point in your life, you have to choose [whether
you] *want to fly around all the time starting over or is it time to move on.
And I felt it was time to move on.*

Neil lives in Missoula, where he owns the Source Health Club.

BROCK OSWEILER
BORN: November 22, 1990, Coeur d'Alene, ID
COLLEGE: Arizona State
POSITION: Quarterback
NFL EXPERIENCE: 2012–present
TEAMS: Denver Broncos (2012–15); Houston Texans (2016–present)

Houston Texans starting quarterback Brock Osweiler's story traces back to
Flathead High School, where he dodged defenders, threw touchdown passes
and was the star of the basketball team.

"You know, Montana is extremely close to my heart. I spent 16 years
there," said Brock Osweiler to ESPN in July 2016. "I was born in Idaho, but
I spent the majority of my time in Kalispell, Montana, so I'll always have
Montana very close to myself. Not a lot of athletes come out of Montana, so
it's something that makes you extremely proud. And you want to represent
your state the right way."

The younger of two brothers, Brock was six feet, four inches by the time he was in seventh grade, and he dominated youth sports in Kalispell throughout his childhood. He spent his summers starring for the Yakima Elite AAU team, one of the best squads in the Pacific Northwest. Whether it was scoring fifty points in a middle school game or pulling off a 360-degree dunk as a fifteen-year-old, Brock, who grew to six feet, seven inches, with size 17 shoes, became known as the confident kid with a single-minded mission to succeed.

Osweiler's gridiron highlights include the longest play in Montana state history, when he threw for 99 yards. "Everyone knew who he was before he got to high school," said Reed Watkins, a teacher at Flathead High School. "He was already playing basketball all over the country."

Russell McCarvel took over as head coach at Flathead High School when Brock was only a sophomore. "Brock and I got together and we spent a lot of time that spring discussing team goals and his goals, expectations," said McCarvel. "Even as a junior, he was one of our captains, which is pretty rare, but he was already at that point, kind of the face of the team, the face of a leader, even the face of the school. At that time, the NFL was a long ways away, but he was obviously going to be a college player."

"All three years that he played for me, freshman, sophomore and junior year, he was first team all-state consensus," said Osweiler's former high school basketball coach, Fred Febach. "I mean, there was no doubt, he was one of the best players in the entire state. And one of the best players and one of the better players to ever come through Montana."

As a sophomore, Brock asked Coach McCarvel to critique his self-made college resume tape. Brock said he wanted to send the tape to the top schools in the nation, including Florida State, Alabama State, Washington and Stanford. "For most kids from Montana, that's just not realistic," said McCarvel. "But I was like, 'Yeah, that's a good idea.'"

After he played college football at Arizona State University, Osweiler was drafted by the Denver Broncos in the second round of the 2012 NFL draft.

"It was kind of funny the first meeting we had with the quarterbacks," said Rick Dennison, offensive coordinator of the Broncos, who was also born in Kalispell. "It's probably pretty rare that two people in this small room of five would be born in a small town in the northwest corner of Montana. I haven't been to Kalispell in a long time, but I still know bits and pieces and he knows the area where we used to hang out. It's kind of fun."

As Peyton Manning's understudy in 2015, Osweiler threw ten touchdown passes with six interceptions for the eventual Super Bowl champion

Broncos. To applaud Osweiler, students at Flathead High School signed a banner bearing his photos as a Brave and a Bronco. It read, "Capturing the Flathead Spirit! Good Luck in Super Bowl XLVIII." The school sent a picture of the banner to Osweiler as he prepared for the game.

The Texans signed Osweiler in March 2016 to a four-year, $72 million contract that included $37 million guaranteed, paying him more per year than Matthew Stafford, Andy Dalton and Alex Smith. "That's even though Osweiler had seven career starts and was benched in January's playoffs in favor of Manning, whose right arm was long past its expiration date," noted a disapproving writer at *Rolling Stone*.

Osweiler struggled through a disappointing season with the Texans in 2016, with plot lines "dominated by his interceptions, errant throws and a lack of touchdowns and decisiveness," according to UPI News.

At season's end, he was fourth in the league with sixteen interceptions and one of the worst passer ratings (55.3). Despite this, the Texans owner praised Osweiler as being "as good as Aaron Rodgers" and vowed to give him another chance in 2017.

MIKE PERSON

BORN: June 17, 1988, Glendive, MT
COLLEGE: Montana State
POSITION: Offensive guard
NFL EXPERIENCE: 2011–present
TEAMS: San Francisco 49ers (2011); Indianapolis Colts (2012);
Seattle Seahawks (2012–13); St. Louis Rams (2013–14);
Atlanta Falcons (2015–16); Kansas City Chiefs (2016–present)

Football taught Mike Person to look forward to the next day and take advantage of what he was given. He earned class A all-state football honors as a junior and senior, was named team MVP as a senior and was selected for the Shrine and MonDak All-Star games.

Yet, it was his training in multiple sports at Dawson County High School in Glendive that molded Person for the National Football League. He was also a two-time state discus champion and lettered twice in basketball.

"You just have to give it your all, and it can't just be during the season," said Person, whose father, Jim Person, played college football at Montana Tech. In addition, Mike Person had two uncles who played at the college level. "Everything that you do helps you in a different sport. Basketball helped my quickness and coordination, and track helped my footwork. You just have to buy in all year because it's not a seasonal thing. The biggest thing is dedication."

He redshirted at Montana State in 2006; in 2008, he earned honorable mention all-conference honors while helping the Bobcats lead the Big Sky in most rushing yards and fewest sacks allowed. He allowed just two and a half sacks and one quarterback pressure all season, started every game at right tackle and was named the team's Most Inspirational Player. The following season, he was named first team all-conference and started every game.

In Person's senior season, he didn't allow a single sack and ended his college career (2007–10) with forty-eight consecutive starts on Montana State's offensive line.

"Growing up in a small town, you're going to have to work hard to get noticed," said Person. "Everything that you do, you have to do everything to the best of your ability for you to even have a chance. Being from Glendive instilled that in me—doing everything that I could, whether it's at work or in practice."

Person was drafted by San Francisco in the seventh round in 2011. "The thing about the NFL is all about if you can stick," said Person.

Person has logged thousands of frequent flier miles. He was let go by the 49ers, signed by the Indianapolis Colts, dropped by the Colts, signed by Seattle, released by the Seahawks and claimed by the Rams. Person said that, similar to most other professions, the NFL is well ordered—his average day is structured with meetings, videos, exercises and practices.

"Monday and Tuesday is basically Saturday and Sunday for us. So I wake up at 6:00 a.m., go in and get a lift, and then start meetings at 8:00 a.m. for four hours. Then we have a walk-through and come in for forty-five minutes. Then we go out for practice. Then we get in the hot tub or cold tub and get any therapy we need and do a review of that practice film after."

He signed with Atlanta prior to the 2015 season. The six-foot, four-inch, 299-pound interior offensive lineman started fourteen games at center and blocked for an offense that ranked seventh in the NFL, averaging 374.1 yards per game. Person made his first NFL start against Philadelphia on September 14, 2015, blocking for an offense that totaled 395 yards. His line support helped Matt Ryan exceed 4,000 passing yards (for the fifth straight season).

The Falcons released Person on October 25, 2016. He was picked up by the Kansas City Chiefs, his sixth team—and the sixth city that the Montana boy has called home since his NFL ride began.

"I'll always be a small-town kid, regardless of if I'm in a big city," said Person. "Everything I've learned was learned in a small town, so that's always going to be there."

Cory Procter

Born: October 18, 1982, Seattle, WA
College: Montana
Position: Offensive guard
NFL Experience: 2005–10
Teams: Dallas Cowboys (2005–9); Miami Dolphins (2010)

Corey Procter attended Gig Harbor High School in the crabbing and fishing village of Gig Harbor, Washington, and was a letterman in football and wrestling.

In football, he was twice named the team MVP and as a senior earned all-league, all-area, all-state and All-Northwest honors. He received a scholarship to play for the University of Montana, where he became a four-year starter at multiple positions on the offensive line, starting forty-two consecutive games, plus five playoff contests.

University of Montana graduate Cory Procter played offensive guard in the NFL from 2005 to 2010. *Courtesy Cory Procter.*

"Coach Joe Glenn was there and I loved it," said Procter. "On my recruiting trip during the winter, the flight coming and the one going out both got canceled. But everybody was crazily accommodating, and I fell in love with the place. In college, I'd go fishing, a little ways up from Rock Creek, and I went to the Bitterroot and fish some of my favorite bends and fishing holes. You'd always catch and find something. St. John's Rud [along the Blackfoot River], and I had a blast and I still miss it."

Procter was signed by the Detroit Lions in 2005 and shortly after signed with the Dallas Cowboys as a backup at guard and center. In his first two seasons at Dallas, he was activated for two games, but he did not play. In 2007, he played in all sixteen games as part of the special teams units.

Some of the bigger hits come on special teams, and it's the constant line of the politically correct version of football today [emphasizing the removal of special teams play]. *The reason that football is so popular is because of the possibility of danger and the chance of seeing such a big news story, almost like a train derailment. Football and train accidents, they can be gruesome, and people take a sick kind of a pleasure in it.*

They've increased the yard distance for the PAT, and I think that is okay because there are better, finer athletes now and why make it so easy? But the league has been targeting players on defense and when you are reluctant to hit somebody, that's where and when injuries do happen. As far as the element of danger, you sign up for that and those possibilities.

In 2008, Procter started eleven games at left guard, replacing injured Kyle Kosier and holding off the mightiest defensive monsters, relentless rushers and sack leaders of the game. "I tried to play locked in to the game but still loose and I got really uptight and played stiff the last few years," said Procter.

I can remember clearly when [coach] *Wade Phillips told me that I had the start and when Kyle came back and forth, and there was a Monday Night Football game against Philly. That year, we started hot and then we went up and down. It was against the Eagles and I started and kicked ass and I played really well, and we made a drive to win at the end, and controlled the game. It felt like Montana and it felt like a cohesive unit. Like a lot of guys, I struggled to find what I had in college, and a lot of guys struggle in the pros—the game is too fast, whatever. In the NFL, it is a little harder because of player contracts, a shorter playing time, guys get cut, the business side, and a lot of that overshadows some of the greatest things you liked about the game. But to have a unit of guys, in sync with each other, and committed, and to have that happening in a game, that reminded me of Montana.*

On May 24, 2010, Procter was signed by the Miami Dolphins, but his stay there was short-lived. During a week eleven game against the Chicago Bears, Procter, who was sprinting downfield for a dump-off pass, fell to the ground without contact by a defender and was immediately in pain. It was determined that he had suffered an ACL tear in his left knee.

"It was a short screen and I was climbing to the second level and I over-pursued and as I was planting left to come back, it was a non-contact injury," said Procter. "The tendon ruptured at the knee cap. It was a freak, weird thing, and it ended up getting infected, and one surgery turned into five. As I was trying to get better, an abscess formed and I had to have several different scopes to get scar tissue out. I was out the whole next season when I should have been ready for training camp. I was rehabbing for a year, and by then you are atrophying in your quads and legs. It's hard. Because football is all you know and that messes with you. Luckily, I had my wife to help me through it—it's heavy."

Procter manages his own beverage company and dabbles in the music scene as a drummer.

"I don't think you ever fully leave it [football]," said Procter. "You are so connected to it for so long, you never really get out, to some sort of degree, appearances and speaking at schools and some of that good stuff. Football has great qualities and there are great relationships that we benefit from. That all carries over to your job and your family and how you look at other things."

CHASE REYNOLDS
BORN: October 22, 1987, Drummond, MT
COLLEGE: Montana
POSITION: Linebacker
NFL EXPERIENCE: 2012–16
TEAM: St. Louis Rams / Los Angeles Rams

Chase Reynolds became the first high school player in Montana history to rush for more than 5,000 yards in a career, leading the Drummond Trojans to back-to-back undefeated class C eight-man state championships (2003–5).

The special teams ace re-signed with the Rams, moving from St. Louis to L.A. in 2016.

"It can be stressful, but I just focused on working hard and being ready for the opportunity when it came," Reynolds, who played in Missoula (2007–10) told the *Los Angeles Times* of NFL free agency. "I obviously just tried to keep my mind straight and just work, not worry too much about the process…and try and stay in shape and be ready for today when I had to report."

Reynolds became a star in Big Sky Country by breaking Montana's career rushing touchdown record as a senior and coming close to its all-time yardage mark. He finished his career with fifty-two rushing scores and 4,067 yards, three shy of Yohance Humphery's career yardage record. He went undrafted out of Montana in 2011 and signed with the Seattle Seahawks during fall training camp. He was released before the season, but the Rams scooped him up and assigned him to their practice squad. Reynolds remained there through the 2012 season.

He made his NFL debut in 2013, playing in all sixteen of St. Louis's games on special teams. Reynolds has appeared in thirty-three games over the past three seasons with the Rams, making twenty-five career tackles with the punt and kickoff coverage units.

Chase Reynolds drew interest from a few teams in the spring of 2016, with Oakland another front-runner, according to the *St. Louis Post-Dispatch*, but re-signing with the Rams was his priority. His one-year contract was above the league minimum of $675,000 for players with three years of active roster experience and could have approached $900,000 with roster bonuses and incentives.

In January 2016, following a league owners' vote, the Rams announced they intended to uproot the franchise and return to the West Coast, where the team had once operated for nearly fifty years. The L.A. Rams had moved to St. Louis in 1995. Knowing a move was imminent whether he returned to the Rams or signed elsewhere, Reynolds and his wife, Kila, moved their three children back to Montana in February 2016. "I've been with them for five years and I just love the guys I work with," Reynolds told the *Post-Dispatch* in September 2016. "It was definitely my preferred option when it came time to re-sign. They gave me a deal and I'm happy to be back."

Reynolds told the *Los Angeles Times* that he splits time in the off-season between "his hometown of Drummond and Missoula, working out at the university and at Pfahler Sport Specific," a gym run by former teammate and Frenchtown native Steven Pfahler.

"I enjoy the outdoors a little bit, something I haven't been able to do in a really long time," said Reynolds. "It is really exciting to be back and to be in Montana for more than a week or two."

Reynolds was the second former Griz to garner a new contract with the Rams in the 2016 offseason. Los Angeles used its franchise tag on cornerback Trumaine Johnson (2008–11) in March, agreeing to pay the cornerback nearly $14 million for the 2016 season.

SHANN SCHILLINGER
BORN: May 22, 1986, Baker, MT
COLLEGE: Montana
POSITION: Defensive back
NFL EXPERIENCE: 2010–13
TEAMS: Atlanta Falcons (2010–13); Tennessee Titans (2013)

Hailing from a town of 1,741 in Montana was no obstacle to the NFL for Shann Schillinger.

"Baker is a small oil town in the eastern part of the state that supports sports and local athletics," said Schillinger. "It's a special place and I wouldn't want to be raised anywhere else. My mom grew up there, and my dad was assistant football coach, track coach and assistant basketball coach, and my uncle was head football coach. Every time [Montana-born] Tim Hauck was playing in an NFL game, we made it a point to have the TV on and made sure to watch him."

A former All–Big Sky first team safety at Montana, Schillinger spent four seasons with the Atlanta Falcons and Tennessee Titans, mostly as a special teams player. He played with former Grizzly defensive end Kroy Biermann in Atlanta.

"Biermann lended me his car and showed me the ropes and he was a big resource for me," said Schillinger.

It was an honor and a privilege to play in the NFL, and I didn't take that lightly. There are thousands who are trying to get your job, and to survive come cut time was exciting, and it was exciting to have hundreds of people from the state of Montana to reach out and congratulate you, like a big family. You could be playing the Broncos and your group of friends could be Broncos fans, but your friends are cheering for you because you are from Montana. When you are in the NFL, Montana people track you and reach out, keep in touch with you and follow you.

Hailing from a town of 1,741 in Montana was no obstacle to the NFL for Shann Schillinger, who played in the league from 2010 to 2013. *Courtesy University of Montana.*

Four years in the NFL altered Shillinger's perception of the game. Football is an American intuition, and like other institutions, it's money-driven and cutthroat.

"It's truly a business," said Schillinger.

> *I knew it going into it and you can't blame it, it's what makes it a great place to work. But it's a dog-eat-dog business. I don't think you can truly get that feeling until you are in it. Good players come and they are gone after two days. My first week, Erik Coleman, a good mentor and teammate on the Falcons, told me, "You are going to get hurt at some point in time and you are going to get cut at some point in time." It was great perception on how the league works and operates. You can't brace for it—it happens. Every day I came to work I did my best. You've got to perform and if you don't the next man up is going to come take your job. After I got cut from the Falcons, on Mondays I would look at the injury reports to see what safeties were hurt and who went down. You almost wanted them to go down so you could get the opportunity. It's extremely, extremely competitive, but obviously I wouldn't trade any of those memories that I have from my four years. I had the opportunity because other guys in front of me at UM paved the way.*

After football, Shillinger immediately took to coaching, which is a family tradition. Shann got his coaching start in 2014 under his older brother, Jace, the NAIA Dickinson State Bluehawks' offensive coordinator, as a special teams and wide receivers assistant. He spent a year in Nebraska assisting special teams coordinator Bruce Read. In 2016, he accepted the safeties coach position at his alma mater, the University of Montana.

"To be here is special to me," said Schillinger. "My father played here and it means a lot to me. I grew up there from a boy to a man. Coaching at UM is my way of giving back to the university. I tell kids in the program that they should not give up hope of the NFL at UM. But it's the opposite. There are opportunities here to play more and there are just as many scouts coming through here."

JEFF SHOATE

BORN: March 23, 1981, San Diego, CA
COLLEGES: Montana; San Diego State
POSITION: Cornerback
NFL EXPERIENCE: 2004; 2007
TEAM: Denver Broncos (2004; 2007)

At five feet, eleven inches tall and 180 pounds, freshman Jeff Shoate made an immediate impact as UM's third corner. The nineteen-year-old tallied thirteen tackles, intercepted a pass, made a memorable rib-breaking hit on Cal Poly's quarterback and managed an impressive 3.14 GPA his first semester.

Shoate, who had a baby boy and new bride back home in San Diego, transferred to San Diego State his second year. He cited his homesickness as the reason he opted not to stick with UM's program.

In the fifth round of the 2004 NFL draft, the Denver Broncos selected Shoate. He saw limited action on defense in 2004, registering three tackles. He was reserved primarily on special teams. He went on the injured reserve list in 2005 after knee surgery before being waived by the Broncos in 2006.

After that, Shoate spent time once more on the Broncos' active roster before being

Former Griz Jeff Shoate earned a ring as a member of the New York Giants' practice squad in Super Bowl XLIII. *Courtesy University of Montana.*

signed to the practice squads of the Ravens, Giants and Patriots. He earned a ring as a member of the Giants' practice squad in Super Bowl XLIII.

THATCHER SZALAY
BORN: January 18, 1979, Kalispell, MT
COLLEGE: Montana
POSITION: Offensive guard
NFL EXPERIENCE: 2002–6
TEAMS: Cincinnati Bengals (2002–4); Baltimore Ravens (2005); Seattle Seahawks (2006)

Born in Kalispell and raised in the Star Meadows area, forty-five miles northwest of Whitefish, Thatcher Szalay spent the summers of his youth working as a sawyer, machete in hand.

Son of a logger, Szalay was reared in the Salish Mountains, the closest neighbor was five miles down the road. "It is wild country," he said. "It produces tough guys. It was always an honor to be able to say that. Whether you are in the United States or in Mexico, there is a general respect for Montana and its wildness and toughness. We have bear attacks and people falling off of climbs and people drowning in the river. Outside of the cities, there is no cell service and you have to be self-reliant. You have to be able to improve and deal with adversity moreso than what other people experience in other states."

As an offensive lineman at UM, he had the size (six feet, four inches, 303 pounds) and the strength (he benched 225 pounds thirty-four times). But landing an NFL contract required every atom of his strength.

"I took it day by day," said Szalay, who signed with the Cincinnati Bengals in 2002. "It was all broke down into four different cuts, starting with one hundred guys, and they get it down to fifty-three by final preseason game. Every week they'd come in and knock off five or ten guys, and there was a guy who notified everyone they were cut, and we called him the Grim Reaper. He would walk by, and thankfully, he never said anything to me. What a lousy job that would be."

Szalay, who was once fined fifty dollars by the Bengals for "throwing people around," nearly landed a starting spot in 2004 in Cincy. He'd played solidly against the Patriots in a preseason game in place of the veteran center. The next practice, he broke his wrist. Two days after that, the center went down for six weeks. He stayed on the practice squad and roster for three seasons.

Thatcher Szalay came close to landing a starting spot in 2004 in Cincinnati and dressed in four games in 2005 for the Baltimore Ravens. He retired after being cut by the Seattle Seahawks the following year. *Courtesy Thatcher Szalay.*

In Cincy, the guys on the offensive line had been together and it was cutthroat. The way the veterans treated drafted players and the way they treated undrafted players was like night and day. Drafted guys make the team regardless of the way they play, because they [the organization] *like him. In preseason, the center would tell me the wrong thing to do, when I was a guard. I had to have smarts and the confidence in myself.*

Cincy was hard because I came from a close, tight family in college and Cincy wasn't that way. Being a hardworking kid from Montana, I had to take a deep breath and try to connect with who I was. In Cincinnati, I couldn't find a place to feel grounded. But it was a major learning experience.

Szalay dressed in four games in 2005 for the Baltimore Ravens and retired after being cut by the Seattle Seahawks the following year.

"I had five years in the league and four of them counted," said Szalay. "You have to have at least four in the league to receive a pension. Seattle wanted me to come back and go to training camp. I ended it on my own terms. But my wife and I had long distance and no stability. I decided that I'm going to be with my wife, buy a house and start a family." The couple has three children.

Szalay is in the midst of his eleventh year as a teacher at Florence-Carlton Middle School.

"I teach all subjects, from English to science. I enjoy it and I take it seriously. Middle school is a tough time, you are coming of age, your body is changing, and it's a time to set yourself apart, to be a leader and not a follower. As a teacher, you need to let them know that you value them enough to help them find success in their lives, which are still so moldable."

JORDAN TRIPP
Born: April 3, 1991, Missoula, MT
College: Montana
Position: Outside linebacker
NFL Experience: 2014–present
Teams: Miami Dolphins (2014); Jacksonville Jaguars (2015);
Seattle Seahawks (2016); Green Bay Packers (2016)

Jordan Tripp's path has been molded by tradition: a Missoula native, his father and grandfather each played for the Montana Grizzles. As a senior in high school, he was named captain of the team and earned all-state and all-conference honors. When Tripp earned a scholarship offer his senior year at a Montana football camp, he accepted it on the spot.

"I wasn't heavily recruited," he said. "I grew up always wanting to play at Montana. If you ever go out there and see a game, the atmosphere is unbelievable. I had talked to some other schools about walking on, but I wanted to play in front of my family."

Tripp's four years were spent studying, competing and bulking up at Missoula's downtown steakhouse, the Depot. He decided that he would not just exist as a player, but that he would thrive. Not only did he enlarge his body mass by more than fifty pounds through hard exercise and astronomical caloric intake, he experienced an incidental growth spurt that advanced him three inches in height. The additional mass and height proved to be advantageous. He finished his Grizzlies career among the all-time tackle leaders, with 335 from 2009 to 2013.

"We don't have a training table like some of the bigger schools, but I got big on nutrition after sophomore year," said Tripp. "I got really serious with it."

"Tripp's lineage goes back three generations, and he's a Loyola High School product, which has a history of good linebackers," said Mick Holien, longtime broadcast voice of Grizzly athletics from 1985 to 2016. "One of

Missoula's Jordan Tripp was drafted in the fifth round by the Miami Dolphins in 2014 and played in thirteen games as a rookie. *Courtesy University of Montana.*

the things I remember of him playing when he was a sophomore at Montana was his leadership. He commands respect. He had this intensity on the field and an infectious smile off of it."

Tripp was drafted in the fifth round by the Miami Dolphins in 2014 and played in thirteen games as a rookie. He then spent 2015 with the Jaguars and played in twelve games. His first NFL start came on December 13, 2015, against the Indianapolis Colts, filling in for one of his mentors, Paul Posluszny, who had fractured his hand the week before. It was the first time a Missoula prep alumni started in the league since "Wild Bill" Kelly in 1930.

Tripp said that football has taught him how to live, how to fight for what he wanted and to pursue things into existence. "You prepare so you're ready, then you don't let the moment take you over," he said. "You control your emotions and do what you've prepared to do."

Tripp came to Seattle as a practice squad member after being released by the Jacksonville Jaguars the week before the start of the 2016 regular season. He was activated in October and made one start on November 27 against the Tampa Bay Buccaneers. Tripp made one tackle before being hurt while—ironically—starting in place of an injured Brock Coyle, his college teammate in Missoula.

"All the work and all the time put in, it's for moments like that [of starting]," said Tripp. "Getting that type of an opportunity is just a huge blessing for sure. If you want to do certain things and you have certain goals, I believe only you are the one who can stop you. You just have to put that in your mind, that there's going to be ups and downs. You have to look at every instance and everything that happens as a lesson."

After being released by the Seahawks in January 2017, he joined the Green Bay Packers' active roster as an inside linebacker.

"I feel like I can contribute," said Tripp. "I'm as versatile as anybody. It doesn't matter where you came from, because when you get to the NFL, everyone is the best."

Joey Thomas

BORN: August 29, 1980, Seattle, WA
COLLEGE: Montana State
POSITION: Cornerback
NFL EXPERIENCE: 2004–8
TEAMS: Green Bay Packers (2004–5); New Orleans Saints (2005);
Dallas Cowboys (2007); Miami Dolphins (2008); Oakland Raiders
(2010)

Joey Thomas was chosen out of Montana State University in the third round of the 2004 NFL draft by the Green Bay Packers. The team chose him with the seventieth pick. Thomas, the seventh selection of the third round, joined Pro Football Hall of Famer Jan Stenerud and longtime NFL offensive lineman Jon Borchardt as the only Bobcats ever chosen in the third round. (Montana State All–Big Sky offensive tackle Brent Swaggert signed a free-agent contract with the San Francisco 49ers late Sunday afternoon following the NFL draft. He was released.)

"Bozeman was a phenomenal time for me and the relationships and the people I met through that program," said Thomas.

The brand of football we played was wide open, and when I went in the third round, it was the beginning of the Big Sky Conference becoming a hotbed of recruiting. Afterwards, guys were coming out rapidly, and I think the draft class I was in has a lot to do with it. It put Big Sky on the map, and that was before guys were already fast-tracked.

It was beautiful going from the city to the country and to see Mother Nature, it was eye-opening. Winter was a shock. If it snows here in Seattle, they shut down the city. In Bozeman, you have a snow day and people are walking around like it's normal, they still function, they still go to class. It was a shock to learn how to maneuver or even walk in the snow, or drive in the snow. My first six months were a shock. But you adapt to it. Bozeman was a blessing. Though, I didn't know it at the time.

Thomas served a backup role in the Packers' defense in his rookie year. In 2005, he unsuccessfully attempted to unseat second-year player Ahmad Carroll for the number two cornerback position. In a career spanning thirty-one professional contests, Thomas started one game in 2005 for the Packers.

"Mental toughness is the best thing you can have as a football player," he said. "The two things I miss are the camaraderie of teammates and the competition of every game day and finding out who is better, me or you? When you get drafted, you are automatically pinned up against each other. Being young, [Ahmad Carroll and I] we didn't understand that. My dad played the same position, and the position is in my blood."

He is currently the head football coach of the Garfield Bulldogs, in Seattle's inner city. When San Francisco 49er quarterback Colin Kaepernick chose not to stand for the national anthem, the entire Bulldogs team decided that they would take a similar stand by taking a knee. Thomas respects the power of football's platform, in which a backup quarterback can kneel during the national anthem and spark debate, outrage and, maybe, change.

"I believe in what they're doing and I believe in the mission," Thomas said. "The relationship between a player and coach is all about trust, and if they are going to walk through a wall for you, they need to know that you care about them as individuals. We spent hours all talking about different issues that were important to them, and they decided that taking a stand would help them better deal with their emotions and better facilitate their emotions. These young men want to make our society and community better than the way they found it."

Jimmy Wilson

Born: July 30, 1986, San Diego, CA
Position: Defensive back
NFL Experience: 2011–15
Teams: Miami Dolphins (2011–14); San Diego Chargers (2015)

San Diego native Jimmy Wilson graduated from the University of Montana in 2010. His time in Montana was fraught with personal and legal entanglements. He pled guilty in Missoula Municipal Court in December 2010 to biting a woman's leg near the intersection of Park Street and Southwest Higgins Avenue. The August 8, 2010 incident occurred just a month after he was cleared by the NCAA to return to play in the fall for the Griz. Wilson, a standout cornerback at UM (2004–6), was arrested in 2007 for the California murder of Kevin Smoot and spent the next two years in prison before eventually being acquitted in a second jury trial. Three years and almost five months after his arrest, Wilson would get back on the field for the Montana Grizzlies.

He played four seasons with the Miami Dolphins as a free safety, defensive back

Jimmy Wilson graduated from UM in 2010 and played four seasons with the Miami Dolphins. Wilson's life has been besieged by personal and legal problems, including two years spent in prison on murder charges he was acquitted of in 2009. *Courtesy University of Montana.*

and safety, as well as a special teams player. Wilson appeared in thirteen games with San Diego in 2015 before the team released him in December. In the off-season, he signed on with Kansas City and Cincinnati, but both stints were short-lived. After entering the league as a seventh-round choice in 2011, Wilson played in seventy-three regular-season games, logged twenty-eight starts and amassed five interceptions.

BIBLIOGRAPHY

Chapter 1

Cleveland Plain Dealer. "NFL Arrives to Stay." December 16, 1945.

Cohen, Stan, Dave Guffey and Mick Holien. *Montana Grizzlies: Odyssey to a National Championship—Illustrated 100 Year History of University of Montana Football*. Missoula, MT: Pictorial Histories Publishing Company, 1965.

Didinger, Ray. *The Eagles Encyclopedia*. Philadelphia, PA: Temple University Press, 2014.

Holien, Mick. *Montana Football Vault*. Atlanta, GA: Whitman Coin Products, 2009.

Illustrated 100 Year History of University of Montana Football. Missoula, MT: Pictorial Histories Publishing Company, 1965.

International News Service. "Freeze Out in Championship." December 16, 1945.

Kearney, Patrick. *The Divide War*. Butte, MT: Butte Books, 2012.

Paige, David. *What Giants They Were*. Chicago, IL: Triumph Books, 2000.

Peterson, Robert W. *Pigskin: The Early Years of Pro Football*. New York: Oxford University Press, 2008.

Reischel, Robert. *Packers Essential: Everything You Need to Know to Be a Real Fan*. Chicago, IL: Triumph Books, 2006.

Reyburn, Susan. *Football Nation: Four Hundred Years of America's Game*. Washington, D.C.: Library of Congress, 2013.

Spokane Daily Chronicle. "Cahoon Back to Coaching," October 12, 1953.

Suburban Times. "Edward Ross Barker" (obituary). September 7, 2012.

Chapter 2

Cohen, Stan, Dave Guffey and Mick Holien. *Montana Grizzlies: Odyssey to a National Championship—Illustrated 100 Year History of University of Montana Football.* Missoula, MT: Pictorial Histories Publishing Company, 1965.

Cook, Kevin. *The Last Headbangers: NFL Football in the Rowdy, Reckless '70s—The Era that Created Modern Sports.* New York: W.W. Norton & Company, 2013.

Holien, Mick. *Montana Football Vault.* Atlanta, GA: Whitman Coin Products, 2009.

Lombardi, Vince, and W.C. Heinz. *Run to Daylight.* Reissue, New York: Simon & Schuster, 2014.

Paige, David. *What Giants They Were.* Chicago, IL: Triumph Books, 2000.

Zagorski, Joe. *The NFL in the 1970s: Pro Football's Most Important Decade.* Jefferson, NC: McFarland & Company, 2016.

Chapter 3

Byrne, Jim. *The $1 League: The Rise and Fall of the USFL.* Upper Saddle River, NJ: Prentice Hall, 1987.

Kluck, Ted. *Three-Week Professionals: Inside the 1987 NFL Players' Strike.* Lanham, MD: Rowman & Littlefield Publishers, 2015.

Monnig, Alex. *Seattle Seahawks.* Chicago, IL: Triumph Books, 2015.

Patoski, Joe Nick. *The Dallas Cowboys: The Outrageous History of the Biggest, Loudest, Most Hated, Best Loved Football Team in America.* Reprint, New York: Back Bay Books, 2013.

Reeths, Paul. *The United States Football League, 1982–1986.* Jefferson, NC: McFarland & Company, 2017.

Seattle Times. "Trying Season." October 3, 1987.

Sports Illustrated. *John Elway: The Drive of a Champion.* New York: Simon & Schuster, 1998.

Chapter 4

ESPN.com, "Mariani's Many Returns." October 20, 2016. http://www.espn.com/id/456823.

Florida-Times Union. "Holmes Surprises at End." August 13, 2016.

NFL.com. "Osweiler's Time to Lead." February 13, 2012. http://ww.nfl.com/id22047576.

St. Louis Post-Dispatch. "Tripp among Re-Signs." September 19, 2016.

ABOUT THE AUTHOR

 rian D'Ambrosio lives in Helena, Montana. He has written several books related to Montana and hundreds of newspaper and magazine articles about music, boxing, history, travel and true crime for myriad publications.

CPSIA information can be obtained
at www.ICGtesting.com
Printed in the USA
LVHW081457150621
690280LV00002B/87